THE NEW GROVE®

Russian Masters 1

GLINKA BORODIN
BALAKIREV
MUSORGSKY TCHAIKOVSKY

David Brown
Gerald Abraham
David Lloyd-Jones
Edward Garden

W. W. NORTON & COMPANY
NEW YORK   LONDON

Copyright © David Brown, Gerald Abraham,
David Lloyd-Jones, Edward Garden 1980, 1986

First published in
The New Grove Dictionary of Music and Musicians®,
edited by Stanley Sadie, 1980

British Library Cataloguing in Publication Data

Russian Masters 1: Glinka, Borodin, Balakirev, Musorgsky,
Tchaikovsky.—(The Composer biography series)
1. Composers—Soviet Union—Biography
I. Brown, David, *1929–* II. The new Grove dictionary
of music and musicians   III. Series
780′.92′2   ML390

ISBN 0-393-31585-1

First American edition in book form with additions 1986 by
W. W. NORTON & COMPANY
500 Fifth Avenue, New York NY 10110

Printed in the United States of America

W. W. Norton & Company, Inc.
500 Fifth Avenue, NY, NY 10110
W. W. Norton & Company Ltd.
10 Coptic Street, London WC1A 1PU

1 2 3 4 5 6 7 8 9 0

Contents

List of illustrations

Illustration acknowledgments

We are grateful to the following for permission to reproduce illustrative material: Novosti Press Agency, London (figs.1, 6, 8, 15-18); Central State Literature and Art Archives of the USSR, Moscow (fig.2); from E. Gordeyeva, ed: *M. I. Glinka: sbornik stat'yey* (Moscow, 1958)/photo, British Library, London (fig.3); Society for Cultural Relations with the USSR, London (fig.4); M. I. Glinka State Central Museum of Musical Culture, Moscow (figs.5, 10, 11, 20); M. E. Saltïkov-Shchedrin State Public Library, Leningrad (fig.7); Theatre Museum, Leningrad (fig.9); Tchaikovsky House Museum, Klin (figs.11 (photo), 13); Archiv für Kunst und Geschichte, Berlin (figs.12, 14); Russian Museum, Leningrad (cover)

General abbreviations

A	alto, contralto [voice]	Mez	mezzo-soprano
addl	additional	movt	movement
aut.	autumn		
		ob	oboe
B	bass [voice]	obbl	obbligato
b	bass [instrument]	orch	orchestra, orchestral
Bar	baritone [voice]	orchd	orchestrated (by)
bn	bassoon	ov.	overture
BWV	Bach-Werke-Verzeichnis		
	[Schmieder, catalogue of	pf	piano
	J. S. Bach's works]	Pol.	Polish
		prol	prologue
c	circa [about]	pt.	part
cl	clarinet	pubd	published
collab.	in collaboration with		
conc.	concerto	qnt	quintet
Cz.	Czech	qt	quartet
db	double bass	R	photographic reprint
		repr.	reprinted
eng hn	english horn	rev.	revision, revised (by/for)
		Russ.	Russian
facs.	facsimile		
fl	flute	S	soprano [voice]
frag.	fragment	str	string(s)
		sum.	summer
hn	horn	sym.	symphony, symphonic
inc.	incomplete	T	tenor [voice]
		transcr.	transcription,
J	Jähns catalogue [Weber]		transcribed (by/for)
Jg.	Jahrgang [year of		
	publication/volume]	U.	University
		v, vv	voice, voices
K	Köchel catalogue [Mozart	va	viola
	no. after / is from 6th edn.]	vc	cello
		vn	violin
L.H.	left hand		
lib	libretto	wint.	winter

Symbols for the library sources of works, printed in *italic*, correspond to those used in *Répertoire International des Sources Musicales*, Ser. A.

Bibliographical abbreviations

Preface

This volume is one of a series of short biographies derived from *The New Grove Dictionary of Music and Musicians* (London, 1980). In their original form, the texts were written in the mid-1970s, and finalized at the end of that decade. For this reprint, they have been re-read and modified by their original authors and corrections and changes have been made; in particular, the Tchaikovsky text has been supplemented in the light of recent research. The bibliographies have been brought up to date.

The fact that the texts of the books in the series originated as dictionary articles inevitably gives them a character somewhat different from that of books conceived as such. They are designed, first of all, to accommodate a very great deal of information in a manner that makes reference quick and easy. Their first concern is with fact rather than opinion, and this leads to a larger than usual proportion of the texts being devoted to biography than to critical discussion. The nature of a reference work gives it a particular obligation to convey received knowledge and to treat of composers' lives and works in an encyclopedic fashion, with proper acknowledgment of sources and due care to reflect different standpoints, rather than to embody imaginative or speculative writing about a composer's character or his music. It is hoped that the comprehensive work-lists and extended bibliographies, indicative of the origins of the books in a reference work, will be valuable to the reader who is eager for full and accurate reference information and who may not have ready access to *The New Grove Dictionary* or who may prefer to have it in this more compact form.

S.S.

MIKHAIL GLINKA

David Brown

CHAPTER ONE

1804–34

I Early years

Mikhail Ivanovich Glinka was the father of the 19th-century Russian nationalist school of composers, and exerted a profound and freely acknowledged influence upon Balakirev and his circle and upon Tchaikovsky. He was born in Novospasskoye (now Glinka), near Smolensk, on 1 June 1804.

It is possible that the Glinkas were Polish in origin, though a branch of the family had been established in the Smolensk region for over 150 years before Mikhail's birth. They were landowners who had developed some broad cultural interests, and Glinka's uncle, who lived only 10 km from Novospasskoye, had his own serf orchestra which included in its repertory some of the overtures and symphonies of Haydn, Mozart, and even Beethoven. Initially Glinka was excluded from such experiences, for immediately after his birth his paternal grandmother took him into her charge, virtually incarcerating him in her own overheated room for the first six years of his life. Thus, besides undermining his constitution and laying the foundations of his lifelong hypochondria, she effectively cut him off from all music except for the folksongs sung in abundance by his nurse, the chant he heard in the village church, and the strident church bell music for which the Smolensk region was famous. The last particularly attracted him, and his earliest 'compositions' were imitations of such bell music on copper basins. The importance of this initial and exclusive musical diet was fundamental: the folksongs sank deep into Glinka's mind so that later he could effortlessly incorporate their shapes into his own melodic invention. At the same time his ear became accustomed to a higher norm of dissonance than contemporary western European composers would have found acceptable, partly through the bell music, and partly through the familiarity he must have acquired in later childhood with the rough *podgolosok* harmonizations which Russian peasants habitually improvised to their folksongs.

On his grandmother's death in 1810, Glinka passed into the care of his parents, and at last began to hear other music. But it was another four or five years before a clarinet quartet by Bernard Crusell suddenly aroused in him a passion for Western music. His interests now shifted primarily to this field, and he was able to broaden his experiences further after 1817, when he was sent to school in St Petersburg. There he excelled at languages, adoring also the natural sciences and any subject that elicited an imaginative response. In general, though, his musical education was thoroughly unsystematic, and, despite the fact that Caterino Cavos, who was to conduct the première of *A Life for the Tsar*, was responsible for music at his school, Glinka gained most of his musical experience outside school in St Petersburg. During his schooldays he had three piano lessons from John Field, and he met and favourably impressed Hummel when the latter was visiting Russia. On leaving school in 1822 he resisted his father's pressures to enter the foreign service, and settled into the life of a musical dilettante in the world of the St Petersburg drawing rooms to which his sociability and skill, both as singer and pianist, readily gained him access.

Glinka had a lifelong attraction towards remote and, to him, exotic places, and in 1823 he persuaded his father to allow him to visit the Caucasus, ostensibly to take the waters at Pyatigorsk and Kislovodsk. The medical results of this treatment were disastrous, but Glinka was deeply impressed both by the scenic wonders of the region and by its festivals and customs. On returning in the autumn, he spent some six months at Novospasskoye; during this time he was able to rehearse his uncle's orchestra, gaining invaluable insights into the craft of orchestration. However, when he returned to St Petersburg in 1824, he settled again into an undirected existence, hindered only by his undemanding employment as an under-secretary in the office of the Council of Communications (1824–8) and by the constant illnesses, real and imaginary, which are diligently chronicled in his *Zapiski* ('Memoirs'). Otherwise he engaged in pleasant, sometimes frivolous, musical pastimes with an ever widening circle of acquaintances, from time to time furnishing these activities with simple compositions. He associated with Pushkin, Griboyedov, Del'vig and other important figures of this very active period of Russian literature, though he seems to have been quite unmoved by the cultural and social ideas that motivated most of them. The only event to disturb his empty life was the shock of falling under suspicion of sheltering his former tutor, Wilhelm Küchelbecker, who had taken part in the abortive Decembrist revolt of 1825. Glinka, who never engaged in politics, retired to the country until the upheaval subsided.

During the 1820s he composed a fair amount of music, even though he had had no formal musical grounding. On leaving school he had received the greatest help from Karl Mayer, a St Petersburg musician whose leisurely but intelligent guidance he declared was of immense value. He inherited no tradition of sophisticated composition, and there was as yet no sign of distinctive national character in his more extended pieces. But the rich cultural life of St Petersburg, comparable with that of any large western European city, provided him with models upon which he could base his early works. During his youth and 20s he was able to make acquaintance with, notably, the operas of the French school and of Rossini, and with a selection of the orchestral and choral masterpieces of Haydn, Mozart and Beethoven. He also constantly attended informal musical gatherings, and throughout his creative life his piano dances and variations reflected this world in their trite melodies or brilliant but empty figuration.

Far more serious intentions are revealed in his orchestral and ensemble music of the 1820s. Here he attempted symphonic composition, soon managing to synthesize conventional sonata structures of no distinction with tame, even banal, melodic material. The achievement of his later music is foreshadowed only in his sometimes deft contrapuntal combinations and decorative counterpoints, and in the skill with which he handled his chosen instrumental forces. Glinka's 'Classical' phase closed with the String Quartet in F. It was a line of development that was unsuitable for him; in any case, in the late 1820s his attention was focussing increasingly upon the styles and techniques of

Italian opera; before leaving for Italy in 1830 he had composed numerous pieces with Italian texts, though they are stiff and sometimes stylistically insecure.

The most accomplished of Glinka's early compositions are to be found among his songs with piano accompaniment. A few are feeble, and in most the narrow confines of a drawing-room aesthetic cramp the invention and expressive scope, but in *Razocharovaniye* ('Disenchantment') – which, like *Pamyat' serdtsa* ('Heart's memory'), contains some striking yet apparently inexplicable premonitions of Schumann – Glinka explores deeper feelings which find even more cogent expression in *Golos s tovo sveta* ('A voice from the other world'), written, it seems, for his sister Pelageya's husband after her death in 1828. Apart from these songs, Glinka's most noteworthy compositions of the 1820s are his six folksong stylizations, miniatures in which the very simple piano accompaniments are usually exactly right for the pseudo-folk melodies which he could so readily invent.

II Italy and Berlin

In May 1830 Glinka left Russia for Italy with Nikolay Ivanov, a tenor of the imperial chapel. After travelling through Germany and taking the waters at Ems and Aachen, they proceeded through Switzerland to Milan, which was to be Glinka's base for the next three years. There Glinka took some lessons in composition from Francesco Basili, who was the director of the Milan Conservatory, but these he soon discontinued because of their academic aridity. He derived more benefit from his acquaintance with Bellini and Donizetti, and he also established a certain local fame as a pianist. To maintain it, he wrote a little piano music. In Milan he also met Mendelssohn, though neither seems to have been much impressed by the other. In September 1831 Glinka and Ivanov set out for Rome, where they met Berlioz. Glinka's ultimate destination was Naples, where he arrived at the beginning of November. The 'electric-sulphurous air' soon proved uncongenial to him, but he acquired a deeper understanding of the art of singing from the teaching of Andrea Nozzari and Joséphine Fodor-Mainvielle. In March 1832 Glinka and Ivanov parted company, the latter remaining to make his début in Donizetti's *Anna Bolena*, while Glinka returned to Milan.

The rest of 1832 was mainly occupied with flirtations, the composition of some insignificant chamber works and with growing disenchantment with Italy. While there, Glinka wrote surprisingly little vocal music either to Italian or Russian texts, though his cavatina *L'iniquo voto* shows that he could now challenge the Italians on their own ground. His instrumental compositions from this period were either confections for the Italian public or else trivia inspired by young ladies who had aroused his passions. Glinka himself recognized their unworthiness and was growing aware that Italian manners did not come naturally to him. 'I could not sincerely be an Italian', he wrote in his *Memoirs* in 1854. 'A longing for my own country led me gradually to the idea of writing in a Russian manner.' After an unhappy visit to Venice in March 1833, he became violently ill, and as a result his voice changed to a resonant high tenor. In August he left Italy for good, spent some time in Vienna, where he heard the orchestras of Strauss and Lanner, and derived great benefit from homeopathic treatment. In October he arrived in Berlin to join his sister Natalya and her husband.

In an endeavour to put his technique of composition in order, Glinka occupied himself in Berlin with five months of intensive study under the distinguished teacher Siegfried Dehn. It was the only systematic course in composition that he ever undertook, and it produced, in addition to a pile of chorale harmonizations and fugal exercises, a Capriccio on Russian themes for piano duet and an unfinished Symphony on two Russian themes. These are certainly the most interesting instrumental works he had yet composed. In the Symphony he again took up a procedure he had first tried in an unfinished symphony in B♭ (*c*1824); this is also based on Russian folksongs, each of which is stated and given a number of varied repetitions. In the Symphony on two Russian themes he used the technique with much more assured inventiveness and technical security, and was already moving towards the 'changing background' procedure which was to prove his most successful method of treating folktunes in an extended composition. The Symphony was avowedly written in a German style, and takes on a progressively more conventional aspect in those passages where Glinka became entangled in contrapuntal procedures which did not come easily to him. He was more consistently successful in the Capriccio, which had no organic structural pretensions (Glinka himself described it as a potpourri). In this work he made only one brief attempt at generating the music through contrapuntal argument, being otherwise content either to rub his tunes together crudely but effectively, or else to furnish them with decorative counterpoints. Elsewhere he used simple variation treatment, but the meretricious tinsel of the solo piano variations has gone. Though the Capriccio is roughly wrought, both it and the Symphony reveal the liveliness of Glinka's mind.

Glinka's quiet but profitable life in Berlin was shattered in March 1834 by the sudden news of his father's death, and he decided to go back to Russia with Natalya and her husband. He intended to return to Berlin, for he was planning to marry a young Jewess, Maria, who was the object of his first serious love affair. Shortly after his return to Russia, however, he transferred his affections to Mariya Petrovna Ivanova, a pretty but shallow girl whom he married a year later, on 8 May 1835. In any case, he was soon utterly absorbed by the composition of his first opera.

CHAPTER TWO

1834–42

I 'A Life for the Tsar'

In 1824 Glinka had briefly thought of writing an opera on Sir Walter Scott's *Rokeby*, and a few tiny fragments of the music have survived. It seems that he did not contemplate another opera until ten years later when, while visiting Moscow in June 1834, he decided upon Zhukovsky's *Mar'ina Roshcha* ('Marina Grove') as a subject and composed several pieces for it. But it was back in St Petersburg a little later, at a weekly gathering of men of letters and a few musicians, that Zhukovsky himself suggested the tale of Ivan Susanin, the Russian peasant who in 1612 or 1613 had, at the cost of his own life, saved the first of the Romanov tsars by leading astray a group of marauding Poles who were hunting him. Glinka's imagination was immediately caught by the subject; 'many themes and even details of their workings flashed into my head at once', he recorded. *Marina Grove* was abandoned, and he worked so quickly on the new opera that his librettist, Baron Georgy Rosen, a writer of German extraction who was secretary to the tsarevich, often had to fit his texts to existing music.

The next two years were happily occupied by the composition of *Ivan Susanin*, though Glinka did find time early in 1836 to set for voice and piano Zhukovsky's new ballad *Nochnoy smotr* ('The night review') as a stark 'fantasia'; its uncompromisingly bleak declamation, sombre but relentless rhythmic tread, and measured dissonance compound a sinister power quite unprecedented in Russian music, and which Glinka never again attempted. Preliminary rehearsals of the opera started early in 1836, and Glinka's work received both the enthusiastic approbation of the performers and also constructive criticism from his friends. After the selfless intervention of Cavos, who had himself written an opera on the same subject in 1815, the work was accepted by the imperial theatres. The tsar himself followed the work's progress with interest, and at the final rehearsals agreed that it should be named *Zhizn' za tsarya* ('A Life for the Tsar') instead of *Ivan Susanin*. On 9 December 1836 the première was given to a glittering audience, who received the opera rapturously. Overnight Glinka was acknowledged as Russia's leading composer.

Although, like earlier Russian composers, Glinka attempted to imbue his music for the opera with a national character, it is in fact less national than has sometimes been supposed. Basically it is a Western opera, harmonically conventional and exhibiting little of that rhythmic vitality which might readily be identified as Russian, drawing a good part of its vocal manners from Italian opera and making use of the large choral scenes and formal ballet of French opera. What is really novel in Glinka's opera is its recitative. All previous Russian operas had used spoken dialogue to link the formal musical movements, but Glinka set every word, devising a flexible and expressive recitative which enables the music to penetrate the whole of the work. This enrichment, coupled with Glinka's melodic inventiveness and instinct for simple yet strong drama, gives the opera its life.

Though in no sense profoundly drawn, the characters are in general alive, and Susanin emerges as a truly heroic figure. The one clear failure is with the Poles, personified musically in their encounters with Susanin by the decorative ballet music to which they dance the formal ballet of Act 2. This music thus becomes their leitmotif, and in his use of this device, both in relation to the Poles and to certain other characters, Glinka was ahead of his time. His grasp of the leitmotif's emotional power is splendidly demonstrated in Act 4 during Susanin's farewell, when, as Susanin's thoughts return to the individual members of his family, there are eight recollections of music that has been associated with them earlier in the opera. The purpose of such recollections is not, however, entirely emotive. Glinka was concerned that the opera should make 'an harmonious whole', and the more than 20 quotations of earlier music that he incorporated into the last stages of the opera do much to give it a satisfying shape.

The one thoroughly national movement is the beautiful Bridal Chorus in Act 3. Elsewhere the national characteristics are found almost exclusively in the opera's melodic content, even though Glinka used only two borrowed melodies in the whole work. Many Russian folktunes share certain characteristic turns of phrase or underlying shapes, and Glinka's early acquaintance with folk music enabled him to incorporate certain of its features into his melodies for *A Life for the Tsar*. One critic recorded that many in the first audiences 'noticed something familiar in it, tried to recall from which Russian song this or that motif was taken, and could not discover the original'. Nevertheless, the integration of national melody with the techniques and forms of Western opera was still imperfect, for often in a movement that starts with a recognizably Russian character, the national element weakens when the extending processes begin (especially when modulation sets in), and disappears completely with the final cadencing. As in the Symphony on two Russian themes, it is clear that Glinka was drawn towards variation procedures as the most satisfactory way of treating his quasi-national melody. Such procedures underlie a number of movements, and are seen most explicitly in the impressive stage picture of the Epilogue (the Slavsya Chorus), which was to be the precedent for similar crowd scenes in later Russian opera.

Unequal in quality and inconsistent in style, *A Life for the Tsar* is nevertheless fashioned by a mind of such freshness and one capable of such imaginative flashes that it succeeds well on the stage. The orchestration is masterly, and already shows something of that characteristically clear quality which was to become a pronounced feature of later Russian scoring.

II 'Ruslan and Lyudmila'

No sooner had *A Life for the Tsar* been produced than Glinka, prompted by the playwright Shakhovskoy, fastened upon Pushkin's poem *Ruslan and Lyudmila* as the subject for his next opera. He had hoped that Pushkin himself might prepare the libretto; but in February 1837 Pushkin died from the wounds received in a duel. At the beginning of 1837, as a result of the success of his first opera, Glinka was appointed Kapellmeister of the imperial chapel. The salary from

1. Mikhail Ivanovich Glinka: lithograph (1837)

the new position was very necessary to pay his debts, for his household economy was chaotic; also his relationship with his wife had deteriorated even while he was still composing *A Life for the Tsar*. His thoughts turned to another subject for an opera, but by the autumn he had again taken up *Ruslan and Lyudmila*. A scenario was worked out by his friend Konstantin Bakhturin 'in a quarter of an hour while drunk', and he had already composed a number of pieces for it and found a librettist in a young army officer and poet, Valerian Shirkov, before he was sent to the Ukraine in May 1838 to select singers for the imperial chapel. After enlisting some recruits (notably from the choir of an enraged Bishop of Poltava), Glinka settled on a friend's estate at Kachanovka; there he continued work on *Ruslan and Lyudmila* and was able to try out his new pieces with his friend's serf orchestra. In September he arrived back in St Petersburg and, being short of funds, set about compiling a collection of musical pieces composed by himself as well as by others. It included three of his best songs from this period, all Pushkin settings, of which the tiny but exquisite *Gde nasha roza?* ('Where is our rose?') set an example for later miniatures in Russian song. Though still living with his wife, he entered openly into an affair with Ekaterina Kern, to whom he dedicated his Valse-fantaisie, and for whom he set Pushkin's *Ya pomnyu chudnoye mgnoven'ye* ('I recall a wonderful moment'). Despite its sentimentality, its tender and impassioned sincerity makes it one of his finest songs. Before the year was out he had proof of his wife's infidelity and had separated from her, and at the end of the year he resigned from the imperial chapel, his interest in which had for some time been declining.

'Ruslan and Lyudmila'

Though Glinka was in the lowest of spirits at the beginning of 1840, the release from the tensions of his marriage and from the professional duties at the chapel ultimately afforded him more time for composition. In January 1840 his mother arrived in the capital and bore him off to Novospasskoye until the scandal of his separation from his wife had subsided. In May he returned to St Petersburg and compiled a set of 12 songs, *Proshchaniye s Peterburgom* ('A farewell to St Petersburg'), on texts by his friend Nestor Kukol'nik, a popular third-rate playwright. None of these songs equalled the quality of his earlier Pushkin settings, though *Poputnaya pesnya* ('Travelling song') had some curiosity appeal as being probably the first ever railway song. By the middle of August, despite his separation from Ekaterina, he was again working on *Ruslan and Lyudmila* after a lapse of some 18 months. Nevertheless, work was to be interrupted yet again, for Kukol'nik requested some incidental music for his new play, *Knyaz' Kholmsky* ('Prince Kholmsky'), and within four weeks, in the most intensive burst of creative activity in his whole life, Glinka composed an overture, four entr'actes and one of the three songs.

Kukol'nik's play was a ludicrous melodrama woven around certain historical figures and events of late 15th-century Muscovy, when the tsar was engaged in conflict with the Order of Livonian Knights and with the religious heresy of the Judaists. For an overture, Glinka provided a neat sonata structure, less distinctive melodically than that for *Ruslan and Lyudmila*, but effective. As in the overtures to both his operas, he used music from the rest of the work to provide the two subjects. In *Prince Kholmsky* he used two of the three vocal pieces, and incorporated the remaining song into the first entr'acte; this is a character study of the Jewess Rachel, one of the principal female characters. The second entr'acte is a musical portrayal of Kholmsky himself, the third a striking march; but the finest of all is certainly the fourth, a brooding and harshly dissonant piece in which, as Tchaikovsky later declared, 'Glinka shows himself one of the most substantial symphonists of our time'.

During 1841 work on *Ruslan and Lyudmila* was fitful. In March Glinka's wife remarried bigamously, and he was compelled to abandon any idea of going abroad while divorce proceedings were instituted. Inspiration flagged until the autumn, when he settled in with his sister Elizaveta and was able to have an uninterrupted winter of work on the opera. Because Shirkov was in the Ukraine, others had to be asked to help with the final assembly of the mass of material Glinka had composed. When he submitted the nearly completed work to the imperial theatres in March 1842, it was accepted without question. Glinka's spirits were raised even further by the deep interest shown towards the opera by Liszt (then on his first Russian visit). All went well with the production until the later stages of rehearsal, when tensions arose between Glinka and the cast over some derogatory remarks about the performers that had been attributed to him. In fact, not all the singers were satisfactory; illness struck down one of the best principals, and the opera's undramatic nature could not be concealed, despite ruthless cutting at the final rehearsals. At the first performance (9 December 1842) the opera was coolly received, though appreciation grew with subsequent performances.

'Ruslan and Lyudmila'

Dramatically, *Ruslan and Lyudmila* is a disaster. Pushkin's fantastic, ironic fairy tale relies heavily upon imaginative and evocative scenes, and its structure is unsuited to the stage. The circumstances in which the scenario was drafted could not aid its coherence, and the haphazard and extended process of composition sealed its fate: Glinka devoted his attention to possible set pieces as they took his fancy, until eventually it transpired that he had written too many. The final process could only be a hasty and expedient stitching together of the patches. The result is an opera in which some major incidents, such as the crucial encounter between the hero Ruslan and the villainous dwarf Chernomor, are hastily passed over in favour of extended irrelevancies such as the whole of Act 3, which has no place in Pushkin's poem. Elsewhere certain events are incomprehensible because some essential part of Pushkin's tale has been omitted. Yet the quality of Glinka's music is often higher than that of *A Life for the Tsar*. Because the subject of *Ruslan and Lyudmila* is not specifically Russian, it did not prompt Glinka again to compose music with affinities to Russian folk music. What it did offer were powerful and varied imaginative stimuli to which Glinka responded with music of striking novelty; this music provided a rich store of materials, manners and techniques upon which later composers could draw. Chernomor's march, for example, was the model for those little musical grotesques that have decorated Russian music not only in Musorgsky but up to Prokofiev and Stravinsky. In the music for Chernomor, Naina and their followers, and for Ratmir, is to be found the source of the orientalism and 'magic' idiom of later Russian music, while Ruslan and Svetozar's court

2. *Autograph MS of the beginning of Finn's ballad from Act 2 of Glinka's 'Ruslan and Lyudmila' composed 1837–42*

elicited from Glinka a pseudo-archaic, heroic manner; this was formed by allying melodic breadth and rhythmic virility to sturdy or dissonant harmony, at times abetted by touches of local colour (notably the combination of the piano and harp to mimic the sound of the gusli).

In other respects *Ruslan and Lyudmila* represents a retreat from *A Life for the Tsar*, for Glinka largely abandoned his flexible recitative manner, and there is only one clear leitmotif, the whole-tone scale associated with Chernomor. When he used this device Glinka did not abandon tonal chords; instead it serves to unstabilize the music harmonically, as a musical embodiment of Chernomor's magic manoeuvres. The whole-tone scale appears for the first time in the coda to the overture, then in the Abduction Scene of Act 1, the finest dramatic scene that Glinka ever wrote. Finally it occurs in the struggle between Ruslan and Chernomor in Act 4, where Ruslan opposes the dwarf's whole-tone assaults with a firm E major, making one of the most imaginative musico-dramatic conceptions in 19th-century music. Elsewhere the music can be merely conventional. The cowardly Farlaf's music derives from Italian *opera buffa*, Lyudmila's cavatina in Act 1 is overburdened with Italianate coloratura, and the dances of Act 3 are but routine ballet music. The characterization, too, is inconsistent. Both Ruslan and Lyudmila are well-rounded characters, but Ratmir and Finn, the magician, diminish in interest as the opera proceeds. Nor is the treatment of atmosphere always satisfactory, for, while Glinka could deftly conjure up enchantment, he signally failed to convey the sensuous elements in Pushkin's poem, evoking sultriness but not a trace of sexual passion. Although one of his stylistic fingerprints, the chromatic flattened 6th, had appeared often in his earlier music, it was in *Ruslan and Lyudmila* that Glinka first used chromaticism at all extensively. However, Glinka applied chromaticism in quite a different manner from Tchaikovsky or Wagner. He rarely used it for emotional purposes (his chromaticism is almost always descending), except to add extra pathos in a coda. Sometimes he used it to produce strident dissonance, but mostly to provide touches of colour.

It is in *Ruslan and Lyudmila* that Glinka's variation treatment of folk melody crystallizes into the changing background technique, another item in the rich legacy of this opera to later Russian composers. This technique is used, for example, in Finn's ballad (see fig.2) and the Head's narrative in Act 2, but is seen to best advantage in the ravishing Persian Chorus that opens Act 3, where the tune remains intact throughout five statements while the orchestral background is completely changed on each repetition. The reflection of the outlines of Russian folksong is less strong than in *A Life for the Tsar*; *Ruslan and Lyudmila* contains more borrowed folk material, though it is mostly of oriental origin. The source for much of the melodic material of the opera appears to have been Ruslan's great aria in Act 2, one of the first pieces to be composed. These thematic affinities help to give the whole work a certain consistency which compensates in part for the fewer quotations of earlier material in the final stages of *Ruslan and Lyudmila* than in *A Life for the Tsar*.

CHAPTER THREE

1843–57

I Paris, Spain and 'Kamarinskaya'

Bitterly disappointed by the cool reception of his opera *Ruslan and Lyudmila* at its first performances, Glinka spent the next year in dejected inactivity. Finally the urge to travel was reawakened, and in June 1844 he set out for Paris. There his spirits revived, and he quickly established a full social life, particularly with his compatriots in the French capital. By far the most important events of his Paris stay were his meetings with Berlioz, whose mordant wit he enjoyed, and whose talk on music in general and on his own works in particular Glinka found very instructive. In March 1845 Berlioz included excerpts from Glinka's operas in one of his 'monster' concerts, and Glinka scored a *succès d'estime* with a concert he himself promoted four weeks later. His pleasure was crowned by an article about him which Berlioz contributed to the *Journal des débats*. Yet even more important for him than this public fame was the opportunity to devote several months to the study of Berlioz's music, including some pieces as yet unpublished. As a result, Glinka's own creative future became clear to him, and he resolved to compose some *fantaisies pittoresques* for orchestra which, 'employing perfect instruments and perfect performing technique', would 'communicate equally with connoisseurs and the ordinary public'. For some time he had been drawn towards

Spain, and he decided to go there: both folk music and visual impressions might provide the stimulus for these pieces, perhaps also for a Spanish opera. In May he left Paris, crossed the Pyrenees, and passed the summer in Valladolid, where Don Santiago Hernandez, the Spanish servant he had engaged in Paris, had relations. In mid-September Glinka arrived in Madrid and set about the first of his *fantaisies pittoresques*, the First Spanish Overture. This is a very attractive piece deployed as a sonata structure, in which a traditional Spanish *jota aragonesa* generates both subjects as a series of varia-tions. The orchestral palette is sparkling, with local colour provided by castanets and by harp and pizzicato strings imitating guitars. An attempt to arrange for a hearing of the work in a concert of his own music proved abortive, and in December he left Madrid for the milder winter climate of Granada. He pursued his leis-urely study of Spanish music, and immersed himself in the customs of the country. On returning to Madrid in March 1846, Glinka and Don Santiago parted com-pany, but the latter was soon replaced by Don Pedro Fernandez, a young music student who was to be Glinka's servant, friend and secretary for the next nine years. After passing the next winter in Seville, Glinka had had enough of Spain, and in June 1847 returned, via Paris, to Novospasskoye.

Apart from the First Spanish Overture, Glinka wrote no music while abroad. He spent the next winter in Smolensk and once again started to compose, producing some songs and piano pieces. After a dinner given in his honour he was drawn into a demanding social life in which he was expected to exhibit his performing talents; wishing to escape from this, he decided in March 1848 to return to Paris. However, on arriving in Warsaw, he heard that his application for a passport had been refused. As a result, he spent much of the next year in the city. It was to prove a rich time for composition, for although a project for a piece on the medieval warrior Il'ya Muromets came to nothing, he did complete three fine songs and two orchestral pieces. The first of the latter works was *Recuerdos de Castilla*, based on four Spanish tunes; dissatisfied with the piece, he expanded it in 1851 into *Souvenir d'une nuit d'été à Madrid*, also known as the Second Spanish Overture. In this piece the sonata pattern of the First Spanish Overture is abandoned in favour of a freer structure in which sections based upon the Spanish tunes are juxtaposed, each being built mostly by simple variation procedures. The result is a kaleidoscopic composition of a striking but unpretentious inventiveness exceeded only by that of the second orchestral piece of Glinka's Warsaw stay, *Kamarinskaya*. Unlike the Spanish Overtures, *Kamarinskaya* is a purely musical conception, in which Glinka's teeming fantasy is released by the perception of a relationship between two otherwise dissimilar Russian folk melodies, the pert *Kamarinskaya* tune and a wedding song. In this piece Glinka's changing background technique receives its most extended use, for the three-bar phrase of *Kamarinskaya* is repeated some 70 times in the course of the work against different accompaniments. The simple audacity of the piece and, above all, the suggestions in its seemingly inexhaustible inventiveness were to exercise a profound influence upon later Russian composers. Tchaikovsky even went as far as declaring that the Russian symphonic school 'is all in *Kamarinskaya*, just as the whole oak is in the acorn'.

II Final years

In November 1848 Glinka returned to St Petersburg, but only six months later he was back in Warsaw. While he was there he wrote three more songs which, like those he had composed in the previous year, confirm the growing influence of Chopin on his music. This is most clearly seen in the richer chromaticism and greater enterprise of his tonal schemes, and in the tendency of the coda to become the climax of the piece rather than merely a formal rounding-off of the structure. Of the Warsaw songs the tender *Adel'* ('Adèle'), one of Glinka's loveliest compositions, and the rumbustious *Zazdravnïy kubok* ('The toasting cup'), both to poems by Pushkin, reveal the extremes of expression which Glinka could command. Perhaps the most fascinating of these late songs is the setting of Gretchen's *Meine Ruh' ist hin* (from a Russian translation of *Faust*), a remarkable piece which must suffer by comparison with Schubert's unforgettable setting but which has its own atmosphere of melancholy rather than pathos. After these, apart from the haunting song *Finskiy zaliv* ('The Gulf of Finland') and the expansion of *Recuerdos de Castilla* into the Second Spanish Overture, Glinka wrote no music of importance. In September 1851 he returned to St Petersburg. During the winter his health deteriorated: spring brought a little improvement, and his spirits were further revived in April by a very successful concert of his music by the Philharmonic Society, which elected him an honorary member. It was at this time that he dictated to Serov his observations on the use of the orchestra.

In June 1852 he set out for western Europe. A fortnight in Paris further improved his health, but in

3. Mikhail Glinka with his sister, Lyudmila Shestakova, in 1852

Toulouse his physical condition compelled him to abandon a planned visit to Spain. Back in Paris he tinkered with a Ukrainian Symphony on the subject of Gogol's Cossack hero Taras Bul'ba, but dropped it when he found that he could not 'get out of the German rut in the development' (*Memoirs*). In the end he remained in Paris nearly two years, living quietly and making frequent visits to the Jardin des Plantes and, his special delight, its menagerie. In March 1854 war broke out between France and Russia; compelled to leave Paris, he was back in St Petersburg in May.

There is no doubt that a great change came over 'Glinka in his last years, and that this served to inhibit his compositional processes. Age was partly to blame, but also the fact that, as he put it, 'when I settle into work, I involuntarily hear the music of others, and this distracts me'. He admitted that the only music that did not bore him was 'Classical' music, in which category he included Bach, Handel and Gluck. Vladimir Stasov, his first biographer, who first met him in 1849, also asserted that he felt an increasing isolation through the constriction of his social circle. Company was certainly necessary to him, and he had often liked to compose while sitting on the fringe of some convivial, even noisy gathering. It is clear that he now sensed that he was near the end of his career, and his last three years were spent in putting his past in order, first by assembling his *Memoirs* in 1854, and then by going through his own compositions and writing out from memory pieces that had been lost. Since his mother's death in 1851 he had grown increasingly close to his sister, Lyudmila Shestakova, and she lavished much care on him during his last years. He worked further on the Ukrainian

Symphony, and in 1855 even started a third opera, *Dvumuzhnitsa* ('The bigamist'), based on a very successful play by Shakhovskoy. He orchestrated a few of his own songs, and also some compositions by other composers. Finally his musical interests fastened upon even earlier music, and he conceived the idea that it would be possible 'to unite Western fugue and the requirements of our music in the bonds of a legitimate marriage' to create a style for church music in which he might compose. In May 1856 he set out for Berlin to study Western contrapuntal techniques with Dehn, who put before him Lassus and Palestrina as models. Despite mountainous labours, there was no sign that he was approaching a successful synthesis before he died. But he never lost faith in this possibility, and his last months were generally quiet and contented.

One tiny product of his time in Berlin was his fifth set of vocal exercises, a final reflection of his lifelong preoccupation with the art of singing; they reveal those ideals of naturalness, clarity and good intonation which he sought in other singers, and himself displayed in his unrivalled performances of his own songs. While in Berlin he also had frequent contact with Meyerbeer, who conducted the Trio from *A Life for the Tsar* at a court concert on 21 January 1857. Soon after the concert Glinka caught a cold; he died within a fortnight, on 15 February. He was buried in Berlin, but in May his body was exhumed and taken back to St Petersburg for its final interment.

CHAPTER FOUR

Style and influence

Glinka was a man of small character, and it is not surprising that his music is not marked by strong individual traits which might have constituted a more vividly or assertively personal style of composition. The principal way in which the stages of his creative course may be defined is through the influences which he successively admitted to his own music. Only a few of his songs were in any way 'personal', and these were among his slighter drawing-room compositions. Like many later Russian composers he depended to an unusual degree on a stimulus to his imaginative process, and this he found not only in poetry and drama, but also in Spanish and Eastern music, and other sources. He responded to these stimuli unpredictably, and his music is consistent neither in style nor in quality.

It is impossible to grasp the extent of Glinka's achievement without taking into account the musical situation into which he was born. During the 18th century the domination of Russian culture by Western styles became absolute. Even Russian folksong types did not escape foreign influence, for in the urban areas there developed the 'town song' in which the national character was contaminated by Western elements, fostering a more regular rhythmic pulse and phrase structure, a greater use of sequence, and melodic contours conditioned by the harmonic practices of Western music.

Although Glinka was intimately acquainted with the purer rural folk music during his early childhood, it was the bastard town tradition and particularly the imported Western styles which monopolized his attention during his schooldays and early manhood in St Petersburg. When, during his three years in Italy, he began to turn his attention seriously to composing music with a genuinely Russian character, he could not dispense with Western compositional techniques any more than could men of the preceding generation, like Cavos and Titov. Nevertheless Glinka was able to go much farther than these men in incorporating elements from indigenous Russian music into his own work, as can be heard in the melodic shapes of *A Life for the Tsar*, which constantly reflect those of folk music.

However, if Glinka's nationalism had offered no more than the melodic fund of his first opera, he would never have become such a potent influence on later Russian music. Also, if he had composed a particularly individual brand of music, it would have influenced only another composer who could have identified with it readily; in any case, the style (and influence) would have passed quickly into history as the musical language evolved. As it is, Glinka's most valuable legacy is not his folk stylizations, but the bold and original concepts of musical language and form that sprang from his remarkable combination of a vivid (and very Russian) musical imagination with a keen-eared intelligence. The latter quality was also revealed throughout his life in his very precise criticisms of performers, especially singers, as well as in the clear texture of his orchestration in which the role of each component in the sound is finely calculated. In compositional matters this sharp musical intelligence and imagination produced music that was not only striking and novel but also completely lucid. Unlike the German, who found it natural to fashion a large-scale design out of a musical fabric woven from small melodic entities and spanned out upon an evolving tonal scheme, the Russian thought more readily in terms of full melodic statements and subsequent variation. It was Glinka whose clear-headed perceptions devised such forms and procedures that could serve as models for later Russian composers.

The full revelation of Glinka's originality and Russianness is in *Ruslan and Lyudmila*, where the rhythm has a recognizably Russian exuberance and where the harmony asserts at times a pungency and a colouristic use of chromaticism quite distinct from conventional Western practices. With its changing background movements, its heroic, magic and oriental idioms, and its element of caricature, *Ruslan and Lyudmila* proved to be the most seminal work in the history of Russian music. Of Glinka's other pieces, only *Kamarinskaya* had a comparable influence; from it, Tchaikovsky said, 'all later Russian composers to the present day (and I, of course, among them) draw, in the most obvious fashion, contrapuntal and harmonic combinations as soon as they have to develop a Russian dance-tune'.

The first composer of major importance to be influenced by Glinka was Balakirev; during Glinka's last years the two composers knew each other well, and Glinka gave Balakirev strong encouragement and approval. In the Overture on the themes of three Russian songs Balakirev followed the precedent of Glinka's First Spanish Overture and applied the changing background method within the structure of a sonata movement. In the oriental fantasia for piano, *Islamey*, he employed the method even more consistently, using a broad formal scheme that closely resembles that of *Kamarinskaya*. Tchaikovsky, too, used the changing background technique in parts of his Second Symphony, notably in the first subject of the finale; later in this same movement he used the whole-tone scale in the bass, following the example of Glinka in Chernomor's music from *Ruslan and Lyudmila*. Rimsky-Korsakov likewise used the whole-tone scale on occasions, and the magic idiom and lyricism in his operas, and the scoring in his earlier works, was directly modelled upon Glinka's styles and practices. In the development of Tchaikovsky's *Romeo and Juliet* there also occurs another feature of Chernomor's music, the alternation around a single held note of two chords which are unrelated except that they have this note in common. This particular harmonic trick was to become a minor fingerprint of Russian harmony.

The stage-picture style of Glinka's two operas established the dramatic manner followed by many later Russian composers. It is to be seen in the greatest of late 19th-century Russian operas, Musorgsky's *Boris Godunov*, most obviously in the Coronation Scene, which is modelled directly on the final scene of *A Life for the Tsar*. Musorgsky was also indebted to this opera for something of his solemn manner (notably in the Monastery and Duma scenes of *Boris Godunov*), and he was a splendid disciple of Glinka as a caricaturist: the rogue monks in *Boris Godunov* and especially the gnome and two Jews in *Pictures at an Exhibition* are the successors to Glinka's Chernomor and Naina; other grotesque musical characterizations are to be found among Musorgsky's songs. Although Borodin also showed a gift for such caricature, it was Glinka's heroic manner that proved of greater importance to him, not only in substantial sections of his opera *Prince Igor*, but also in the Second Symphony. He also used the whole-tone scale prominently in his song *Spyashchaya knyazhna* ('The sleeping princess'), and his free use of unresolved 2nds both in this song and elsewhere in his work was probably fostered by such examples of dissonance in Glinka's work.

Besides the influence of his music, Glinka provided the next generation of Russian composers with an example of creative independence to fortify their moral courage in their individual researches for their own musical personalities; even more important, he furnished not only these, but Russian composers of later generations, with an abundance of musical attitudes and procedures upon which they could draw to fertilize their own creative processes. Thus, although their works might be very different in musical style from anything Glinka wrote, they would never have been written in the way they were but for his example. Prokofiev and especially Stravinsky exhibit the same clarity of sound that Glinka had established in his orchestration, and both were masters of caricature. Stravinsky openly admired Glinka, and Dyagilev, after hearing the first part of *Apollon musagète*, commented that 'one feels it is in part Glinka and part 16th-century Italian'. Stravinsky himself explicitly recognized his debt by giving one third of the dedication of his opera *Mavra* to the composer in whose tradition the work was consciously composed.

WORKS

Edition: *M. I. Glinka: Polnoye sobraniye sochineniy*; ed. V. Ya. Shebalin and others (Moscow, 1955–69) [G]
(all published in St Petersburg unless otherwise stated)

Numbers in right-hand margins denote references in the text.

STAGE
(all productions in St Petersburg; * = full score, † = vocal score)

Title	Description	Libretto	Composed	Published	Produced	Remarks	G	
Rokeby	opera	Scott	1824	—	—	sketches for entr'acte only	xvii, 139	9
Mar'ina Roshcha [Marina Grove]	opera	V. Zhukovsky	1834	—	—	sketches; used in Zhizn' za tsarya	—	9
Zhizn' za tsarya [A Life for the Tsar]	opera, 4, epilogue	G. Rosen	1834–6	*1881, ov. only 1858; †1856 or 1857	9 Dec 1836	ov, arr. pf 4 hands, G v, 106; pt. of epilogue arr. solo pf. G vi. 255	*xii/a, b, suppl. †xiii	2, 8, 9–12, 14, 17, 19, 27, 29, 31, 77, 78, 83, 147, 164, 168, 169, 170, 209
Moldavanka i tsiganka [The Moldavian girl and the gypsy girl]	aria with chorus	—	1836	Moscow, 1947	20 April 1836	for K. Bakhturin's play	vii, 3	
Scene at the monastery		N. Kukol'nik	1837	*1881 †1856 or 1857	30 Oct 1837		—	
Knyaz' Kholmsky [Prince Kholmsky]	incidental music	—	1840	1862	12 Oct 1841	ov., 3 songs and 4 entr'actes for Kukol'nik's tragedy; Evreyskaya pesnya used as no.2 of Proshchaniye s Peterburgom, 1840: other 2 songs arr. 1v, pf, G x. 271, 273	vii, 37	15–16
Tarantella	stage piece, I. Myatlev reciter, chorus, orch		1841	1862	25 Jan 1841		viii, 5	
Ruslan i Lyudmila [Ruslan and Lyudmila]	opera, 5	Pushkin, Kukol'nik, V. Shirkov, N. Markevich, M. Gedeonov	1837–42	*1878, ov. only 1858; †1856	9 Dec 1842	pt. of Finn's ballad and pt. of Lyudmila's scena arr. pf. 1852, G vi. 251, 254	*xiv/a, b, suppl. †xv	12, 14–20, 21, 30, 31, 61, 64, 83, 91, 159, 169–70, 194
Dvumuzhnitsa [The bigamist]	opera	A. A. Shakhovskoy	1855	—	—	sketches, lost	—	27

ORCHESTRAL

Title	Composed	Published	Remarks	G	
Overture, D	c1822–6	Moscow, 1955		i, 129	
Overture, g	c1822–6	Moscow, 1955		i, 85	
Andante cantabile and rondo	c1823	Moscow, 1955		i, 3	
Symphony, Bb	c1824	Moscow, 1969	inc.	xvii,142	7
Symphony on two Russian themes	1834	Moscow, 1948	inc.	i, 193	7, 8, 12
Valse-fantaisie, b	1839–56	1878	orig. for pf, 1839; orchd 1845, lost; reorchd 1856	ii, 213	
Capriccio brillante	1845	1858	on the Jota aragonesa; also known as First Spanish Overture	ii, 3	22, 23, 30, 196
Kamarinskaya	1848	1860	arr. pf 4 hands (1856)	ii, 105	21, 23, 30, 31, 92
Recuerdos de Castilla	1848	Moscow, 1956	expanded into Souvenir d'une nuit d'été à Madrid, 1851 (1858); also known as Second Spanish Overture. G ii, 143	ii, 71	23, 24, 196
Polonaise, F	1855	1856	on a Spanish bolero theme	ii, 185	
Concerto for orchestra, Eb		Moscow, 1969	inc.	xvii, 185	

INSTRUMENTAL

Title	Composed	Published	Remarks	G	
Variations on a theme of Mozart, Eb, pf/harp	1822	by 1856	theme from Die Zauberflöte; orig. lost, but written down from Lyudmila Shestakova's memory	vi, 13, 20	4, 6, 22
Septet, Eb, ob, bn, hn, 2 vn, vc, db	c1823	Moscow, 1957	inc.	iii, 3	
Str qt, D	1824	Moscow, 1948	inc.	iii, 67	
Variations on an original theme, F, pf	c1824	Moscow, 1878	—	vi, 1	
Sonata, pf, va	1825–8	Moscow, 1932	2 movts only	iv, 3	
Variations on the song Sredi dolinï rovnïye [Among the gentle valleys], a, pf	1826	1839		vi, 51	
Variations on a theme from Cherubini's Faniska, Bb, pf	1826 or 1827	1839		vi, 55	
Variations on Benedetta sia la madre, E, pf	1826	by 1829		vi, 26, 39	
[5] nouvelles quadrilles françaises, pf	?1826	by 1829		vi, 267	
Cotillon, Bb, pf	by 1828	1829		vi, 67	
Mazurka, G, pf	by 1828	1829		vi, 70	
[4] nouvelles contredanses, pf	by 1828	1829		vi, 71	
Nocturne, Eb, pf/harp	1828	Moscow, 1878		vi, 62	

Title	Date	Publication	Remarks	Vol.
Finskaya pesnya [Finnish song], D, pf	1829	1830		vi. 77, 78
Trot de cavalerie, G, pf 4 hands	1829 or 1830	Moscow, 1878		v. 3
Trot de cavalerie, C, pf 4 hands	1829 or 1830	Moscow, 1878		v. 7
Str qt, F	1830	Moscow, 1878	arr. pf 4 hands, 1830 (Moscow, 1878), G v. 63	iii. 125 4
Proshchal'niy val's [Farewell waltz], G, pf	1831	1834		vi. 117
Rondino brillante on a theme from Bellini's I Capuleti e i Montecchi, Bb, pf	1831	Milan, 1832		vi. 104
Variazioni brillanti on a theme from Donizetti's Anna Bolena, A, pf	1831	Milan, 1831		vi. 79
Variations on 2 themes from the ballet Chao-Kang, D, pf	1831	Milan, 1831		vi. 93
Divertimento brillante on themes from Bellini's La sonnambula, Ab, pf, 2 vn, va, vc, db	1832	Milan, 1832		iv. 29
Impromptu en galop-on the barcarolle from Donizetti's L'elisir d'amore, Bb, pf 4 hands	1832	Milan, 1832		v. 9
Serenata on themes from Anna Bolena, Eb, pf, harp, bn, hn, va, vc, db	1832	Milan, 1832		iv/suppl.
Gran sestetto originale, Eb, pf, str qnt	1832	Milan, 1832		iv. 81
Trio pathétique, d, pf, cl, bn	1832	Moscow, 1878		iv. 173
Variazioni on a theme from I Capuleti e i Montecchi, C, pf	1832	Milan, 1832		vi. 118
Variations on Alyab'yev's Solovey [The nightingale], e, pf	1833	1841		vi. 135
3 fugues, pf:	1833 or 1834			
3-pt., Eb		Moscow, 1885		vi. 147, 149
3-pt., a		by 1844		vi. 151, 154
4-pt., D		Moscow, 1885		vi. 157
Mazurka, Ab, pf	1833 or 1834	1834		vi. 160
Mazurka, F, pf	1833 or 1834	1834		vi. 161
Capriccio on Russian themes, A, pf 4 hands	1834	Moscow, 1904		v. 19 7–8
Motif de chant national, C, pf	?1834–6	Moscow, 1969		xvii. 227
Mazurka, F, pf	?1835	c1836		vi. 162
[5] contredanses, pf	1838	1839		vi. 166
Waltz, Eb, pf	1838	1839		vi. 164
Waltz, Bb, pf	1838	1839		vi. 170
La couventine, contredanses, pf	1839	1839	orig. for orch, lost	vi. 188
Grande valse, G, pf	1839	1839	orig. for orch, lost	vi. 175
Polonaise, E, pf	1839	1839	orig. for orch, lost	vi. 184

35

Title	Composed	Published	Remarks	G
La séparation, nocturne. f, pf	1839	1839		vi. 204
Le regret, nocturne, pf	1839	—	inc., lost; used in no.11 of Proshchaniye s Peterburgom, 1840	—
				14
Valse-fantaisie, b, pf	1839	1839	orchd 1845, lost; reorchd 1856 (1878)	vi. 193
Galopade, Eb, pf	1838 or 1839	1839		vi. 174
Bolero, d, pf	1840	1840	arr. 1v, pf as no.3 of Proshchaniye s Peterburgom, 1840	vi. 208
Tarantella, a, pf	1843	1850	on the Russian song Vo pole beryoza stoyala [In the field there stood a birch tree]	vi. 217
Mazurka, c, pf	?1843	1843		vi. 219
Privet otchizne [A greeting to my native land], pf	1847	?1855		
1 Souvenir d'une mazurka, Bb				vi. 220
2 Barcarolle, G				vi. 225
3 Prière, A			arr. 1v, pf, 1855	vi. 232
4 Thème écossais varié			based on the Irish tune The Last Rose of Summer	vi. 240
Polka, d, pf	1849	Moscow, 1878		vi. 250
Mazurka, C, pf	1852	Moscow, 1878		vi. 256
Polka, Bb, pf 4 hands	1840–52	1852	conceived 1840, written down 1852	v. 47
Detskaya pol'ka [Children's polka], Bb, pf	1854	1861		vi. 257
Las mollares, G, pf	?1855	1856	transcr. of Andalusian dance	vi. 264
Leggieramente, E, pf	—	Moscow, 1969		xvii. 170

5, 22, 27, 28

VOCAL
(all for 1v, pf unless otherwise stated; • = full score, ° = vocal score)

Title	Translation	Composed	Published	Text	G
Moya arfa	My harp	1824; orig. lost, written down 1855	1862	Scott, trans. K. Bakhturin	x. 1
Ne iskushay menya bez nuzhdi 1v, pf	Do not tempt me needlessly	1825	before 1854	E. Baratïnsky	x. 2, 6
2vv, pf					ix. 23
Pleurons, pleurons sur la Russie, prologue on the death of Alexander I and the accession of Nicholas I. T, SATB, pf, db		1826	Moscow, 1894	Olidor	xvi. 17

Title	Translation / description	Text	Composed	Published	Ref
Akh ti, dushechka, krasna devitsa	Ah, my sweetheart, thou art a beautiful maiden	folksong	1826	c1830	x. 18
Bedniy pevets	The poor singer	V. Zhukovsky	1826	1829 or 1830	x. 10
Utesheniye	Consolation	Uhland, trans. Zhukovsky	1826	1830	x. 14, 16
Bozhe sil vo dni smyateniya. A. T. B. pf	O God, preserve our strength in the days of confusion	biblical	1827 or 1828	Moscow, 1878	ix. 28
Chto, krasotka molodaya	Why do you cry, young beauty	A. Del'vig	1827	c1830	x. 40
Gor'ko, gor'ko mne	Bitter, bitter it is for me	A. Rimsky-Korsakov	1827	1831	x. 28
Pamyat' serdtsa	Heart's memory	K. Batyushkov	1877	1829	x. 19
Ya lyublyu, ti mne tverdila [also known as Le baiser with Fr. text by S. Golitsïn (1854)]	'I love' was your assurance	A. Rimsky-Korsakov	1827	before 1854	x. 24
Pour un moment [also pubd with Russ. text, Odin lish' mig (1855)]		S. Golitsïn	1827 or 1828	1834	x. 35, 38
Skazhi zachem	Tell me why	Golitsïn	1827 or 1828	1829	x. 31
Mio ben ricordati A. T. pf			1827 or 1828	1829	ix. 43
S. pf				1878	x. 63
A. ignobil core. B. male chorus, orch, inc.			1828 or 1834	Moscow, 1969	xvii. 205
Due canzonette italiane:					
1 Ah, rammenta, o bella Irene			1828	Moscow, 1891	x. 73
2 Alla cetra					x. 76
Come di gloria al nome. SATB, str			1828 or 1829	Moscow, 1960	ix. 71
Dovunque il guardo giro. B, pf			1828	Moscow, 1955	x. 58
Ho perduto, il mio tesoro. T, pf			1828	1864	x. 47
La notte omai s'appressa. SATB, str, inc.			1828	Moscow, 1969	xvii. 196
Mi sento il cor trafiggere. T, pf			1828	1864	x. 42
O Dafni che di quest'anima. S, pf			1828	Moscow, 1955	x. 68
Pensa che questo instante. A, pf			1828	Moscow, 1955	x. 56
Piangendo ancora rinascer suole. S, pf			1828	Moscow, 1955	x. 61
Pur nel sonno. S, pf			1828	1864	x. 52
Sogna chi crede d'esser felice. A, T, T, B, str			1828	Moscow, 1954	ix. 92
Tu sei figlia. S, pf			1828	1864	x. 50
Akh ti, noch' li, nochenka	O thou black night	Del'vig	1828	1831	x. 97, 98
Dedushka, devitsi raz mne govorili	The maids once told me, grandfather	Del'vig	1828	1829	x. 89, 90

5

Title	Translation	Text	Composed	Published	G	
Molitva, S, A, T, B, pf	Prayer	Pushkin	1828	Moscow, 1878	ix, 35	
Ne poy, krasavitsa, pri mne	Sing not, thou beauty, in my presence	Pushkin	1828	1831	x, 92	
Razocharovaniye	Disenchantment	Golitsïn	1828	1851	x, 82, 85	5
Zabudu l' ya	Shall I forget	Golitsïn	1828	1832	x, 94	
Golos s tovo sveta	A voice from the other world	Schiller, trans. Zhukovsky	1829	1832	x, 100	5
Noch' osennyaya, lyubeznaya, 7 studies, A, pf	O gentle autumn night	A. Rimsky-Korsakov	1829	1831	x, 96	
			1829 or 1830	1864	xi, 13	
Il desiderio [also known as Zhelaniye]		F. Romani	1832	Milan, 1834	x, 104, 108	
L'iniquo voto, S, pf		Pini	1832	Milan, 1833	x, 123	6
Pobeditel'	The conqueror	Uhland, trans. Zhukovsky	1832	Moscow, 1835	x, 112	
Venetsianskaya noch', 6 studies, S, pf	Venetian night	I. Kozlov	1832	Moscow, 1835	x, 117, 119	
			1833	Moscow, 1952	xi, 39	
Dubrava shumit	The leafy grove howls	Schiller, trans. Zhukovsky	1834	1856	x, 139, 144	
Ne govori: lyubov proydyot	Say not that love will pass	Del'vig	1834	1843	x, 133	
Ne nazïvay eyo nebesnoy [orchd 1855, G viii, 119]	Call her not heavenly	N. Pavlov	1834	Moscow, 1834	x, 151	
Tol'ko uznal ya tebya	I had but recognized you	Del'vig	1834	Moscow, 1834	x, 159	
Ya zdes', Inezil'ya	I am here, Inezilla	Pushkin, after B. Cornwall	1834	by 1850	x, 161	
Exercises for smoothing and perfecting the voice			1835 or 1836	1903	xi, 59	
Nochnoy smotr, fantasia, orchd c1836–40, G viii, 93; reorchd 1855, G viii, 107	The night review	Zhukovsky	1836	?1838	x, 165	9–10
Comic canon a 4, collab. V. Odoyevsky			1836	1837	—	
Velik nash Bog, polonaise, SATB, orch	Our God is great	Pushkin, Zhukovsky, P. Vyazemsky, M. Wielhorski, V. Sollogub	1837	*Moscow, 1881 †Moscow, 1878	*xvi, 47	
Kheruvimskaya, 6-pt. chorus	Cherubim's song	biblical	1837	Moscow, 1878	—	
Gde nasha roza?	Where is our rose?	Pushkin	1837	1839	x, 182, 183, 185	14
Stansï	Stanzas	Kukol'nik	1837	1838	x, 173	

Title	Translation	Text author	Composed	Published	Ref	Note
Gimn khozyainu, cantata, T, orch, inc.	Hymn to the master	N. Markevich	1838	1903	viii, 141	14
Gude viter	The wind blows	V. Zabella	1838	1839	x. 188	
Ne shchebechi, soloveyku	Sing not, o nightingale	Zabella	1838	1839	x. 186	
Nochnoy zefir	The night zephyr	Pushkin	1838	1839	x. 190	
Somneniye, A, harp, vn [also for 1v, pf, G x, 176]	Doubt	Kukol'nik	1838	1839	ix, 108, 113	14
V krovi gorit ogon' zhelan'ya	The fire of longing burns in my heart	Pushkin	1838	1839	x. 180	
Vi ne pridyote vnov, S, S, pf	You will not return	Glinka	1837 or 1838	1854	ix, 49	
Esli vstrechus' s toboy	If I shall meet you	A. Kol'tsov	1839	1840	x. 199	
Priznaniye	Declaration	Pushkin	1839	c1858	x. 280	
Svadebnaya pesnya [also known as Severnaya svezda (The North Star)]	Wedding song	E. Rostopchina	1839	1862	x. 194	
Zatsvetet cheremukha	The bird-cherry tree is blossoming	Rostopchina	1839	1862	x. 197	
Kak sladko s toboyu mne bit'	How sweet it is to be with you	P. Rindin	1840	1843	x, 277	
Proshchal'naya pesnya vospitannits Ekaterinskovo Instituta, S, SSA, orch	Farewell song of the pupils of the Ekaterinsky Institute	P. Obodovsky	1840	*Moscow, 1903	*xvi, 69	
Proshchaniye s Peterburgom	A farewell to St Petersburg	Kukol'nik	1840	†Moscow, 1878 1840		15
Romans 1 Romans	Romance				x. 206	
2 Evreyskaya pesnya [from Knyaz' Kholmsky]	Hebrew song				x. 209	
3 Bolero [orig. for pf, 1840]					x. 211	
4 Cavatina					x. 215	
5 Kolïbel'naya pesnya [arr. 1v, str, 1840 (Moscow, 1924), G ix, 120]	Cradle song				x. 220	
6 Poputnaya pesnya	Travelling song				x. 226	15
7 Fantasia					x. 232	
8 Barcarolle					x. 240	
9 Virtus antiqua					x. 245	
10 Zhavoronok	The lark				x. 250	
11 K Molli [based on unfinished nocturne Le regret, pf, 1839]	To Molly				x. 254	
12 Proshchal'naya pesnya, 1v, TBB, pf	Song of farewell				x. 259	
Ya pomnyu chudnoye mgnoven'ye	I recall a wonderful moment	Pushkin	1840	1842	x. 201	14
4 vocal exercises			1840 or 1841	Moscow, 1963	xi. 54	
Lyublyu tebya, milaya roza	I love you, dear rose	I. Samarin	1842	1843	x, 281	
K ney	To her	Mickiewicz, trans. Golitsin	1843	1843	x, 283	

Title	Translation	Text	Composed	Published	G	
Milochka	Darling		1847	1848	x, 287	
Ti skoro menya pozabudesh' [orchd 1855 (Moscow, 1885), G viii, 133]	Soon you will forget me	Yu. Zhadovsky	1847	1848	x, 290	
Zazdravnaya pesnya, 1v, chorus	Toasting song		1847	Moscow, 1960	ix, 5	
Tyazhka pechal' i grusten svet	Meine Ruh' ist hin	Goethe, trans. E. Huber	1848	1848	x, 302	24
Slishu li golos tvoy	When I hear your voice	Lermontov	1848	?c1850	x, 294	
Zazdravniy kubok	The toasting cup	Pushkin	1848	1848	x, 296	24
Adel'	Adele	Pushkin	1849	1850	x, 316	24
Meri	Mary	Pushkin, after B. Cornwall	1849	1850	x, 322	
Rozmowa	Conversation	Mickiewicz	1849	Warsaw, 1849	x, 309	
Finskiy zaliv [also known as Palermo]	The Gulf of Finland	Obodovsky	1850	1851	x, 326	
Proshchal'naya pesnya dlya vospitannits obshchestva blagorodnikh devits, SSAA, orch	Farewell song for the pupils of the Society of Genteel Maidens	M. Timayev	1850	*Moscow, 1903 †Moscow, 1880	*xvi, 105	24
Kosa, 1v, SATB, orch	The scythe	A. Rimsky-Korsakov	1854	1855	*viii, 51 †ix, 131	
Molitva, 1v, SATB, orch [orig. for pf, 1847]	Prayer	Lermontov	1855	1855	*viii, 65 †ix, 6	
Ne govori, chto serdtsu bol'no	Say not that it grieves the heart	Pavlov	1856	1856	x, 335	
Ekteniya pervaya, SATB	First litany		?1856	Moscow, 1878		
Da ispravitsya molitva moya, T, T, B	Let my prayer be fulfilled		?1856	Moscow, 1878		
Gimn voskreseniya, T, T, B	Resurrection hymn		1856 or 1857	Moscow, 1969	xviii, 112	
A school of singing			1856 or 1857	Moscow, 1953	xi, 65	27

ORCHESTRATIONS OF WORKS BY OTHER COMPOSERS

Shterich: Waltz on a theme from Weber's Oberon, pf, 1829 (Moscow, 1968), G xviii, 1 27

Hummel: Souvenir d'amitié, nocturne op.99, pf, 1854 (Moscow, 1968), G xviii, 13 27

Dargomïzhsky: Likhoradushka [Fever], song, 1855 (Moscow, 1968), G xviii, 86

Alyab'yev: Solovey [The nightingale], song, 1856 (Moscow, 1889), G xviii, 89 27

For a complete list of works, including the titles of fragmentary and lost compositions, see Brown

BIBLIOGRAPHY

M. Glinka: 'Zametki ob instrumentovke' [Notes on orchestration], 'Prilozheniye instrumentovki k muzïkal'nomu sochineniyu' [The application of orchestration to musical compositions], *Muzïkal'niy i teatral'niy vestnik* (1856), no.2, p.21; no.6, p.99

V. Stasov: 'M. I. Glinka', *Russkiy vestnik* (1857)

L. Shestakova, ed.: 'M. I. Glinka: zapiski', *Russkaya starina*, i (1870), 380, 474, 562: ii (1870), 56, 266, 372, 419–62 (Eng. trans., 1963)

O. Fouque: *Michel Ivanovitch Glinka d'après ses mémoires et sa correspondance* (Paris, 1880)

V. S. [V. Stasov], ed.: *Zapiski M. I. Glinki i perepiska evo s rodnïmi i druz'yami* [Glinka's memoirs and correspondence with his relations and friends] (St Petersburg, 1887)

V. Stasov: 'M. I. Glinka: novïye materialï dlya evo biografii' [New material for his biography], *Russkaya starina*, lxi (1889), 387

N. Findeyzen: *Mikhail Ivanovich Glinka: evo zhizn' i tvorcheskaya deyatel'nost'* [His life and creative activity] (St Petersburg, 1896)

——: *Katalog notnïkh rukopisey, pisem i portretov M. I. Glinka, khranyashchikhsya v rukopisnom otdelenii imperatorskoy publichnoy biblioteki v S-Peterburge* [Catalogue of music manuscripts, letters and portraits of Glinka, contained in the manuscript section of the Imperial Public Library in St Petersburg] (St Petersburg, 1898)

N. Findeyzen, ed.: *M. I. Glinka: polnoye sobraniye pisem* [Complete collection of letters] (St Petersburg, 1907)

M. Calvocoressi: *Glinka: biographie critique* (Paris, 1911)

M. Montagu-Nathan: *Glinka* (London, 1916/*R*1977)

O. von Riesemann: 'Die Musik in Russland vor Glinka', 'Michael Iwanowitsch Glinka', *Monographien zur russischen Musik*, i (Munich, 1923), 1–59, 61–226

A. N. Rimsky-Korsakov, ed.: *M. I. Glinka: zapiski* (Moscow and Leningrad, 1930)

G. Abraham: 'Glinka and his Achievement', *Studies in Russian Music* (London, 1935), 21

M. Calvocoressi and G. Abraham: *Masters of Russian Music* (London, 1936) [incl. G. Abraham: 'Michael Glinka', 13–64]

G. Abraham: '*A Life for the Tsar*', '*Ruslan and Lyudmila*', 'Glinka, Dargomïzhsky and *The Rusalka*', *On Russian Music* (London, 1939), 1–51

B. Asaf'yev: *M. I. Glinka* (Moscow, 1947)

T. Livanova, ed.: *M. I. Glinka: sbornik materialov i stat'yey* [Collection of material and articles] (Moscow, 1950)

A. Ossovsky, ed.: *M. I. Glinka: issledovaniya i materialï* [Researches and material] (Leningrad and Moscow, 1950)

E. Kann-Novikova: *M. I. Glinka: novïye materialï i dokumentï* [New material and documents] (Moscow, 1950–55)

41

A. Orlova and B. Asaf'yev, eds.: *Letopis' zhizni i tvorchestva Glinki* [Record of Glinka's life and work] (Moscow, 1952)

T. Livanova and V. Protopov, eds.: *Glinka: tvorcheskiy put'* [Creative path] (Moscow, 1955)

A. Orlova, ed.: *Glinka v vospominaniyakh sovremennikov* [Glinka in the reminiscences of his contemporaries] (Moscow, 1955)

R. Petzoldt: *Michail Glinka: Sein Leben in Bildern* (Leipzig, 1955)

E. Gordeyeva, ed.: *M. I. Glinka: sbornik stat'yey* [Collection of articles] (Moscow, 1958) [incl. complete bibliography of Russian titles]

V. A. Kiselyov and others, eds.: *Pamyati Glinki 1857–1957: issledovaniya i materialï* [In memory of Glinka 1857–1957: research and material] (Moscow, 1958)

V. Protopopov: *'Ivan Susanin' Glinki* (Moscow, 1961)

A. S. Lyapunov, ed.: *M. I. Glinka: Literaturnïye proizvedeniya i perepiska* [Writings and correspondence] (Moscow, 1973–7)

D. Brown: *Glinka: a Biographical and Critical Study* (London, 1974/ *R*1985)

R. Taruskin: 'Glinka's Ambiguous Legacy and the Birth Pangs of Russian Opera', *19th Century Music*, i (1977–8), 142

——: 'How the Acorn Took Root: a Tale of Russia', *19th Century Music*, vi (1982–3), 189

ALEXANDER BORODIN

Gerald Abraham

David Lloyd-Jones

CHAPTER ONE

Life

I Early life

Alexander Porfir'yevich Borodin was born at St Petersburg (now Leningrad) on 12 November 1833. He was the illegitimate son of the elderly Prince Luka Stepanovich Gedianov (more correctly Gedianishvili) by the 24-year-old Avdot'ya Konstantinovna Antonova, who later married a retired army doctor named Kleinecke. In accordance with common practice, the child was registered as the lawful son of one of his father's serfs, Porfiry Borodin. His mother, beautiful and intelligent, was comfortably off and educated him at home together with a girl cousin, a circumstance that made him a somewhat girlish boy and perhaps helped to mould his nature to its peculiar tenderness and gentleness. As a child he learnt German (from his mother's housekeeper) and French (from a governess); at 13 he began to learn English from a certain John Roper. Later, after a year in Italy, he was able to write scientific essays in Italian. At the age of eight he showed interest in the music and instruments of a military band and was able to reproduce what he had heard at the piano, so his mother engaged a bandsman to give him flute lessons. At nine he developed a precocious calf-love and composed a polka for piano, entitled *Hélène* after the object of his affection. In 1846 his mother took a boarder of her son's age, Mikhail

Shchiglev (later a well-known music teacher), and the boys shared tutors and began a friendship of many years; they had piano lessons from a German named Pormann, a poor though methodical teacher. The boys played the symphonies and overtures of Haydn, Beethoven and Mendelssohn as piano duets, attended Gungl's concerts at Pavlovsk in the summer and the university concerts in the winter. Shchiglev taught himself to play the violin, Borodin the cello, in order to take part in chamber music, and Borodin composed for them in 1847 a so-called 'concerto' for flute and piano and a little trio for violins and cello on themes from *Robert le diable*; a little later came sonatas for flute and cello with piano. At the same time the young Borodin developed an interest in elementary chemistry, making fireworks and so on, and experimenting with galvanism.

In 1850 Borodin entered the Medico-Surgical Academy, where his closest friends were the German students. There he studied botany, zoology, crystallography, anatomy and, above all, chemistry, which became a passion. In his third year he became a student of the chemistry professor N. N. Zinin, who allowed him to work in his laboratory although he sometimes had to reproach him for giving too much time to music. With Shchiglev and two brothers Kirillov (one of whom afterwards became the well-known operatic bass 'Vasil'yev I') Borodin formed a small music group, part of a larger circle that met to play and hear string quintets at the flat of an amateur cellist, Gavrushkevich; there Borodin was usually a listener, being a poor cellist, but he occasionally took part in order to make up a five, playing with special pleasure in the quintets of Boccherini, Onslow and the russianized German Franz

Xaver Gebel, in whose music Borodin 'detected the influence of Russian Moscow'.

On 6 April 1856 Borodin finished the academy course *cum eximia laude*; he was immediately appointed assistant in general pathology and therapy, and posted for practical experience to the second military hospital as a house surgeon, an occupation that left him little time for music. In August 1857 he accompanied a senior oculist to an international ophthalmic congress in Brussels, and also visited Paris. On 17 March 1858 he read a paper, 'On the Action of Ethyl-iodide on Hydrobenzamide and Amarine', to the physico-mathematical section of the Russian Academy of Sciences and it was printed in the bulletin for that year; this was his first published work. On 15 May he received a doctorate for his dissertation *On the Analogy of Arsenical with Phosphoric Acid* and spent the whole summer at Soligalich in the Kostroma government, analysing the mineral waters and studying their medicinal properties. In the autumn of 1859 he was again sent to western Europe to continue his studies. Before he left Russia (13 November) he met for the second time (the first had been three years earlier) the young Musorgsky; but Borodin's three years' absence abroad prevented the ripening of acquaintance. He spent most of his time at Heidelberg, where his friends included Mendeleyev, Sechenov and Botkin, working with the German chemist Erlenmeyer. In July 1860 he made a trip down the Rhine and visited Rotterdam, and in September enjoyed a holiday in Italy with Mendeleyev, visiting Genoa and Rome, after which Borodin went on alone to Paris. In 1861 he and Mendeleyev visited Freiburg to hear the famous organ and attended an international congress at Karlsruhe.

In May 1861 Borodin made the acquaintance at Heidelberg of a 29-year-old Russian lady, Ekaterina Sergeyevna Protopopova, sent to Germany for treatment for tuberculosis; she was a brilliant pianist, an admirer of Chopin, Liszt and Schumann (particularly the last) and she quickly converted Borodin, then under the spell of Mendelssohn, to her tastes. Their friendship developed quickly, and during a visit to Baden-Baden ripened to love; on 22 August they became engaged. At Mannheim they heard *Der fliegende Holländer*, *Tannhäuser* and *Lohengrin* for the first time, and were overpowered by the brilliance of Wagner's orchestration. In October Ekaterina had to go to Italy because of her poor health; Borodin accompanied her to Pisa, intending to leave her there, but was invited by two eminent Italian chemists to stay on and work. They remained at Pisa, or rather at Viareggio, until August 1862, and their idyll was not seriously disturbed by a young girl, Giannina Centoni, who fell in love with Borodin; he 'made a daughter of her' and they corresponded for seven or eight years. Music was not neglected: Borodin and Ekaterina played Bach on the organ of Pisa Cathedral; he even played the cello in the opera orchestra, and during summer 1862 composed the Piano Quintet in C minor and the Tarantella in D major for piano duet. (Two years earlier, at Heidelberg, he had written his String Sextet in D minor in Mendelssohnian style 'to please the Germans'.)

In September 1862 Borodin returned to St Petersburg and on 20 December was appointed reader in chemistry in the Medico-Surgical Academy (becoming full professor on 28 April 1864). From 1863 he also lectured on chemistry in the Institute of Forestry, and in 1863–5 he further augmented his income by translating scientific books for the publisher Wolf. In the same year the new laboratory of the Medico-Surgical Academy, near the Alexandrovsky Bridge, was opened, and Borodin, who had married Ekaterina on 29 April, was given quarters in the same building. There he spent the rest of his life, except for his long summer vacations, and there for ten years he continued his investigation of the products of the condensation of the aldehydes of valerian, enantol and vinegar.

II Productive years
Immediately after his return to Russia in the autumn of 1862 Borodin had met Balakirev and had renewed his acquaintance with Musorgsky. Under the former's influence and guidance he at once began the composition of a symphony in E♭, the greater part of the first movement of which was sketched by December 1862; the first sketches for the finale date from May 1863, the scherzo from 1864 and the Andante from a holiday at Graz between June and August 1865 (these dates and that of the meeting with Balakirev were given by the composer's widow during her last illness; there is reason to believe some of them to be too early). The symphony was completed early in 1867; on 7 March 1868 it was given a trial run-through with other new Russian works, under Balakirev, for the benefit of the directors of the Russian Musical Society, and made a very bad impression owing to innumerable errors in the parts; the first public performance (on 16 January 1869), also under Balakirev, was more successful.

In the meantime Borodin had embarked on other

compositions: some unfinished variations for piano on a Czech theme sent him by Balakirev (January 1867), the earliest of his mature songs, *Spyashchaya knyazhna* ('The sleeping princess') and an 'opera-farce' *Bogatïri* ('The Bogatïrs') to a libretto by V. A. Krïlov, with music partly original, partly adapted from Rossini, Meyerbeer, Offenbach, Serov and others (late summer and autumn of 1867). *The Bogatïrs* was produced anonymously at the Bol'shoy Theatre, Moscow, on 18 November 1867, but failed completely; Borodin was not present. (It was revived at the Moscow Chamber Theatre in the 1933–4 season, and in 1936 provided with a fresh libretto by Demyan Bednïy which was soon officially condemned.) In 1868 came more songs, *Morskaya tsarevna* ('The sea princess'), *Pesnya tyomnovo lesa* ('Song of the dark forest'), *Fal'shivaya nota* ('The false note'), all to his own verses, and a setting of L. A. Mey's translation of Heine's *Vergiftet sind meine Lieder*; he also began an opera based on Mey's drama *Tsarskaya nevesta* ('The Tsar's Bride'). During the summer and autumn of the same year his otherwise exceptionally happy married life was disturbed by the infatuation of the 22-year-old Anna Kalinina, sister of the composer N. N. Lodï-zhensky, which – needlessly but understandably – aroused Ekaterina's jealousy; Borodin was touched by Anna's adoration but faithful to Ekaterina. Before long he seems to have been completely disillusioned about Anna; indeed *The False Note* is probably an expression of that disillusionment. His domestic life was yet more firmly anchored in 1869 by the adoption of a seven-year-old girl, Liza Balaneva (afterwards the wife of his scientific pupil and colleague, A. P. Dianin, and mother of his biographer and editor of his collected letters).

During the period from December 1868 to March 1869 Borodin deputized anonymously for his friend Cui as music critic of the *Sanktpeterburgskiye vedomosti*; his articles are reprinted in Stasov's book.

The success of the E♭ Symphony at its public performance led to the beginning of a second symphony (in B minor) during the first two or three months of 1869. But Borodin was still more anxious to compose an opera. *The Tsar's Bride* dissatisfied him, but on 30 April Stasov sent him a scenario (given in Braudo) of a three-act opera based on the 12th-century prose–poetic epic *Slovo o polku Igoreve* ('The story of Igor's army', a work believed by some authorities to be an 18th-century forgery). Borodin spent the summer in the gathering of materials and study of literary sources and in September began the composition, working desultorily at separate numbers for which he wrote the words at the same time; in March 1870 he abandoned it owing to its lack of dramatic interest and transferred some of the music already composed to the B minor Symphony, the first movement of which was completed in autumn 1871. The finale, too, was sketched out by the beginning of November of that year. At the beginning of 1872 he was invited by the director of the imperial theatres to collaborate with his friends Rimsky-Korsakov, Musorgsky and Cui in the composition of a four-act opera-ballet *Mlada*, with a libretto by V. A. Krïlov; Borodin undertook the fourth act, using some of the music originally composed for *Prince Igor*, but the project was soon abandoned.

Borodin's musical work was constantly subordinated to his professional activities, which were increased in 1872 by the foundation of the medical courses for women, in which he took a leading part; for the rest of his life these involved not only additional lecturing in chemistry but considerable administrative work as treasurer. At about the same time he found that his work on aldehydes was being anticipated by German chemists who had much better laboratory equipment, and in 1873 he returned to his earlier subject, amarine. From 1874 onwards his laboratory work consisted less of original research than of supervision of student work, a more arduous and less interesting task to which he nevertheless devoted most of his time, tremendous energy and even at times his private purse.

Towards the end of 1874 Borodin's interest in *Prince Igor* was revived; the Polovtsian March was composed, and the next summer the famous dances as well as several other numbers. In winter 1874–5 he sketched his String Quartet in A 'suggested by a theme of Beethoven's' (from the B♭ Quartet op.130); it was 'almost finished' by January 1877, but really completed only in August 1879. In autumn 1876 Borodin was surprised by the news that the Russian Musical Society wished to perform his new symphony; he was unable to find the score and, though ill in bed, had to reorchestrate the first and last movements. The two middle movements were found and the symphony was conducted by Nápravník on 10 March 1877, though, owing to the heavy, brassy scoring, it had little success. (The scoring, particularly of the scherzo, was lightened later and the work in its new form successfully played under Rimsky-Korsakov at a Free School concert on 4 March 1879; at the next concert, a week later, the Polovtsian Dances from *Prince Igor* were performed for the first time.)

4. *Alexander Porfir'yevich Borodin*

III   Final decade

During the summer of 1877 Borodin visited a number of German universities in order to study their chemical laboratory arrangements; while at Jena in July he took the opportunity to visit Liszt at Weimar and was received most cordially. From this year dates the recitative and cavatina, 'Medlenno den' ugasal' ('Slowly the daylight fades'), in *Prince Igor*, inspired by yet another of the passionate young women whose love he returned platonically. But the opera made slow progress, in spite of the pressure and even active assistance of Rimsky-Korsakov, who performed separate numbers from time to time at concerts of the Free School of Music. After autumn 1881 *Prince Igor* appears to have been neglected altogether for about five years. Even some of the little time Borodin had for composition was frittered away in jests that were never published, perhaps never even written down: quadrilles on themes from Rimsky-Korsakov's *Pskovityanka*, a waltz on one of Varlaam's songs in *Boris Godunov*, a set of lancers in the church modes and so on. One of these jests, a polka that he played to a 'Chopsticks' accompaniment, caught the fancy of Rimsky-Korsakov, Cui and Lyadov, who in 1878 produced a whole collection which, with three more pieces by Borodin himself, was published as *Paraphrases*. More surprisingly, Liszt was so pleased with this 'merveilleuse oeuvre' that he contributed a short piece of his own to the second edition.

It was because of Liszt, too, that Borodin's music now began to be heard in western Europe. On 20 May 1880 the E♭ symphony was performed with great success at Baden-Baden, and that year Borodin wrote a short orchestral piece, which contributed more than anything else to his early fame, the musical picture *V sredney Azii* ('In Central Asia'), one of 12 pieces commissioned from various Russian composers to accompany a series of *tableaux vivants* illustrating the events of the first 25 years of the reign of Alexander II. In gratitude he dedicated this to Liszt, whom he met again in June 1881 at Magdeburg at the festival of the Allgemeiner Deutscher Musikverein and also visited at Weimar. In 1883 he published in the journal *Iskusstvo* an article 'List u sebya doma v Veymare' ('Liszt in his Weimar home').

Musorgsky's death in March 1881 moved Borodin to a beautiful setting of Pushkin's poem *Dlya beregov otchizni dal'noy* ('For the shores of thy far native land'), and that summer he completed a second string quartet, in D major; but during the 1880s it became increasingly difficult for him to spare time for music. His wife's constant ill-health frequently obliged her to stay in the healthier climate of Moscow, and much time was wasted in railway journeys between the capitals. Above all, there was, as he acknowledged in a letter to his wife, 'the difficulty of being at one and the same time both a Glinka and a Stupishin [a civil servant], scientist, commissioner, artist, government official, philanthropist, father of other people's children, doctor and invalid. . . . You end by becoming only the last'. In June 1885 an attack of cholera seriously undermined his health and was to be the main cause of the heart disease of which he died.

At the same time Borodin's fame was spreading in western Europe. The Belgian Countess of Mercy-Argenteau had the First Symphony performed at Verviers (1884) and Liège (1885). On her initiative his songs and three excerpts from *Prince Igor* were provided with French translations, and he was made a member of the French Société des Auteurs, Compositeurs et Editeurs, with Saint-Saëns and Bourgault-Ducoudray as his sponsors. The A major Quartet was played in Paris in 1884. In 1885 he showed his gratitude to the countess by dedicating to her a set of piano pieces, *Petit poème d'amour d'une jeune fille*, afterwards published as a *Petite suite* (some new, some dating from the late 1870s), and to the young Belgian conductor Jadoul a piano scherzo in A♭ (published as an arrangement of a non-existent orchestral version). During August and September of that year he visited Belgium as the countess's guest, on his way calling again on Liszt at Weimar and also spending a short time in Paris. He declined invitations to conduct Russian concerts at the Antwerp Exhibition, but heard his works performed at Liège, Antwerp and Brussels, and was fêted everywhere. He expressed renewed gratitude to the countess in a song of French words, *Septain*, published by Muraille of Liège. After only three months in Russia, in the course of which he made a successful début as a conductor with the amateur orchestra of the Medical Academy on 13 December, he returned to Belgium with Cui to spend Christmas at Argenteau, and the two composers enjoyed further triumphs at Liège and Brussels.

During 1886 Borodin worked on a long-contemplated third symphony, in A minor. It was destined to remain unfinished, for the year was, as he said, 'a very hard one'. First his mother-in-law was very ill; then on 15 June he was again summoned to Moscow by telegram to his wife, who was twice 'literally on the point of death and saved only by a miracle': even after this she could neither walk nor lie down, and had to sleep sitting in an armchair. Nevertheless in November he contributed a *Serenata alla spagnola* to a string quartet on the theme B–LA–F written with Rimsky-Korsakov, Lyadov and Glazunov as a name day present for M. P. Belyayev, who had recently founded his publishing house and the series of Russian Symphony Concerts mainly for the sake of their works. At the beginning of 1887 Borodin returned to *Prince Igor* and composed several numbers, including the overture and the chorus of Russian prisoners in Act 2, which he played to friends but never wrote down except in fragmentary sketches. On the morning of 27 February he improvised at the piano some new material for the Third Symphony. That evening he attended a fancy-dress ball organized by the professors of the Medical Academy for their families and friends; in Russian national dress, with red shirt and high boots, he was in very good humour, laughing and joking, when at midnight he fell and died of heart failure in a few seconds. His wife survived him by only five months (she died on 9 August) during which she dictated to S. N. Kruglikov some reminiscences that were heavily drawn on by V. V. Stasov in the biography he published two years later.

Works

I Introduction to the music

When, in 1906, Sir Henry Hadow declared of Borodin
that 'no musician has ever claimed immortality with
so slender an offering', he was basing his judgment
on the 20 or so works that were thought at that
time to be the sum of the composer's output. In the
intervening years Soviet research has discovered and
published a further 20 titles which, although of slighter
value, have helped to fill out the formerly sketchy early
period of Borodin's career and, in a few instances,
revealed some charming chamber compositions of genuine artistic worth. It is nevertheless a measure of the
quality and enduring appeal of Borodin's finest works
that this substantial increase has in no way invalidated
Hadow's assessment.

Borodin's earliest attempts at composition were essentially by-products of his own amateur music-making;
and the arrangements or free adaptations of Mozart,
Haydn, Bellini, Donizetti and others that he made for
musical gatherings soon gave way to attempts at original
composition. In these he was strongly influenced by the
salon music of the day such as the sentimental, quasi-
folksongs and dances of Gurilyov, Varlamov, Vilboa
and others, and the four early songs (three of them with
cello obbligato) are convincing imitations of these fashionable contemporaries. The string trio in G minor on

the folksong *Chem tebya ya ogorchila* betrays the more characterful influence of Glinka. In this, although he used the variation form too rigidly, Borodin showed clear signs (in the pizzicato *scherzando* fourth variation, for instance) of an individual talent flexing its muscles.

The end of the 1850s brought a noticeable change in Borodin's style. A greater involvement with the cello at amateur chamber music gatherings, combined with the period of scientific study spent in Germany, appears to have released in him a new vein of lyricism and an interest in formal design, qualities which in his eyes found their fullest contemporary expression in the music of Mendelssohn. Although Borodin's confessed admiration for this composer was to be superseded by more positive influences in the years to come, an unmistakably Mendelssohnian quality can be found in a number of his more mature works, notably the chamber music of the 1870s. Nowhere is this influence to be felt more strongly than in the String Quintet in F minor (two cellos) and the Piano Trio in D (the finale of which was never composed), where hardly a dissonance is to be found to disturb the pervading mood of serenity and euphony. Another aspect of the same influence that was to prove enduring can be detected in Borodin's increasing interest in light, mercurial scherzos, though in this the example of Berlioz came to play an equally important part. The most substantial and highly developed of these early works is the Piano Quintet in C minor, which displays the usual lyricism, smoothness of texture and neatness of design of this period, but at the same time exhibits a new, heartfelt, elegiac quality and, in the finale, a rough-hewn Russian strength that give the first clear indication that, of all the Russian nationalist composers, it was Borodin who was to prove Glinka's spiritual heir.

II Orchestral works

It is customary to refer to the works that Borodin composed before his return to Russia (1862) as belonging to the pre-Balakirev period; and certainly the First Symphony in E♭, which was composed during the five years following Borodin's meeting with Balakirev in 1862, bears witness to an astonishing growth of assurance and technical mastery. Even though he was working under the close, almost tyrannical guidance of his mentor, it is hard to exaggerate the boldness of Borodin's decision to embark on a full-length symphony at a time when he had so little experience of extended forms and none at all of orchestration. Yet, in the event, the First Symphony's technical shortcomings – its understandably stiff handling of sonata form, excessive reliance on sequences and pedal points and, notably in the finale, all too obvious influence of Schumann – are swept aside by the work's freshness, charm and exuberance. Already fully characteristic of the composer are the serenely peaceful Andantino end of the first movement, the ingeniously phrased scherzo, with its linking phrases of 2nds and metrically irregular, folky trio, and the rich, passionate cantilena of the Andante slow movement. The orchestration, which owes not a little to the example and treatise of Berlioz, is assured, colourful and imaginative; it should therefore be stressed that this is entirely Borodin's work and that there is not a grain of truth in the statement 'revue par N. Rimsky-Korsakov et A. Glazounov' to be found in all editions of the score other than the first of 1882.

Similarly, the differences in text and indications of scoring between the earlier piano duet reduction and the full score, which led some commentators to suspect editorial interference, are merely the result of Borodin's revision of the score before publication.

The Second Symphony in B minor was begun almost immediately after the première of the first in 1869, but because of his preoccupation with *Prince Igor* it was not finally completed until 1876. This delay brought with it a positive gain, for it was during this period that Borodin reached the height of his powers; he never surpassed the achievement of this symphony in which all the individual facets of his creative personality became fused to produce one of the boldest and most colourful symphonies of the 19th century. Viewed in the context of Russian music, it can be considered as a more mature, symphonic counterpart to Glinka's *Ruslan and Lyudmila*. The first movement, for instance, inhabits the same epic, legendary world, but with an added dimension of granite-like strength and concision, launched by the grim, purposeful eight-note motto theme which is coloured by its minor 2nd and juxtaposition of major and minor 3rd. The scherzo is a tour de force of orchestral dexterity and syncopation, while the trio introduces the note of oriental languor that was to become one of Borodin's most appealing characteristics. The slow movement, an even richer descendant of that of the First Symphony, shows a mastery of free rondo form flanked by a poetic horn invocation, and leads directly into the festive, orchestrally resplendent finale. Above all, the Second Symphony has one of the hallmarks of a great symphony: four movements of contrasting mood, colour and tempo that nevertheless form a whole with an underlying unity. As with the First Symphony, the second was much revised by Borodin, and it is certain that he incorporated several technical improvements suggested by Rimsky-Korsakov when preparing the full score for publication in October 1886. As the symphony was in early proof stage when Borodin died, Rimsky-Korsakov, assisted by Glazunov, agreed to see the score through the press. The greater part of his so-called editorial work, therefore, merely involved the duties of a proof corrector, but Rimsky is himself responsible for certain features of the resulting publication. The metronome marks throughout the work are his (in this connection it should not be forgotten that he conducted the highly successful second performance of the symphony in close collaboration with Borodin), and he further added four tempo indications to the Andante. However, in no single instance did he introduce an alteration of rhythm, melody or harmony, and it is regrettable that in designating Rimsky-Korsakov and Glazunov as editors of the symphony, the publisher perpetuated the mistaken belief that the orchestration is not in all essentials the work of Borodin.

The unfinished Third Symphony presents no such problems, for its posthumous publication in 1888 is perfectly accurate in its statement that it was finished and orchestrated by Glazunov. Glazunov completed and orchestrated the first movement partly from sketches left by Borodin and partly from memory. For the second, he fulfilled the composer's known intentions by orchestrating the scherzo for string quartet composed in 1882 (later published in the *Les vendredis* collection), and by composing a trio from the music of the episode of the merchant's narration of the defeat of Igor's army, which Borodin had discarded from Act 1 of his opera in 1879. There are fragmentary sketches for a slow movement (variations on an Old Believer chant) and finale but, although he also had his memory of Borodin's piano extemporizations of these to draw on, Glazunov wisely refrained from undertaking so major a task of reconstruction. Much of the quiet, almost pastoral lyricism and contrapuntal quality of the charming first movement of the Third Symphony can be accounted for by the fact that this music was originally planned in 1883–4 as a string quartet. In spite of its moments of energy and strength it is pervaded by a serenity, sometimes tinged with melancholy, which strongly evokes the Russian countryside. Glazunov was solely responsible for the beautiful coda. The piquant scherzo in 5/8 has gained much from Glazunov's resourceful scoring in Borodin's style, but Borodin would probably have introduced the noble melody of the trio with greater subtlety. Despite its unfinished state, the Third Symphony's two movements make a satisfying unity in performance and are fully representative of Borodin in his more relaxed, lyrical mood.

Borodin's only other orchestral work is the formally admirable and wholly delightful 'musical picture' *In Central Asia*, in which a peaceful, diatonic Russian melody and a rhythmically more supple oriental theme are restated, in varying harmonizations and scoring, against a pervading ostinato evoking the journey of a caravan across the steppes, and eventually combined. Although some commentators have suggested that both themes are genuine folktunes, there is evidence to the contrary in the form of sketches for the oriental theme and from the reminiscences of M. M. Kurbanov, who quoted Borodin as saying that he fashioned the two themes with their contrapuntal combination in mind.

III Songs

Although Borodin's output of songs is sadly small and inevitably overshadowed by Musorgsky's more distinctive achievement, the 12 songs of his maturity (most of which were written to his own texts), nevertheless constitute an attractively varied group. In *Spyashchaya knyazhna* ('The sleeping princess') he created an atmosphere of brooding stillness and a *Ruslan*-inspired world of legend by means of persistent unresolved 2nds and the whole-tone scale in a way that was to influence Debussy, Ravel and Stravinsky. However, already in this first song Borodin showed himself more concerned with the accompaniment than with the vocal line, which is stiffer and more rhythmically unadventurous than might be expected. Similar means are used in a closely related song, *Morskaya tsarevna* ('The sea princess'), to portray the insidious charm and seductiveness of Borodin's version of the Lorelei and to evoke a general nautical background. Outstanding among the songs, however, is *Pesnya tyomnovo lesa* ('Song of the dark forest'), in which the feeling of elemental power and epic grandeur of Russian folk legend are evoked by a pervading use of unison, at first combined with dissonant seconds and then briefly expanding into block harmonies at the climax. In this song Borodin came closest to the uncompromising realism of Musorgsky, partly because of the frequent changes of time signature, and it is a measure of his own satisfaction with it that he chose to rework it for inclusion in the second scene of Act 1 of *Prince Igor*, only to reject the whole episode at a later state as being too discursive. The ballad *More* ('The sea'), cast in free rondo form, is Borodin's most ambitious song, in which a turbulent and unusually elaborate main section contrasts with a more characteristic barcarolle-like episode. Once again, his essentially instrumental leanings are betrayed by the excessively syllabic declamation of the vocal line. Although clearly modelled on Schumann's *Ich grolle nicht*, his setting of Pushkin's *Dlya beregov otchizni̇̆ dal'noy* ('For the shores of thy far native land') is deeply moving and perhaps the most immediately appealing of his songs. His only orchestral song, a setting of Nekrasov's amusing poem *U lyudey-to v domu* ('Those folk'), describing the contrasting ways of life of the rich and the poor, is a comic character study in the Musorgsky vein and deserves to be better known.

IV Instrumental music

In 1875 Borodin reported to a friend that he was working on his First String Quartet in A 'to the horror of Stasov and Modest [Musorgsky]'. The horror expressed by his friends was occasioned by the fear that Borodin was surrendering himself to the charms of teutonically academic 'pure' music in a way that was inconsistent with the tenets of the St Petersburg nationalist composers. In the event Borodin succeeded admirably in fusing a style of quartet writing derived from Beethoven and Mendelssohn with a wholly individual and, at times, discernibly 'Russian' quality. Probably no work of his gives the lie more clearly to the charge of inspired dilettantism that is still sometimes brought against him than this First Quartet, for its craftsmanship is as impeccable as the understanding it displays of the innermost resources of each instrument. The first movement is Borodin's most extended single movement and, although its prevailing tone is lyrical, it contains a remarkable variety of mood and texture and is notable for its contrapuntal resourcefulness. The Andante con moto is unmistakably Slavonic in its combination of elegy and passionate rhapsody and even the fugal *misterioso* middle section is not without individuality and expressive character. The delicate trio of the *Queen Mab*-like scherzo is a tour de force of original harmonic writing for the first violin and cello, while the second violin is required to produce what must be one of the earliest uses of the left-hand pizzicato effect. The finale is perhaps more conventionally energetic but it makes a fitting conclusion to this most engaging of quartets.

The far shorter, better-known, Second Quartet in D is dedicated to the composer's wife and known to be a nostalgic evocation of the happy period of their first meeting in Heidelberg. The quartet's narrow emotional range, its Romantic languor and the pervading blandness of its textures run the danger of being considered cloying, yet Borodin avoids this by virtue of the music's latent muscularity. The quartet's popularity is largely due to the luxuriant richness of the third movement Nocturne, which has suffered innumerable arrangements by others. True to his instrument, Borodin gave the lion's share of this haunting love-song without words to the cello, and the movement ends with one of his characteristic ecstatic, climbing *perdendosi* sequences.

Borodin's contribution to piano literature is negligible. The seven short numbers that constitute the *Petite suite*, a collection of separate pieces that he had written over a period of some five years, hardly rise above the level of agreeable salon music. The late Scherzo in A♭, however, is far more distinctive and the last in a varied line of playful scherzos. It makes an excellent encore to a concert programme, and was regularly used as such by Rakhmaninov. Borodin never made the orchestration of it that is advertised on the first edition, but Glazunov, when making his 1889 orchestration of the *Petite suite*, incorporated it into the concluding Nocturne.

V   Stage music

Borodin's archives in the Leningrad Public Library contain his detailed manuscripts of the eight numbers that he wrote in 1872 for the fourth act of the collective opera-ballet *Mlada*. Apart from Rimsky-Korsakov's arrangement and orchestration of nos.5–7 as the *Finale from the Opera-ballet Mlada* nothing has been published to show the quality and importance of this music, so that a study of the *Mlada* numbers offers a most promising field for research. When the venture was abandoned, Borodin reworked most of the material for inclusion in *Prince Igor*; thus nos.1 and 3 became the opening C major chorus and the eclipse episode in the Prologue, no.4 the Act 3 trio, and no.8 the closing chorus of the opera. No.2, the duet between Yaromir and the High Priest, is an exception, for although some of the material is familiar from *Prince Igor* it constitutes an unknown yet extended scene packed with fine music fully scored by Borodin. The scene draws on one of the few sections that had already been composed for *Prince*

5. Autograph MS of the opening of Yaroslavna's scene with chorus from Borodin's 'Prince Igor', composed 1869–70

Igor – Yaroslavna's arioso – but also includes the music that was later remodelled as the first version of Igor's aria.

No discussion of Borodin can fail to show the extent to which most of his compositions were bound up with the protracted creation of his most substantial achievement, the opera *Prince Igor*. The main reason why the opera remained unfinished and largely unorchestrated when he died after 18 years of intermittent labour on it was undoubtedly his attitude to composition as a part-time occupation. But much of the blame can also be laid at the door of his foolhardy decision to fashion his own libretto from the early Russian chronicle on which the opera is based (*The Story of Igor's Army*), and his failure to complete this basic task before embarking on the actual composition. It is for this reason, as much as for any shortcomings of Borodin as a composer of dramatic music, that the opera as it is now known appears so tableauesque and disjointed (the character of Vladimir Galitsky for instance, his fine aria notwithstanding, remains enigmatic and inconsequential); and why, in spite of its abundant musical richness, it has never gained a secure place in the repertory outside Russia. Borodin's attitude towards opera was strongly conservative in his predilection for melody and closed forms, and it is therefore not surprising that the chief appeal of *Prince Igor* lies in the quality of its individual numbers rather than in its whole shape or ability to involve an audience in the narrative. Thus Yaroslavna's two wonderfully touching arias, Igor's noble aria of remorse and longing and Vladimir's more conventional but ardent cavatina are the lyrical centrepieces of a loose design that also includes a number of fine choral scenes crowned by the barbaric splendour of the Polovtsian Dances. Though Borodin was especially proud of the subordinate comic scenes of the gudok players Skula and Eroshka, these seem less successful if only because their humour is largely expressed in arid recitative and thus is more verbal than musical.

The most considerable task that faced Rimsky-Korsakov (who had already begun to edit the opera for performance during Borodin's lifetime) and Glazunov when they undertook the task of completing the opera was the sketchy state of the third act in which Igor escapes from his Polovtsian captors. Despite considerable ingenuity on their part, the resulting pasticcio fails to carry conviction both musically and dramatically, and consequently the act is sometimes omitted in performance. Glazunov's greatest achievement was his reconstruction of the fine overture from his memory of Borodin's piano extemporizations of it; both he and Rimsky were obliged to orchestrate about half the opera. Although Glazunov left an interesting account of the extent of their editorial labours, it will not be known in precise detail how much they embellished or deviated from Borodin's original conception until the Soviet musicologist Pavel Lamm's manuscript edition of the vocal score, showing as far as is possible what Borodin wrote, is published.

WORKS

(published in St Petersburg unless otherwise stated)

Numbers in right-hand margins denote references in the text.

STAGE

Title	Genre	Libretto	Composed	Performed	Publication/MS	Remarks	67–70
Bogatïri [The Bogatïrs]	opera-farce, 5 scenes	V. A. Krïlov	1867	Moscow, Bol'shoy, 18 Nov 1867	USSR-Lob, US-STu	loosely based on excerpts from operas by Rossini, Meyerbeer, Offenbach, Serov, Verdi, Hérold and others; largely orchd by E. N. Merten; 2 choral excerpts ed. A. Nefedov (Moscow, 1977)	50
Tsarskaya nevesta [The Tsar's Bride]	opera	Borodin, after L. A. Mey	1867–8			sketches only; lost	50, 51
Mlada	opera-ballet, 4	Krïlov, after scenario by S. A. Gedeonov	1872		USSR-Lil, Lsc, Mcm	Act 4 only; other 3 acts by Rimsky-Korsakov, Cui and Musorgsky; finale (nos.5–7) arr. and orchd Rimsky-Korsakov (Leipzig, 1892); choral excerpt from finale ed. A. Nefedov (Moscow, 1977)	51, 67, 69, 117
Knyaz' Igor' [Prince Igor]	opera, prol. 4	Borodin, after scenario by V. V. Stasov	1869–70, 1874–87	St Petersburg, Mariinsky, 16 Nov 1890	Leipzig, 1889	unfinished; completed and partly orchd by Rimsky-Korsakov and Glazunov; 4 choral excerpts, not in orig. vocal score, ed. A. Nefedov (Moscow, 1977)	32, 51, 52, 54, 56, 57, 61, 62–3, 64, 67, 68, 69–70

ORCHESTRAL

Symphony no.1, E♭, 1862–7, arr. of orig. version pf 4 hands (c1877), score (1882) — 60–64; 49, 51, 54, 55, 60–61, 62, 81, 166

Symphony no.2, b, 1869–76, arr. of orig. version pf 4 hands (c1877), score (1887) [score seen through press by Glazunov and Rimsky-Korsakov] — 32, 51, 61–2

V sredney Azii [In Central Asia], musical picture, 1880 (Hamburg, 1882), arr. pf 4 hands (1882) — 54–5, 63

Symphony no.3, a, 1882, 1886–7 (Leipzig, 1888) [1st and 2nd movs only: ed., orchd and arr. pf 4 hands by Glazunov] — 56, 57, 62–3

CHAMBER

Concerto, D-d, fl, pf, 1847, lost — 46, 58, 59

Trio, G, 2 vn, vc, 1847, lost [based on themes from Meyerbeer's Robert le diable] — 46

Trio, G, 2 vn, vc, c1850–60, frag., USSR-Lit — 46

Quartet, D, fl, ob, va, vc, 1852–6 (Moscow, 1949) [based on works by Haydn]

String Quintet, f, 1853–4 (Leningrad, 1960) [coda of finale unfinished]

Grand Trio, G, 2 vn, vc, 1859–62, 1st and 2nd movts (Moscow, 1949) [3rd movt unfinished]

Trio, g, 2 vn, vc, ?1860 (Moscow, 1946) [based on folksong 'Chem tebya ya ogorchila', 'How I did grieve thee'] — 58–9

Cello Sonata, c, 1860 [based on a theme from Bach's unacc. Vn Sonata BWV1001]

String Sextet, d, 1860–61, 1st and 2nd movts (Moscow, 1946) [3rd and 4th movts lost; sketch for finale, Lsc] — 48

Piano Trio, D, 1860–61 (Moscow, 1950) [3 movts only] — 59

Piano Quintet, c, 1862 (Moscow, 1938) — 48, 59

String Quartet no.1, A, 1874–9 (Hamburg, 1884) — 52, 56, 65–6

String Quartet no.2, D, 1881 (Leipzig, 1888) — 55, 66

Scherzo, D, str qt, 1882 (Leipzig, 1899) [incl. as no.3 in the 2nd set of pieces for str qt Les vendredis, collab. Glazunov, Rimsky-Korsakov and others; later used in Sym. no.3] — 62

Serenata alla spagnola, d, str qt, 1886 (Leipzig, 1887) [for the qt 'B-la-f', collab. Lyadov, Glazunov and Rimsky-Korsakov] — 57

PIANO

For solo pf unless otherwise stated; for details of musical jokes and fragmentary pieces see S. A. Dianin (1955). — 66–7

Polka Hélène, d, pf 4 hands, 1843 (Moscow, 1946) [orig. for solo pf] — 54

Fantasia on a theme of Hummel, ?1849 (1849) — 45

Le courant, study, Ab, ?1849 (1849)

Adagio patetico, Ab, ?1849 (1849)

Scherzo, bb, 1852. lost

Allegretto, Db, pf 4 hands, 1861, USSR-Lit [arr. of 3rd movt of Str Qnt]

Scherzo, E, pf 4 hands, 1861. Lsc

Tarantella, D, pf 4 hands, 1862 (Moscow, 1938) — 48

Polka, Marche funèbre, Requiem and Mazurka, pf 3 hands, ?1874–8; 1st 3 pieces (Hamburg, 1879), Mazurka pubd posth. (Leipzig, 1893) [for the collection Paraphrases, collab. Lyadov and others] — 54

Petite Suite, 1885 (St Petersburg, 1885). orchd Glazunov (St Petersburg, 1889) — 56, 67

Scherzo, Ab, 1885 (St Petersburg, 1885) [orchd Glazunov for inclusion in the Petite Suite] — 56, 67

VOCAL

(for 1v, pf, unless otherwise stated)

Misera me! Barbaro sorte (anon.), T, B, pf, c1850, USSR-Lit, unfinished — 58, 64–5

Bozhe milostivïy [Merciful God] (aria), 1852–5, Lit — 58

Chto ti rano, zoren'ka [Why art thou so early, dawn?] (S. Solov'yov), 1852–5, freely adapted by P. A. Lamm (Moscow, 1947)

Das schöne Fischmädchen (Heine, trans. D. Kropotkin), c1854 (Moscow, 1947) [with vc obbl] — 58

Razlyubila krasna devitsa [The pretty girl no longer loves me] (Vinogradov), c1854 (Moscow, 1947) [with vc obbl] — 58

Slushayte, podruzhen'ki, pesenku moyu [Listen to my song, little friend] (E. von Kruse), c1854 (Moscow, 1947) [with vc obbl] — 58

Spyashchaya knyazhna [The sleeping princess] (Borodin), 1867 (Moscow, 1870), orchd Rimsky-Korsakov (Moscow, 1904) — 32, 50, 64

Pesnya tyomnovo lesa [Song of the dark forest] (Borodin), 1868 (St Petersburg, 1873), arr. male chorus, pf, and orchd by Glazunov (St Petersburg, 1893) — 50, 64

Morskaya tsarevna [The sea princess] (Borodin), 1868 (St Petersburg, 1873) — 50, 64

Fal'shivaya nota [The false note] (Borodin), 1868 (Moscow, 1870) — 50

Otravoy polni moi pesni [My songs are poisoned] (Heine, trans. L. A. Mey), 1868 (Moscow, 1870) — 50

More [The sea] (Borodin), 1870 (Moscow, 1870), orchd 1884, Lsc, unfinished: orchd Rimsky-Korsakov (Moscow, 1906) — 65

Serenada chetiryokh kavalerov odnoy dame [Serenade of four cavaliers to one lady] (Borodin), 4 male vv, c1870 (Leipzig, 1889)

Iz slyoz moikh [From my tears] (Heine, trans. Mey), 1870–71 (St Petersburg, 1873)

Arabskaya melodiya [Arabian melody] (trad., trans. Borodin), 1881 (Leipzig, 1888) — 55, 65

Dlya beregov otchizni dal'noy [For the shores of thy far native land] (Pushkin), 1881 (Leipzig, 1888), orchd Glazunov (Leipzig, 1912)

U lyudey-to v domu [Those folk] (Nekrasov), 1v, orch, 1881 (Leipzig, 1890), arr. 1v, pf by G. O. Dütsch (Leipzig, 1890) — 65

Spes' [Pride] (A. K. Tolstoy), 1884–5 (Leipzig, 1890)

Septain (G. Collin), 1885 (Liège, 1885), trans. Borodin as Chudniy sad [The magic garden] (St Petersburg, 1887) — 56

Slava Kirillu! Slava Mefodiyu! [God save Kirill! God save Methodius!] (anon.), 4 ?male vv, c1885, Lit, unfinished

BIBLIOGRAPHY

A. P. Dianin: 'Alyeksandr Porfir'yevich Borodin: biograficheskiy ocherk i vospominaninya' [Biographical sketch and reminiscences], *Zhurnal russkovo fiziko-khimicheskovo obshchestva*, xx/4 (1888), 1 [incl. complete list of Borodin's scientific publications]

V. V. Stasov: *Alyeksandr Porfir'yevich Borodin: evo zhizn', perepiska i muzïkal'niye stat'i* [Life, correspondence and articles on music] (St Petersburg, 1889)

V. A. Chechott: *A. P. Borodin: ocherk muzïkal'noy deyatel'nosti* [An essay on his musical activities] (St Petersburg, 1890)

A. Habets: *Alexandre Borodine d'après la biographie et la correspondance publiées par M. Wladimir Stassoff* (Paris, 1893; Eng. trans., 1895/R1975)

A. K. Glazunov: 'Zapiski o redaktsii *Knyazya Igorya* Borodina' [Notes on the editing of *Prince Igor*], *RMG*, iii (1896), 155

E. M. Braudo: *A. P. Borodin: evo zhizn' i tvorchestvo* [Life and works] (Petrograd, 1922)

M. D. Calvocoressi: 'Borodin Revised', *MT*, lxv (1924), 1086

N. Findeyzen: 'Borodin's Musical Legacy', *MMR*, lvii (1927), 34, 74

S. A. Dianin, ed.: *Pis'ma A. P. Borodina* [Borodin's letters] (Moscow and Leningrad, 1928–50)

G. Khubov: *A. P. Borodin* (Moscow, 1933)

G. Abraham: *Studies in Russian Music* (London, 1935) [incl. 'Borodin as a symphonist', 102; 'Prince Igor', 119]

M. D. Calvocoressi and G. Abraham: *Masters of Russian Music* (London, 1936) [incl. M. D. Calvocoressi: 'Alexander Borodin', 155]

G. Abraham: *On Russian Music* (London, 1939) [incl. 'The History of *Prince Igor*', 147; 'Borodin's Songs', 169]

A. Dmitriyev: 'Iz tvorcheskoy laboratorii A. P. Borodina' [From Borodin's creative laboratory], *SovM* (1950), no.10, p.81

——: 'K istorii sozdaniya operï A. P. Borodina *Knyaz' Igor*'' [The history of the composition of *Prince Igor*], *SovM* (1950), no.11, p.82; see also suppl. incl. vocal score of 1st version of Igor's aria

L. A. Solovtsova: *Kamerno-instrumental'naya muzïka A. P. Borodina* [Borodin's instrumental chamber music] (Moscow, 1952, 2/1960)

S. A. Dianin: *Borodin: zhizneopisaniye, materialï i dokumentï* [Biography, materials and documents] (Moscow, 1955, rev. 2/1960; Eng. trans. [without the materials and documents but with an additional study of Borodin's music], 1963)

V. A. Vasina-Grossman: *Russkiy klassicheskiy romans XIX veka* [The Russian 19th-century classical romance] (Moscow, 1956) [incl. 'Romansï Borodina', 214]

73

N. A. Listova: 'Iz istorii sozdaniya operï *Knyaz' Igor'* A. P. Borodina' [The history of the composition of *Prince Igor*], *Soobshcheniya Instituta istorii iskusstv*, xv (1959), 36–75

D. Lloyd-Jones: 'The Bogatyrs: Russia's First Operetta', *MMR*, lxxxix (1959), 123

——: 'Borodin in Heidelberg', *MQ*, xlvi (1960), 500 [incl. photostat of Borodin's pf duet in E]

——: 'Borodin's Early Compositions', *The Listener*, lxiii (1960), 773

——: 'Borodin on Liszt', *ML*, xlii (1961), 117

A. N. Sokhor: *Alyeksandr Porfir'yevich Borodin: zhizn', deyatel'nost', muzïkal'noye tvorchestvo* [Life, works, musical compositions] (Moscow, 1965)

V. A. Kiselyov and others, eds.: 'Novïye pis'ma Borodina' [Some new Borodin letters], *Muzïkal'noye nasledstvo*, iii, ed. M. P. Alexeyev and others (Moscow, 1970), 208–39

V. A. Kiselyov: 'Stsenicheskaya istoriya pervoy postanovki *Knyazya Igorya*' [The history of the first performance of *Prince Igor*], *Muzïkal'noye nasledstvo*, iii, ed. M. P. Alexeyev and others (Moscow, 1970), 284–352

G. L. Golovinsky: *Kamernïye ansambli Borodina* [Borodin's chamber music] (Moscow, 1972)

G. Abraham: 'Arab Melodies in Rimsky-Korsakov and Borodin', *ML*, lvi (1975), 313; repr. in *Essays on Russian and East European Music* (Oxford, 1984)

D. Lloyd-Jones: 'Towards a Scholarly Edition of Borodin's Symphonies', *Soundings*, vi (1977), 81

R. C. Ridenour: *Nationalism, Modernism, and Personal Rivalry in Nineteenth-century Russian Music* (Ann Arbor, Mich., 1981)

R. Taruskin: *Opera and Drama in Russia as Preached and Practiced in the 1860s* (Ann Arbor, Mich., 1981)

M. Bobéth: *Borodin und seine Oper Fürst Igor: Geschichte-Analyse-Konsequenzen* (Munich and Salzburg, 1982)

MILY BALAKIREV

Gerald Abraham

Edward Garden

CHAPTER ONE

Life

I 1837–55

Mily Alexeyevich Balakirev was born in Nizhny-Novgorod (now Gor'kiy) on 2 January 1837. The son of a minor government official, he received his first music lessons from his mother and at the age of four could reproduce tunes at the piano. His normal education began at the Nizhny-Novgorod Gymnasium. When he was ten his mother took him to Moscow during the summer holidays for a course of ten lessons with John Field's pupil, Alexander Dubuque, who made him work at Hummel's A minor concerto. After his mother's death the boy was transferred from the Gymnasium to the Alexandrovsky Institute, where he boarded. His musical education was continued by a German musician, Karl Eisrich, one of whose duties was to play the piano and arrange the regular musical evenings at the house of a wealthy local land-owner, Alexander Ulïbïshev, author of well known books on Mozart and Beethoven. Balakirev was indebted to Eisrich for his introduction to the music of Chopin (the E minor Concerto) and Glinka (the trio from *A Life for the Tsar*), both of which impressed him profoundly, and for a general widening of his musical experience. At 14 he helped Eisrich in preparing an amateur performance of Mozart's Requiem. Having been introduced to Ulïbïshev, he was soon engaged as Eisrich's assistant and in his patron's house was given opportunities to hear much chamber music and even Beethoven symphonies played by the small and very poor orchestra of the local theatre under Eisrich's direction. He also had the use of Ulïbïshev's excellent music library. At 15 he himself was allowed to rehearse Beethoven's First, Fourth and Eighth Symphonies. From the same year date his earliest extant compositions, the first movement of a septet for strings, flute, clarinet and piano, and a *Grande fantaisie* on Russian airs for piano and orchestra op.4 (dated '12 December', old style).

In 1853 Balakirev left the Alexandrovsky Institute and, with his friend P. D. Boborïkin (afterwards a novelist, who introduced him in a book as 'Valerian Gorshkov'), entered the University of Kazan as an unmatriculated student of mathematics. He soon made a mark in local society as a pianist, and by taking pupils was able to augment his extremely limited finances. His holidays were spent either at Nizhny-Novgorod or on Ulïbïshev's country estate at Lukino, where he played numerous Beethoven sonatas to help his patron with his book. At Kazan he made the acquaintance of visiting musicians, among them the amateur pianist-composer Ivan Laskovsky, a War Ministry official, for whose works he preserved a lifelong admiration, and the pianists Seymour-Sheath and Anton Katski, with the latter of whom he considered taking lessons in St Petersburg. From this period (1854–61) date the piano fantasy on themes from *A Life for the Tsar*, an attempt at a string quartet (Quatuor original russe), three songs which were first published in 1908 and the first movement of a piano concerto in F♯ minor.

II   1855–60

In the late autumn of 1855 Ulïbïshev took Balakirev to St Petersburg where he introduced him to Glinka and other musical notabilities. Balakirev had by then decided on a musical career. In December he appeared as pianist at a concert at Kronstadt; on 24 February 1856 he made his St Petersburg début at a university concert, playing the solo part in the first movement of his concerto, with great success; and on 3 April he gave a concert of his own at which he played, among other works, a new nocturne and scherzo of his own and the piano part in the Allegro of the Octet op.3, perhaps a revised version of the Septet. Glinka thought highly of his talent, though he considered his composition technique defective – there were then no musical textbooks in Russian and Balakirev's German was inadequate – and gave him two themes from his Spanish collection, on which he was asked to write a Fandango-étude; Balakirev also based his Spanish Serenade on one of the themes. Before leaving Russia for the last time in May 1856, Glinka exacted a promise that no one but Balakirev should be entrusted with his four-year-old niece's musical education and also gave him yet another Spanish theme, a march; this Balakirev used the following year as one of the themes of his Overture on a Spanish March (originally intended as the overture to a drama *The Expulsion of the Moors from Spain*), published only in revised form in 1887. From 1855–6 dates a piano sonata in B♭ minor (op.5), the second movement of which reappeared in revised form first as Mazurka no.5 and later as the second movement of the sonata in the same key of nearly 50 years later; another theme from op.5 figures as the middle section of the Scherzo no.2 (1900).

Although he was now sufficiently well known to be invited to appear in February 1858 as soloist in Beethoven's E♭ major Concerto before the Tsar and his family, Balakirev was still in extreme poverty and supported himself mainly by piano lessons, sometimes giving nine a day, and playing at aristocratic *soirées*. His benefactor Ulïbïshev had just died, leaving him 1000 rubles, two violins and the whole of his music library. In April he fell ill with encephalitis, which left him for the rest of his life subject to severe headaches and constant disorders of the stomach and nerves. He was cared for by Dmitry Stasov, brother of the famous art critic and historian Vladimir Stasov, and during his illness made the acquaintance of the young guards officer and amateur composer Musorgsky. He had already met another composing officer, the 22-year-old Cui; both these young men soon accepted him as their mentor. On his recovery he completed the Overture on three Russian themes (first performed at a St Petersburg University concert on 2 January 1859).

It was during 1858 that Balakirev again began to write songs, and by the end of 1859 had completed 14. The publisher Denotkin took the first 12, offering – but apparently not paying – 15 rubles for each; these were Balakirev's first works to appear in print (1858–9). In the summer of 1858 he also began an overture and incidental music for *King Lear*. Some of the entr'actes, for which Vladimir Stasov sent him English themes, were written by July; the overture was not begun until 31 December, completed in sketch only on 25 September 1859 and orchestrated during the next five days. The last piece of the *King Lear* music, the Procession for Lear's entry in Act I, was not finished till February 1861. The *King Lear* music was revised and fresh numbers added in 1902–5.

III 1861–6
Balakirev often found difficulty in completing large-scale works. A second piano concerto was begun in the summer of 1861, if not earlier – the slow movement was thematically connected with a requiem which was occupying him at the same time – but the first movement was not finished until the following summer and the work was then laid aside for nearly 50 years. Even at this period Balakirev suffered fits of acute depression when (as in June 1861) he was indifferent to music, longed for death and contemplated the destruction of all his manuscripts. He also expended much time and energy on his little group of disciples, particularly Musorgsky, Rimsky-Korsakov (from November 1861) and Borodin (from November or December 1862), all three of whom composed symphonies under his immediate and constant direction. Another activity which took up much of his time was the Free School of Music opened in St Petersburg on 30 March 1862 by Gavriil Lomakin, in rivalry with the new official Conservatory; the original idea was Balakirev's and he became Lomakin's assistant. One of the school's activities was the giving of public concerts, at first by the choir of student-amateurs; in 1863 Balakirev began to share the conducting with Lomakin, taking the orchestral pieces, which soon thrust the choral part into the background, and the concerts became a highly important platform for the bringing out of new works by Balakirev and his

group, as well as compositions by the Western composers they particularly admired – Berlioz, Schumann and (a little later) Liszt.

In the summer of 1862 Balakirev, instead of staying as usual at Nizhny-Novgorod, spent two or three months in the Caucasus – most of the time at Essentuki. He was so impressed by the Caucasus that he returned there the following year, first to Pyatigorsk at the beginning of June, where he noted down Circassian tunes, then to Tiflis and Baku, where he collected Georgian and Persian melodies. One of the first direct reflections of these Caucasian impressions was the setting of Pushkin's *Gruzinskaya pesnya* ('Georgian song'), but a quasi-oriental vein had appeared in other songs *–Pesnya Selima* ('Song of Selim'), *Pesnya zolotoy rïbki* ('Song of the golden fish') – before these visits. For a time (1864) he contemplated an opera on the legend of *Zhar-ptitsa* ('The firebird') and composed a certain amount of music in the 'Caucasian' vein, but the project had to be abandoned for want of a suitable libretto. Earlier in 1864 he completed a less ambitious work, the Second Overture on Russian Themes, which was performed at a Free School concert on 18 April. This was published in 1869 as a musical picture *1000 let* ('1000 years'), alluding to the founding of the Russian state by Rurik in 862; in 1884 it was revised and re-orchestrated, and in 1890 published (with a misleading prefatory note) as a symphonic poem *Rus'*, the ancient name for Russia. The three folksongs introduced in the Overture appeared also in the *Sbornik russkikh narodnïkh pesen* ('Collection of Russian folksongs') which Balakirev had compiled between 1861 and 1865 partly from his own discoveries during summer trips up and down the Volga

from Nizhny-Novgorod, partly from fresh harmonizations of songs in the collections published by Pratsch,
Kashin and Kirsha Danilov; Balakirev's *Collection* was
published by Johansen in 1866. Yet another work begun
at this period (August 1864) made use of both Russian
and oriental folk music – a Symphony in C major, of
which considerable fragments of the first movement,
scherzo and finale existed by 1866.

One duty which occupied Balakirev from time to time
for many years was the editing and publication of
Glinka's works on behalf of the dead composer's sister,
Lyudmila Shestakova. In June 1866 at her request he
visited Prague to arrange the production there of
Glinka's operas, but the outbreak of the Seven Weeks'
War and the Prussian invasion drove him to Vienna and
thence home by way of Budapest. In January 1867 he
returned to Prague; the performances of *A Life for the
Tsar*, under Smetana, horrified him, but after five weeks
of quarrels, intrigues by Smetana and his party, and
intensive rehearsals, he was able to give *Ruslan* (16, 17
and 19 February) and *A Life for the Tsar* (22 February)
with great success. During this second visit to Prague
Balakirev finished the sketch and began the orchestration of an Overture on Czech themes begun the
previous year when, in Vienna, he had come across
Beneš Kulda's little study of folklore, *Svadba v národě
českoslovanském* ('Marriage among the Czechoslovak
people'; Prague, 1859) from which he took three tunes.
The Overture was performed on 24 May at a Free
School concert given in honour of the Slav visitors who
had come to Russia for the All-Russian Ethnographical
Exhibition in Moscow, and it was in writing of this
concert that Stasov coined the phrase *moguchaya*

kuchka ('mighty handful') which became the nickname of the Balakirev group of composers. (They never called themselves, nor were they ever called in Russia, The Five.) In 1905 the Czech Overture was revised, rescored and published as a symphonic poem.

IV 1867–74
Balakirev's tactless and despotic character and his fiery advocacy of musical nationalism had gained for him many enemies not only in Prague but also in St Petersburg, particularly in the 'German' and academic circles of the Conservatory and Russian Musical Society and among their supporters in the press, and sometimes strained his relations with his own group. But at this period his triumph seemed complete. In the autumn of 1867 he succeeded Anton Rubinstein as conductor of the Russian Musical Society symphony concerts (though six of the concerts that season were conducted by Berlioz) and in February 1868 he became director of the Free School in place of Lomakin. Another summer visit to the Caucasus (Vladikavkaz and Kislovodsk) had important artistic results but was embittered by the knowledge that the Grand Duchess Helena Pavlovna, the imperial patroness of the Russian Musical Society, was trying to oust him from the conductorship. She was at first unsuccessful, but Balakirev's tactlessness and his championship of his own group and their Western idols Liszt, Schumann and Berlioz caused so much offence that he was obliged to resign in May 1869. Immediately after this his father's illness and death (on 15 June) at Klin obliged him to spend several months in Moscow and the neighbourhood. Here he formed a close friendship with Nikolay Rubinstein and

with Tchaikovsky, the latter of whom had been moved to public protest by the Russian Musical Society scandal. In Moscow on 21 August Balakirev began an oriental fantasy, for piano, entitled *Islamey*, which he completed in St Petersburg on 25 September; it was dedicated to Nikolay Rubinstein, who played it for the first time at a Free School concert in St Petersburg on 12 December. Balakirev considered *Islamey* as a 'sketch' for a projected symphonic poem on Lermontov's *Tamara*, which he had begun a year or so before.

Balakirev now put all his energy into the work of the Free School, giving five subscription concerts in the winter of 1869–70 in open rivalry with the Russian Musical Society. But he drew no salary from the school, which received no official subsidy, and he now had to support his two sisters. A concert at Nizhny-Novgorod in September 1870, from which he hoped much, brought him a profit of only 11 rubles: a double blow to his finances and his self-esteem. Early in 1871 he passed through a mental and spiritual crisis; his friends found in him 'no trace of his former self', and he appeared inwardly lifeless. He came under the influence of a soothsayer and, from a freethinker, became – and remained for the rest of his life – a bigoted and eccentrically superstitious Orthodox Christian. In August of that year it was even rumoured among his friends that he had gone out of his mind; he avoided them and seemed quite indifferent to music. A little later he pulled himself together and prepared a series of five Free School subscription concerts for the winter of 1871–2; four were actually given, but with the fourth (on 15 April 1872) the available funds were exhausted. In July, desperate, he took a post as overseer in the goods department of the Warsaw Railway, which brought him a salary of 80 rubles a month; in his spare time he gave music lessons. But he soon lost his railway post and was obliged to support himself entirely by teaching, though after a time he was appointed supervisor of the musical classes in two schools. Balakirev remained nominally director of the Free School until the spring of 1874 when – as he never appeared there – he was asked to resign in favour of Rimsky-Korsakov. For four years, until the summer of 1876, he kept away from his old friends and took no part in musical life.

V 1874–94

Then, under the influence of Lyudmila Shestakova, he began to revive: working a little at the symphonic poem *Tamara*, making a duet arrangement of Berlioz's *Harold en Italie*, interfering in Rimsky-Korsakov's management of the Free School, resuming (now with Rimsky-Korsakov and Lyadov) his editorial work on Glinka's scores. In October 1881 he agreed to resume the direction of the Free School, which Rimsky-Korsakov had resigned. He also took over the conducting of the concerts once more, completed *Tamara* during July–September 1882, and performed it at a Free School concert on 19 March 1883. In the meantime (on 15 February 1883), after 16 months of string-pulling by influential Orthodox friends, notably the folksong enthusiast T. I. Filippov, Balakirev was appointed director of the Imperial Court Chapel with Rimsky-Korsakov as his assistant. As early as the summer of 1881 Balakirev had been entrusted with editorial responsibility for a fresh harmonization of the liturgy.

Balakirev's service in the court chapel was mostly administrative; he and Rimsky-Korsakov carried out numerous reforms, particularly in the education and living conditions of the choirboys, in whom Balakirev took a paternal interest, frequently helping them financially from his own resources (to which purpose he devoted fees for private recitals and for occasional compositions). He appeared from time to time as an orchestral conductor, notably at concerts to collect funds for the Glinka memorial at Smolensk and at the unveiling of the memorial on 6 June 1885, but his compositions during this period were few: one or two short religious choruses, the fourth Mazurka (1886), the piano piece 'Au jardin' (1884), based on a melody from his early Octet and dedicated to Henselt on the occasion of the jubilee of the latter's musical activity (1888). The following year he created a scandal by his public refusal to participate in the celebration of another such jubilee – Anton Rubinstein's – on the ground that Rubinstein had done nothing but harm to Russian music. In 1890 his relations with Rimsky-Korsakov, long strained, came to an almost complete breach, but in compensation for the loss of old friends through death or estrangement, he had gathered about him a new group of younger men of whom the most distinguished was the composer Lyapunov, his devoted disciple from 1884 onward.

In October 1894 Balakirev made his last public appearance as a pianist, playing Chopin's B♭ minor Sonata in Warsaw on the occasion of the erection of the Chopin memorial at Zelazowa Wola, a project in which he had taken a leading part. In the autumn of the same year he retired from the Imperial Chapel, with a pension of 3000 rubles a year.

VI 1895–1910

Freed from administrative and financial worries, in 1895 Balakirev actively resumed composition. During 1895–6 he composed ten songs. Since 1893 he had been working on the C major Symphony, laid aside for a quarter of a century, and he completed it in 1897; it was conducted by the composer at a Free School concert on 23 April 1898, his last appearance on the platform. In 1897 he was appointed a member of a commission of the Imperial Russian Geographical Society for the publication of Russian folksongs in performing editions; his own contribution was the provision of piano accompaniments to songs collected in the Arkhangel and Olonets Governments in 1886 by G. O. Dyutsh and F. M. Istomin; he also published the same 30 songs as little pieces for piano duet (1898). From the period 1898–1905 date the majority of Balakirev's shorter piano pieces (Scherzos nos.2 and 3, Nocturnes nos.2 and 3, the later mazurkas and so on). Ten more songs date from 1903–4.

Balakirev was now living in complete retirement, ignored and forgotten by almost everyone outside his immediate circle. In 1904 he composed a cantata for soloists, chorus and orchestra in commemoration of the centenary of Glinka's birth, with quotations from Glinka's music; it was not performed until two years later on the occasion of the unveiling of the Glinka memorial in St Petersburg (16 February 1906). In 1905 came a piano sonata in B♭ minor, of which the second movement – written earlier than the rest – was also published separately as Mazurka no.5. In 1908 he finished his Second Symphony, in D minor, using the material of a scherzo conceived as early as 1862 and

6. *Mily Alexeyevich Balakirev, c1910*

destined in 1866 for the First Symphony; it was played (under Lyapunov) at a Free School concert on 23 April 1909. During the winter of 1908–9 he wrote a suite of three pieces for piano duet and then took up his Second Piano Concerto, in E♭ major, recast the already complete first movement and added a second, based on the Requiem theme in accordance with its original intention; the composition of the finale was interrupted by two pieces of work he had undertaken for a concert in February 1910 in commemoration of the centenary of Chopin's birth: the orchestration of a suite of four of Chopin's piano pieces and a re-orchestration of his boyhood favourite, the E minor Concerto. He had long suffered from heart disease, and he was not well enough to attend the Chopin concert, though he was at a rehearsal. His end was hastened by catching cold, with resultant pleurisy, and he died early in the morning of 29 May. The finale of the E♭ Concerto was completed and orchestrated by Lyapunov.

CHAPTER TWO

Works

Balakirev's importance in the history of Russian music
is twofold – as leader and as composer. It was Balakirev,
even more than Glinka, who set the course for the
development of Russian orchestral music and lyrical
song during the second half of the 19th century. He
learned from Glinka certain methods of treating Russian
folksong instrumentally, a great deal of his bright, trans-
parent orchestral technique and many elements in his
basic idiom; but he developed and expanded even what
he learnt from Glinka – his orientalism, though still a
conventional compromise between Near-Eastern melody
and rhythm and Western harmony and technique, is a
more convincing convention than Glinka's – and he was
able to fuse it satisfactorily with the then advanced
Romantic idioms of the contemporary West, the idioms
of Chopin and Schumann, Berlioz and Liszt (Wagner
offered him nothing he could absorb; indeed he seems to
have been almost completely uninterested in opera except for Glinka's *Ruslan*). This idiom and technique he
transmitted to the men around him – particularly to
Borodin and Rimsky-Korsakov, but also in no small
measure to Musorgsky and even Tchaikovsky – partly
by enthusiastically introducing them to the music that
aroused his own enthusiasm, partly by the example of
his own works, partly by direct and at first persistent
interference in their compositions. He suggested literary

subjects, gave them folk themes to work on, dictated the very keys of their compositions (generally his favourite ones with five-flat or two-sharp signatures), watched over the progress of their work literally bar by bar, frequently altering, sometimes even composing fresh passages when their work displeased him. It was natural that they should rebel against his benevolent tyranny as they grew to artistic maturity; none of them succumbed as fatally to his influence as Lyapunov did a quarter of a century later.

Balakirev stands nearest to Glinka in his early overtures on Russian and other folktunes, in which he developed the technique of incessant variation within a framework suggesting sonata form, employed in *Kamarinskaya*. In the *King Lear* music he leans rather on the Schumann of *Manfred* and on Berlioz. These works survive only in later forms, purged of certain harmonic and orchestral crudities. The pianistic and orchestral methods of Liszt – particularly the *Totentanz* and *Ce qu'on entend sur la montagne* – first make themselves felt in *Islamey* and *Tamara*, two works which in turn exercised an important influence on Debussy and Ravel through their general *facture*, their rhythmic subtleties and their plastic handling of tiny thematic particles.

The works of Balakirev's last period differ very little in manner from his earlier music, despite the quarter of a century that separates them. There is a slight advance in technical polish, a slight loss of creative exuberance; but the C major Symphony, and the scherzo and finale of the D minor, would probably have been little different if they had been written in the 1860s. The quantity of later piano music, however, tends not only to borrow

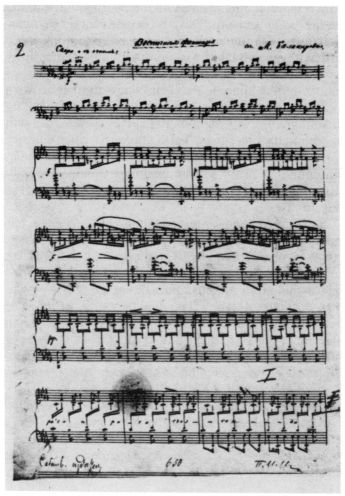

7. *Autograph MS of the opening of the second version of Balakirev's oriental fantasy for piano, 'Islamey', composed in 1902*

earlier material but to repeat mannerisms and to admit a weaker *salon* element. Only the experimental B♭ minor Sonata reaches the level of *Islamey*, although by rather different ways. Balakirev's piano writing, whether fairly easy or extremely difficult (as in *Islamey*, which he was unable to play himself, excellent pianist though he was), is always beautifully written for the instrument, taking advantage of every register, lyrical yet percussive, with exceptionally widespread left-hand parts. His transcriptions are generally in the Liszt tradition, sometimes amounting to fresh artistic creations; this is especially true of his duet transcriptions of folksongs, simple as they are.

Balakirev's songs are predominantly lyrical. His favourite poet was Lermontov, and some of his best songs – *Song of Selim, Song of the Golden Fish* – are settings of Lermontov, though his masterpiece in this field is his music for Pushkin's *Georgian Song*. He was also particularly happy with Kol'tsov and, in his later years, with the Slavophile Khomyakov. In the emotional warmth of his best songs and in the feebler lyricism of others he is reminiscent of Glinka, but his voice parts are often less singable than Glinka's and the piano part is often very important, e.g. *Georgian Song, Song of the Golden Fish, Pustïnya* ('The wilderness'), *Bezzvezdnaya polnoch'* ('Starless midnight coldly breathed'). In a different vein, his setting of Mey's *Zapevka* is hardly distinguishable from his beautifully contrived folksong arrangements.

WORKS

Numbers in the right-hand column denote references in the text.

THEATRICAL

Title	Description	Composed	Publication/MS	
King Lear	Incidental music to Shakespeare's tragedy			80–81, 92
1st version		1858–61	USSR *Lsc*	
2nd version		1902–5	Leipzig, 1902–6	82
Zhar-ptitsa [The firebird]	Opera, fragments only	1864	*Lsc*	

CHORAL

(*unaccompanied unless otherwise stated*)

86, 87

Title	Translation	Forces	Text	Composed	Publication/MS; Remarks
Pesnya: Zholtiy list	Song: The yellow leaf trembles	3-vv chorus	Lermontov	c1860–70	*Lsc*, sketches only; arr. 1v, pf, 1903–4 (Leipzig, 1904)
6 anthems:		Mixed chorus	Biblical	c1880–90	Moscow, 1900
1 So svyatimi upokoy	Rest with the holy ones				
2 Svishe prorotsi	From heaven the prophets				
3 Da vozraduyetsya dusha tvoya	Thy soul is regenerated				
4 Kheruvimskaya pesn'	Song of the Cherubim				
5 Da molchit vsyakaya plot'	All flesh is silent				
6 Dostoyno	It is worthy				
Khristos voskrese	Christ is risen	Female or children's vv	Biblical	c1887	St Petersburg, 1888 Moscow, 1906; arr. mixed chorus (Moscow, 1906)
Gimn v chest' v.k. Georgiya Vsevolodovicha	Hymn in honour of the Grand Duke Georgi Vsevolodovich	Mixed chorus	V. Likhachov	1889	St Petersburg, 1904
Umchalos' vremya zolotoye: proschal'naya pesn' vipusknikh vospitannits Polotskovo zhenskovo uchilishcha dukhovnovo vedomstva	The golden time has flown away: leaving song of the pupils of the Polotsky Ecclesiastical Girls' College	3 female vv	A. Yherova	1891	St Petersburg, 1891

95

Title	Translation	Composed	Forces	Text	Publication/MS; Remarks	
Gimn v chest' avgusteyshey pokrovitel'nitsi Polotskovo zhenskovo uchilishcha, imperatritsi Marii Fyodorovni	Hymn in honour of the most august patroness of the Polotsky Girls' College, the Empress Mariya Fyodorovna	1898	4 female vv, pf	Yasherova	Lsc	
Pod sen'yu shchedroy blagostini: gimn dlya zhenskovo khora	Beneath the shadow of Thy overflowing mercy: hymn for women's chorus	1899	Female vv	Likhachov	St Petersburg, 1899	
Molitva russkikh: gimn dlya zhenskovo khora	The prayer of the Russians: hymn for women's chorus	1899	Female vv	Pushkin	Moscow, 1899; arr. mixed chorus (Moscow, 1899)	
Gimn Khvala vsederzhitelyu bogu	Hymn: Praise to Almighty God	1902	4 female vv	M. Samo-chernova	Lil	
Tebe mi gimn poyem, o shkola dorogaya: shkol'niy gimn dlya zhenskovo ili detskovo khora	We sing you a hymn, o dear school: school hymn for women's or children's chorus	1902	Female or children's vv	P. Lebedinsky	St Petersburg, 1902	88
Kantata na otkritiye pamyatnika M.I. Glinke v Peterburge	Cantata for the unveiling of the memorial to M.I. Glinka in St Petersburg	1902-4	S, chorus, orch	V. Glebov	Leipzig, 1904	
Proshchay navsegda, nash priyut nezabvenniy: 2-ya proshchal'naya pesn' vospitannits Polotskovo zhenskovo uchilishcha dukhovnovo vedomstva	Farewell for ever, our unforgettable haven: second leaving song of the pupils of the Polotsky Ecclesiastical Girls' College	1908	3 female vv	N. Zabelina-Bekarevich	St Petersburg, 1908	

ORCHESTRAL

92

op.	Title	Composed	Publication/MS	Remarks	
4	Grande fantaisie on Russian folksongs, pf, orch	1852	Lsc	Arr. 2 pf (Moscow, 1954)	78
1	Concerto, f♯, pf, orch	1855-6	Lil	1 movt only; arr. 2 pf (Moscow, 1954)	78, 79
—	Overture on a Spanish march theme				79
	1st version	1857	Lsc	—	
	2nd version	1886	Moscow, 1887	—	

96

op.	Title	Composed	Publication/MS	Remarks	
—	Polonaise-fantaisie	1857	Lsc	Unfinished	30, 80
—	Overture on the themes of three Russian songs				
	1st version	1858	Lsc	—	
	2nd version	1881	Moscow, 1882	Balakirev's arr. pf 4 hands (Moscow, 1882)	
—	Concerto, E♭, pf, orch	1861–2, 1906–9	Leipzig, 1911	Unfinished; completed by Lyapunov	81, 90
—	Second Overture on Russian themes				
	1st version	1863–4	St Petersburg, 1869	Pubd as musical picture 1000 let [1000 years]	82
	2nd version	1884	St Petersburg, 1890	Pubd as symphonic poem Rus'; repubd with minor alterations (Leipzig, 1907)	82
—	Symphony no.1, C	1864–6, 1893–7	Leipzig, 1899	Balakirev's arr. 2 pf (Leipzig, 1899)	83, 88, 90, 92
—	Overture on Czech themes				
	1st version	1867	Lil	—	83
	2nd version	1905	Leipzig, 1906	Pubd as V Chekhii [In Bohemia]	84
—	Tamara, sym. poem	1867–82	Moscow, 1884	—	85, 86, 92
—	Symphony no.2, d	1900–08	Leipzig, 1908	Scherzo sketched c1864, orig. intended for Symphony no.1; Balakirev's arr. 2 pf (Leipzig, 1908)	88, 90, 92
—	Suite, b: Préambule, Quasi valse, Tarantella	1901–8	Lsc	Unfinished; completed by Lyapunov	
—	Suite on pieces by Chopin: Préambule, Mazurka, Intermezzo, Finale	1909	Leipzig, 1909	Based on Chopin's Etude, d, Mazurka, B♭, Nocturne, g, Scherzo, d	90

CHAMBER

op.	Title	Composed	Publication/MS	Remarks	
—	Septet, fl, cl, 2 vn, va, vc, pf	1852	—	Lost	78, 79
2	String quartet (Quatuor original russe)	1854–6	Lsc	Unfinished	78
3	Octet, fl, ob, hn, 2 vn, va, vc, pf	1855–6	Moscow, 1959	1st movt and fragments of scherzo only, perhaps rev. of Septet; scherzo adapted for Scherzo no.2, pf, 1900	79, 87
—	Romance, vc, pf	1856	Lsc	—	

PIANO

Edition: *M. A. Balakirev: polnoye sobraniye sochineniy dlya fortepiano*, ed. K. S. Sorokin (Moscow, 1951–4) [B]

(for solo pf unless otherwise stated)

88, 92, 94

Title	Composed	Publication/MS	Remarks	B	
Fantasia on themes from Glinka's *Zhizn' za tsarya*					78
1st version	1854–5	*Lsc*	—	—	
2nd version	1899	Leipzig, 1899	—	iii/1, 6	
Sonata no.1, bb, op.5	1855–6	Moscow, 1949	3 movts only, adapted from an early Bol'shaya sonata, op.3; pt. of 1st movt used later in Scherzo no.2, 1900, 2nd movt rev. as 2nd movt of Sonata, 1900–05, and as Mazurka no.5, 1900	i/2, 93	79, 80
Nocturne no.1, bb					
1st version	1856	*Lsc*	—	—	79
2nd version	1898	St Petersburg, 1898	—	ii, 117	
Fandango-étude	1856	*Lsc*	Rev. as *Ispanskaya serenada*, 1902	—	79
Scherzo no.1, b	1856	St Petersburg, 1863	—	ii, 3	79
Polka, f#	1859	St Petersburg, 1859	—	i/1, 30	
Impromptu, f	c1850–60	*Lsc*	—	—	
Mazurka no.1, Ab					
1st version	1861	St Petersburg, 1861	—	ii, 240	
2nd version	c1884	Moscow, 1884–5	—	ii, 55	
Mazurka no.2, c#					
1st version	1861	St Petersburg, 1861	—	ii, 248	
2nd version	c1884	Moscow, 1884–5	—	ii, 62	
Na Volge [On the Volga], pf 4-hands	c1863	Moscow, 1948	—	iii/1, 288	
Zhavoronok [The lark]					
1st version	c1864	Mainz, 1872	Based on Glinka's song	—	
2nd version	1900	Mainz, 1900		iii/1, 58	
Islamey, oriental fantasy					31, 85, 92, 93, 94
1st version	1869	Moscow, 1870	—	—	
2nd version	1902	Hamburg, 1902	—	i/1, 3	
Au jardin. Db	1884	Moscow, 1885	—	i/1, 36	87
Mazurka no.3, b	1886	Moscow, 1886	—	ii, 64	87
Mazurka no.4, Gb	1886	Moscow, 1886	—	ii, 73	
Pustïnya [The wilderness]	1898	Leipzig, 1898	Arr. of no.2 of Balakirev's 10 songs, 1895–6	iii/1, 3	88
30 russkikh narodnïkh pesen [30 Russian folksongs], pf 4-hands	1898	St Petersburg and Leipzig, 1898	Arr. of Balakirev's 2nd collection, 1898	iii/1, 169	

Title	Composed	Published	Notes	Ref	Pages
Dumka, eb	1900	Leipzig, 1900	—	i/1, 43	
Mazurka no.5, D	1900	Leipzig, 1900	Used in Sonata, 1900–05	ii, 82	79, 88
Scherzo no.2, bb	1900	Leipzig, 1900	Uses pt. of incomplete scherzo for Octet, 1855–6, and pt. of 1st movt of Sonata op.5, 1855–6	ii, 21	80, 88
Valse di bravura no.1, G	1900	Leipzig, 1900	—	ii, 141	
Valse mélancholique no.2, f	1900	Leipzig, 1900	—	ii, 161	
Sonata, bb	1900–05	Leipzig, 1905	2nd movt adapted from 2nd movt of Sonata op.5, 1855–6, and also pubd separately as Mazurka no.5, 1900	i/2, 3	79, 88, 94
Berceuse, Db	1901	Leipzig, 1901	—	i/1, 58	
Gondellied, a	1901	Leipzig, 1901	—	i/1, 49	
Nocturne no.2, b	1901	Leipzig, 1901	—	ii, 124	88
Scherzo no.3, F#	1901	Leipzig, 1901	—	ii, 39	88
Valse-impromptu no.3, D	1901	Leipzig, 1901	—	ii, 170	
Tarantella, B	1901	Leipzig, 1901	—	i/1, 65	
Capriccio, D	1902	Leipzig, 1902	—	i/1, 83	
Ispanskaya melodiya [Spanish melody]	1902	Leipzig, 1902	—	iii/1, 30	
Ispanskaya serenada [Spanish serenade]	1902	Leipzig, 1902	Rev. of Fandango-étude, 1856	iii/1, 37	79
Mazurka no.6, Ab	1902	Leipzig, 1902	—	ii, 94	88
Nocturne no.3, d	1902	Leipzig, 1902	—	ii, 132	
Toccata, c#	1902	Leipzig, 1902	—	i/1, 106	
Tyrolienne, F#	1902	Leipzig, 1902	—	i/1, 118	
Waltz no.4 (Valse de concert), Bb	1902	Leipzig, 1902	—	ii, 180	
Chant du pêcheur, b	1903	Leipzig, 1903	—	i/1, 129	
Humoresque, D	1903	Leipzig, 1903	—	i/1, 134	
Phantasiestück, Db	1903	Leipzig, 1903	—	i/1, 159	
Rêverie, F	1903	Leipzig, 1903	—	i/1, 149	
Waltz no.5, Db	1903	Leipzig, 1903	—	ii, 197	
Waltz no.6, f#	1903–4	Leipzig, 1904	—	ii, 213	
La fileuse, bb	1906	Leipzig, 1906	—	i/2, 69	
Mazurka no.7, eb	1906	Leipzig, 1906	—	ii, 106	
Novellette, A	1906	Leipzig, 1906	—	i/2, 57	
Waltz no.7, g#	1906	Leipzig, 1906	—	ii, 223	
Impromptu	1907	Leipzig, 1907	Based on Chopin's Preludes, eb and B	iii/1, 47	
Esquisses (Sonatina), G	1909	Leipzig, 1910		i/2, 81	
Suite, pf 4-hands: Polonaise, Little song without words, Scherzo	1909	Leipzig, 1909	Orig. sketches c1850–60, Lsc	iii/1, 246	90

SONGS

(all for 1v with pf acc.; published in St Petersburg unless otherwise stated)

Title	English version	Text	Composed	Publication: Remarks	
Tri zabïtïkh romansa [Three forgotten songs]:					
1 Tï plenitel'noy negi polna	Thou art so captivating	A. Golovinsky	1855	Leipzig, 1908	78
2 Zveno	The link	V. Tumansky			
3 Ispanskaya pesnya	Spanish song	M. Mikhaylov			80
20 songs:					
1 Pesnya razboynika	Brigand's song	A. Kol'tsov	1858	1858	
2 Oboymi, potseluy	Embrace, kiss	Kol'tsov	1858	1858	
3 Barkarola	Barcarolle	A. Arsen'yev, after Heine	1858	1858	
4 Kolïbel'naya pesnya	Cradle song	Arsen'yev	1858	1858: arr. chorus, orch/pf, 1898	
5 Vzoshol na nebo mesyats yasnïy	The bright moon	M. Yatsevich	1858	1859	
6 Kogda bezzabotno, ditya, ti rezvish'sya	When thou playest, carefree child	K. Vil'de	1858	1859	
7 Rïtsar'	The knight	Vil'de	1858	1859	
8 Mne li, molodtsu razudalomu	I'm a fine fellow	Kol'tsov	1858	1859	
9 Tak i rvetsya dusha	My heart is torn	Kol'tsov	1858	1859	
10 Pridi ko mne	Come to me	Kol'tsov	1858	1859	
11 Pesnya Selima	Song of Selim	Lermontov	1858	1859	82, 94
12 Vvedi menya, o noch, taykom	Lead me, o night	A. Maykov	1859	1859	
13 Yevreyskaya melodiya	Hebrew melody	Lermontov, after Byron	1859	1861	
14 Isstupleniye	Rapture	Kol'tsov	1859	1861	
15 Otchevo	Why	Lermontov	1860	1861	
16 Pesnya zolotoy rïbki	Song of the golden fish	Lermontov	1860	1861	82, 94
17 Pesnya starika	Old man's song	Kol'tsov	1865	1865	
18 Slïshu li golos tvoy	When I hear thy voice	Lermontov	1863	1865	
19 Gruzinskaya pesnya	Georgian song	Pushkin	1863	1865; orchd c1860–70 (Moscow, 1885)	82, 94
20 Son	The dream	Mikhaylov, after Heine	1864	1865; orchd 1906 (Moscow, 1907)	

10 songs:

No.	Title	Text (first line)	Text (author)	Composed	Publication/MS	Remarks	
1	Nad ozerom	Over the lake	A. Golenishchev-Kutuzov	1895–6	Moscow, 1896		88
2	Pustïnya	The wilderness	A. Zhemchuzhnikov		Arr. pf, 1898		94
3	Ne penitsya more	The sea does not foam	A. K. Tolstoy		—		
4	Kogda volnuyetsya zhelteyushchaya niva	When the yellow cornfield waves	Lermontov		—		
5	Ya lyubila evo	I loved him	Kol'tsov		—		
6	Sosna	The pine-tree	Lermontov		Orig. sketches, 1861, *Lil*		
7	Nachstück		A. Khomyakov		—		
8	Kak naladidi: durak	The putting-right	L. Mey		—		
9	Sredi tsvetov pori osenney	'Mid autumn flowers	I. Axakov		—		
10	Dogorayet rumyanïy zakat	The rosy sunset fades	V. Kul'chinsky		—		

10 songs:

No.	Title	Text (first line)	Text (author)	Composed	Publication/MS	Remarks	
1	Zapevka	Prologue	Mey	1903–4	Leipzig, 1904		88
2	Son	The dream	Lermontov		Orchd 1906, *Ml*		94
3	Bezzvezdnaya polnoch'	Starless midnight coldly breathed	Khomyakov		—		94
4	7 noyabrya	7th November	Khomyakov		—		
5	Ya prishol k tebe s privetom	I came to thee with greeting	A. Fet		—		
6	Vzglyani, moy drug	Look, my friend	V. Krasov		—		
7	Shepot, robkoye dïkhan'ye	A whisper, a timid breath	Fet		—		
8	Pesnya: Zholtïy list	Song: The yellow leaf trembles	Lermontov		Orig. sketches for 3-vv chorus, c1860–70, *Lsc*		
9	Iz-pod tainstvennoy kholodnoy polumaski	Under the mysterious mask	Lermontov		—		
10	Spi!	Sleep!	Khomyakov	1909	Leipzig, 1911		
	Zarya	Dawn	Khomyakov	1909	Leipzig, 1911		
	Utyos	The rock	Lermontov				

CHORAL TRANSCRIPTIONS
(all unaccompanied unless otherwise stated)

Title	Text	Forces	Transcribed	Publication/MS	Remarks
Kolibel'naya pesnya [Cradle song]	N. Kukolnik	SAATTBB	c1887	Moscow, 1900	Arr. of Glinka's song
Mazurka	Khomyakov	SATTBB	c1887	Moscow, 1898	Arr. of Chopin's Mazurkas op.6 no.4, e♭, and op.11 no.4, A♭

Title	Text	Forces	Transcribed	Publication/MS	Remarks
Venetsianskaya noch' [Venetian night]	Kozlov	SATB	c1887	Moscow, 1897	Arr. of Glinka's song
Kolibel'naya pesnya	Arsen'yev	2 female or children's vv, orch/pf	1898	Moscow, 1898	Arr. of no.4 of Balakirev's 20 songs; arr. mixed chorus, orch/pf c1880–90, Lsc
Dve bïlinï [Two legends]:	Folksongs	SATB	1902	Moscow, 1902	Nos.6 and 8 in Balakirev's 30 russkikh narodnïkh pesen [30 Russian folksongs]
1 Nikita Romanovich					
2 Korolevichi iz Krakova [The king's sons from Kraków]					
Eko serdste [Oh! my heart]	Folksong	SATB	1902	Lil	No.27 in Balakirev's 30 russkikh narodnïkh pesen

PIANO TRANSCRIPTIONS

Edition: *M. A. Balakirev: polnoye sobraniye sochineniy dlya fortepiano,* ed. K. S. Sorokin (Moscow, 1951–4) [B]

(all for solo pf unless otherwise stated)

Beethoven: Cavatina from Str Qt, op.130, 1859 (St Petersburg, 1859), B iii/1, 150

——: Allegretto from Str Qt, op.59 no.2, 1862 (Moscow, 1954), B iii/1, 153

——: Str Qt, op.95, 2 pt, 1862 (St Petersburg, 1875), B iii/2, 165

Berlioz: Introduction to La fuite en Egypte, 1864 (St Petersburg, 1864), B iii/1, 142

——: Harold en Italie, pf 4 hands, 1876 (Paris, 1879)

Chopin: Romance from Pf Conc., op.11, 1905 (Leipzig, 1905), B iii/1, 158

Dargomïzhsky: 2 excerpts from Rogdana, pf 4 hands, 1908 (St Petersburg, 1908)

Glinka: Kamarinskaya, pf 4 hands, 1863 (St Petersburg, 1863); 2nd version, solo pf, 1902 (Moscow, 1902), B iii/1, 87

——: Jota aragonesa, solo pf and pf 4 hands, 1864 (St Petersburg, 1864), B iii/1, 291; rev. 1900 (Mainz, 1900), B iii/1, 64

——: Knyaz' Kholmsky [Prince Kholmsky], pf 4 hands, 1864 (St Petersburg, 1864)

——: Noch' v Madride [Night in Madrid], solo pf and pf 4 hands, 1864 (St Petersburg, 1864)

——: Quartet, F, pf 4 hands, 1877 (Moscow, 1878)

——: Chernomor's march from Ruslan i Lyudmila, collab. Liszt, 1890 (Moscow, 1890)

——: Ne govori [Do not speak], 1903 (Leipzig, 1903), B iii/1, 102

L'vov: Overture to Undina, pf 4 hands, 1900 (Leipzig, 1901)

Paganini: Vn Caprice op.1 no.3, c1872, Lsc

A. S. Taneyev: 2 Valse-caprices, A♭, C♭, 1900 (Leipzig, 1900), B iii/1, 121, 131

Zapol'sky: Rêverie, c1900 (St Petersburg, c1900), B iii/1, 110

OTHER ARRANGEMENTS

Chopin: Mazurka op.7 no.7, arr. str orch, 1885 (Leipzig, 1904)

——: Pf Conc. op.11, orchd and partly rewritten, 1910 (Leipzig, 1910)

Dargomïzhsky: Paladin [The knight-errant], arr. 1v, orch, c1860–70, Lil

—: 2 excerpts from Rogdana, arr. 1v, pf, c1870–72 (St Petersburg, 1872)

Glinka: Bolero: O deva chudnaya moya [O my beautiful maid], arr. 1v, orch, c1860–70, Lil

—: Nochnoy smotr [Midnight review], arr. 1v, orch, 1860 (Moscow, 1906)

—: Oriental dances from Ruslan i Lyudmila, arr. 1 orch, 1868 (Leipzig, 1878)

L'vov: Overture to Undina, orchd 1900 (Leipzig, 1901)

Orchestrations of other short works and parts of works by Cui, Dargomizhsky, Glinka, Gussakovsky and Liszt

FOLKSONG COLLECTIONS

Sbornik russkikh narodnikh pesen [Collection of Russian folksongs], 82–3
1865–6 (St Petersburg, 1866); ed. E. Gippius (Moscow, 4/1957)

30 russkiikh narodnikh pesen [30 Russian folksongs], 1898 (Leipzig, 88, 94
1898); arr. pf 4 hands, 1898, nos.6, 8 and 27 also arr. chorus, 1902

EDITIONS

F. Chopin: *Sonate pour piano et violoncelle, op.65* (Leipzig, 1907)

F. Chopin: *Premier trio pour pianoforte, violon et violoncelle, op.8* (Leipzig, 1908)

I. Laskovsky: *Oeuvres complètes pour piano* (St Petersburg, 1858–9)

V. Odoyevsky: *Berceuse* (Moscow, 1895)

M. Wielhorski and F. Liszt: *Lyubila ya* [Loved I him] (Moscow, 1887)

Balakirev assisted with the preparation of Berlioz's Te Deum for publication (Leipzig, 1901), edited a selection of Tausig's piano compositions (Leipzig, 1903–4, 1907) and also produced editions of many of Glinka's works, a list of which is contained in Garden (1967). 339ff.

BIBLIOGRAPHY

R. Newmarch: 'Mily Balakireff', *SIMG*, iv (1902–3), 157

B. Grodsky: *M. A. Balakirev: kratkiy ocherk evo zhizni i deyatel'nosti* [A short essay on his life and works] (St Petersburg, 1910)

V. Karatïgin: 'M. A. Balakirev', *Apollon* (1910), no.10, p.48

V. Karenin: Obituary, *Russkaya mïsl'* (1910), 191

S. M. Lyapunov: 'M. A. Balakirev', *EIT* (1910), no.7, p.40; no.8, p.31

M. D. Calvocoressi, ed.: 'Balakirew: lettres inédites à M. D. Calvocoressi', *Revue musicale mensuelle*, vii/7 (1911), 1

G. I. Timofeyev: 'M. A. Balakirev v Prage: iz evo perepiski' [Balakirev in Prague: from his correspondence], *Sovremennïy mir* (1911), no.6, pp.147–86

S. M. Lyapunov, ed.: *Perepiska M. A. Balakireva s P. I. Chaykovskim* [Balakirev's correspondence with Tchaikovsky] (St Petersburg, 1912)

G. Timofeyev: 'M. A. Balakirev', *Russkaya mïsl'* (1912), no.6, p.38; no.7, p.55

S. M. Lyapunov, ed.: 'Perepiska M. A. Balakireva i N. A. Rimskovo-Korsakova' [Balakirev's correspondence with Rimsky-Korsakov], *MS* (1915–16), no.1, p.114; no.2, p.89; no.3, p.75; no.6, p.56; no.7, p.86; (1916–17), no.1, p.81; no.2, p.33; no.3, p.78; no.4, p.53; no.7–8, p.56

G. Abraham: 'Balakirev's Symphonies', *ML*, xiv (1933), 355

——: 'Balakirev: a Flawed Genius', *Studies in Russian Music* (London, 1935), 311ff

V. Karenin, ed.: *Perepiska M. A. Balakireva s V. V. Stasovïm* [Balakirev's correspondence with Stasov], i (Moscow, 1935) [incl. G. L. Kiselyov: 'Perepiska Balakireva i Stasova kak muzïkal'no-istoricheskiy material' [Balakirev's correspondence with Stasov as source material on music history], pp.xiiff]

M. D. Calvocoressi: 'Mily Balakiref', M. D. Calvocoressi and G. Abraham: *Masters of Russian Music* (London, 1936), 97–146

V. Muzalevsky: *M. A. Balakirev: kritiko-biograficheskiy ocherk* (Leningrad, 1938)

G. Abraham: 'Balakirev's Music to *King Lear*', *On Russian Music* (London, 1939), 193ff

——: 'Balakirev's Piano Sonata', *On Russian Music* (London, 1939), 205ff

——: 'Balakirev's Symphonies', *On Russian Music* (London, 1939), 179ff

A. Kandinsky: *Simfonicheskiye proizvedeniya M. Balakireva* [Balakirev's symphonic compositions] (Moscow and Leningrad, 1950)

A. S. Lyapunova: 'Glinka i Balakirev', *SovM* (1953), no.2, p.75

Bibliography

M. Montagu-Nathan, ed.: 'Balakirev's Letters to Calvocoressi', *ML*, xxxv (1954), 347

I. Belza, ed.: *Izistorii russko-cheshskikh muzïkal'nïkh svyazey* [From the history of Russo–Czech musical relations] (Moscow, 1955), 25 [incl. 23 letters from Balakirev to Boleslav Kalenský]

V. A. Kiselyov, ed.: *M. A. Balakirev: perepiska s N. G. Rubinshteynom i s M. P. Belyayevïm* [Balakirev's correspondence with Rubinstein and Belyayev] (Moscow, 1956)

V. A. Vasina-Grossman: 'Russkiy romans vo vtoroy polovine XIX veka: romanisï Balakireva i Kyui' [The Russian song in the second half of the 19th century: the songs of Balakirev and Cui], *Russkiy klassicheskiy romans XIX veka* (Moscow, 1956), 137–73

V. A. Kiselyov and A. S. Lyapunova, eds.: *M. A. Balakirev: perepiska s notoizdatel'stvom P. Yurgenson* [Balakirev's correspondence with Jürgenson's publishing house] (Moscow, 1958)

V. A. Kiselyov: *Avtografï M. A. Balakireva i materialï, svyazannïye s evo deyatel'nost'yu v fondakh gosudarstvennovo tsentral'novo muzeya muzïkal'noy kul'turï imeni M. I. Glinki* [Balakirev's autographs and other materials connected with his activities, contained in the archives of the Glinka Central Museum of Musical Culture, Moscow] (Moscow, 1959)

Yu. A. Kremlyov and others, eds.: *Mily Alexeyevich Balakirev: issledovaniya i stat'i* [Research and articles] (Leningrad, 1961) [incl. articles on an autograph song for *The Firebird*, the symphonic works, an unrealized opera project, Balakirev's journeys to Warsaw, the piano music, the creative relationship between Balakirev and Lyapunov, the choral works and the ballads and songs]

——: *Mily Alexeyevich Balakirev: vospominaniya i pis'ma* [Reminiscences and letters] (Leningrad, 1962) [incl. letters to his father, Filippov, Timofeyev, Chernov, Zhemchuzhnikov, Bulich, Tchaikovsky, Bourgault-Ducoudray; list of pubd letters; reminiscences by Kul'chinsky, Lalayeva and others]

A. S. Lyapunova, ed.: 'Perepiska M. A. Balakireva i N. A. Rimskovo-Korsakova' [Correspondence between Balakirev and Rimsky-Korsakov], *N. Rimsky-Korsakov: literaturnïye proizvedeniya i perepiska*, v (Moscow, 1963), 17–210

R. Davis: 'Henselt, Balakirev and the Piano', *MR*, xxviii (1967), 173–208

E. Garden: *Balakirev: a Critical Study of his Life and Music* (London, 1967)

I. Kunin: *Mily Alexeyevich Balakirev: zhizn' i tvorchestvo v pis'makh i dokumentakh* [Life and works in letters and documents] (Moscow, 1967)

A. S. Lyapunova and E. E. Yazovitskaya: *Mily Alexeyevich Balakirev:*

letopis' zhizni i tvorchestva [Chronicle of his life and works] (Leningrad, 1967)

E. Garden: 'Balakirev's Personality', *PRMA*, xcvi (1969–70), 43

A. S. Lyapunova, ed.: *M. A. Balakirev – V. V. Stasov: perepiska,* i *1858–80,* ii *1881–1906* [Correspondence] (Moscow, 1970–71)

M. Smirnov: *Fortepiannïe proiz vedeniya kompozitorov Moguchye' kuchki* [The piano works of the Mighty Handful] (Moscow, 1971)

W. Szekalow: 'Wanda Landowska, Balakiriew i Taniejew', *Ruch Muzyczny*, xix (1975), 16

M. K. Černy: 'Smetana a Balakirev', *HRo*, xiii (1976), 239

N. Luzum: 'Romansy Balakireva', *SovM* (1976), no.12, p.133

E. Garden: 'Three Russian Piano Concertos', *ML*, lx (1979), 166

A. Lischke: 'Un complément inédit à la correspondance de Balakirev: trente-quatre lettres à Alexandre Bernardi', *RdM*, lxvii (1981), 35

R. C. Ridenour: *Nationalism, Modernism and Personal Rivalry in Nineteenth-century Russian Music* (Ann Arbor, 1981)

E. Garden: 'Balakirev's Influence on Musorgsky', *Musorgsky In Memoriam, 1881–1981* (Ann Arbor, 1982), 11

——: 'The Influence of Balakirev on Tchaikovsky', *PRMA*, cvii (1982), 86

R. Taruskin: 'How the Acorn Took Root: a Tale of Russia', *19th Century Music*, vi (1982–3), 189

E. Garden: 'Balakirev: the Years of Crisis (1867–76)', *Russian and Soviet Music: Essays for Boris Schwarz* (Ann Arbor, 1984), 145

——: 'Russian Folksong and Balakirev's 1866 Collection', *Soundings*, xi (1984), 52

——: 'Sibelius and Balakirev', *Slavonic and Western Music: Essays for Gerald Abraham* (Ann Arbor and Oxford, 1985), 215

MODEST MUSORGSKY

Gerald Abraham

CHAPTER ONE

Life

Modest Petrovich Musorgsky (or Moussorgsky), the most strikingly individual Russian composer of the later 19th century, was born in Karevo, Pskov district, on 21 March 1839. He was the youngest son of a well-to-do landowner, but had peasant blood, his paternal grandmother having been a serf. According to a not altogether reliable autobiographical sketch written in 1881, under his nurse's influence he became familiar with Russian folk tales, and it was mainly this contact with the spirit of the life of the people which impelled him to improvise music before he had learnt even the most elementary rules of piano playing. His mother gave him his first lessons, and he made such progress that at the age of seven he could play short pieces by Liszt. When he was nine he performed a Field concerto before a large audience in his parents' house, and in August 1849 he began to have piano lessons with Anton Herke, a pupil of Henselt. His general education was continued first at a preparatory school, then with a tutor, and in 1852 he entered the Cadet School of the Guards in St Petersburg, where, according to his elder brother, he was particularly interested in history and German philosophy. During his first year at the Cadet School he composed a *Porte-enseigne polka*, dedicated to his schoolfellows, which was published at his father's expense. He was in the school choir, and the religious instructor, Father Krupsky, encouraged him to study the church music of Bortnyansky and other Russian composers of the early 19th century. The piano lessons with Herke ended in 1854. Musorgsky had learnt nothing of harmony or composition; nevertheless in 1856 he tried to write an opera based on Victor Hugo's *Han d'Islande*. The same year he left the Cadet School and entered the Preobrazhensky Regiment of Guards. Borodin, who met him at this period, described him as an elegant piano-playing dilettante.

In 1857 Musorgsky made the acquaintance of Dargomïzhsky, already an established composer, and César Cui, like himself a young military officer who dabbled in composition; through them, in turn, he met Balakirev and Stasov. Before long he induced Balakirev, his senior by only three years, to give him lessons in musical form, based mainly on Beethoven's symphonies (which they played in four-hand arrangements) but also on compositions by Schubert, Schumann, Glinka and others. From this period date a song, *Gde tï, zvezdochka?* ('Where art thou, little star?'), and a *Souvenir d'enfance* for piano; in 1858 he wrote more songs, piano sonatas in E♭ major and F♯ minor, and the introduction to an opera based on Ozerov's play *Edip v Afinakh* ('Oedipus in Athens'), a project abandoned in 1860. During the summer of 1858 he passed through a nervous or spiritual crisis and on 17 July he resigned his commission; work with Balakirev was resumed later in the year and in November he composed two scherzos for piano, one in C♯ minor, the other in B♭ (he orchestrated the latter with Balakirev's assistance). A visit to Moscow in the summer of 1859 fired his patriotic imagination and provided him with one of the deepest experiences of his youth. He wrote to Balakirev, 'You know I have been a cosmopolitan, but now I have undergone a sort of re-birth: I have been brought near to everything Russian'. But this mood was not reflected in his next composi-tions, a mildly Schumannesque *Impromptu passionné* for piano, suggested by two characters in Herzen's novel *Who is to Blame?*, and a projected cantata, *Marsh Shamilya* ('Shamil's march') for tenor and bass, chorus and orchestra. On 23 January 1860 his Scherzo in B♭ was conducted by Anton Rubinstein at a concert in St Petersburg of the newly founded Russian Musical Society.

The year 1860 was marked by another nervous crisis. Musorgsky wrote, 'During the greater part of this time, from May to August, my brain was weak and in a state of violent irritability'. But in the autumn he announced his recovery and his intention to put all his 'musical sins' in order and begin a new period of his creative life. He may already have toyed with the idea of an opera based on Gogol's story *Vecher nakanune Ivana Kupala* ('St John's eve'), and he now seems to have thought of using material originally intended for this in a setting of the witches' sabbath scene on the Bare Mountain from a play *Ved'ma* ('The witch') by an army comrade, Baron Georgy Mengden. Shortly afterwards, in the winter of 1860–61, he produced an Allegro in C for four hands, a duet transcription in C minor of his C♯ minor Scherzo, the beginnings of two movements of a Symphony in D and an 'essay in instrumentation', *Alla marcia notturna*. That his nervous irritability was not entirely calmed appears from his petulant complaints that Balakirev was 'keeping him in leading-strings' and from his rejection of an opportunity to have the temple scene from his

Oedipus performed by the Russian Musical Society. (The scene was, however, given a concert performance in the Mariinsky Theatre, St Petersburg, on 18 April 1861, under K. N. Lyadov.)

The emancipation of the serfs in March 1861 involved Musorgsky in family difficulties. He was obliged to spend a great part of the next two years in the country, assisting his only surviving brother in the management of the family estate of Karevo. The D major Symphony came to nothing, and both Stasov and Balakirev regretfully agreed that 'Musorgsky is almost an idiot'. Yet he had already written the characteristic *Intermezzo in modo classico* (inspired by a country scene) in its original form for piano solo (winter 1860–61), and in the summer of 1863 he composed two songs, *Pesn' startsa* ('Old man's song') – a setting of 'An die Türen will ich schleichen' from Goethe's *Wilhelm Meister* – and a translation of Byron's *Song of Saul before the Battle*, all of which announce the imminence of artistic maturity. *Tsar' Saul* ('King Saul') may have been written under the influence of Serov's opera *Judith*, which Musorgsky had recently heard; under the combined impact of *Judith* and the reading of Flaubert's *Salammbô* he began in the autumn of 1863 to write the libretto of an opera on *Salammbô*, interweaving his own verses with borrowings from Heine and Russian poets, and taking his stage directions wholesale from Flaubert. The music of *Salammbô*, on which he worked intermittently until the summer of 1866, includes a certain amount of self-borrowing from *Oedipus*, but some of it, in turn, was later transferred with little alteration to *Boris Godunov*.

Financial straits now obliged Musorgsky to enter the

civil service. On 13 December 1863 he was posted to the chief engineering department of the Ministry of Communications, with the rank of collegiate secretary, and on 1 February 1864 he was appointed assistant head clerk of the barracks section of the department. This period of service lasted less than four years; on 13 December 1866 he was promoted to the rank of titular councillor, but on 10 May 1867 he was dismissed from the Ministry. Even before entering the service and beginning *Salammbô* Musorgsky had settled again in St Petersburg (autumn 1863) in conditions that, under the influence of Chernïshevsky's recently published novel *Chto delat'?* ('What is to be done?'), had suddenly become popular among the younger Russian intellectuals: he joined a commune with five other young men, living in the same flat and ardently cultivating and exchanging advanced ideas on art, religion, philosophy and politics. One member of the commune, V. A. Loginov, provided him with the theme of his *Duma* ('Rêverie') for piano. *Salammbô* was one of the books read by the commune and, according to Stasov, it was during the years of communal life that Musorgsky absorbed those views (put forward above all in the writings of Chernïshevsky and Dobrolyubov) on 'artistic truth' and the necessity of subordinating art to life, which he spent his remaining years in working out. The earliest evidence of the new tendency was the first version of the song *Kalistratushka*. Further essays in the same direction were the two piano pieces *Iz vospominaniy detstva* ('From memories of childhood'), written in April 1865 after his mother's death. That last event was the probable cause of Musorgsky's first serious bout of dipsomania, which ended in an attack of delirium

8. Modest Petrovich Musorgsky: portrait (1881) by I. E. Repin

tremens necessitating his removal from the commune to his brother's flat in the autumn of 1865.

Work on *Salammbô* seems to have been abandoned in the summer of 1866, although *Porazheniye Sennakheriba* ('The destruction of Sennacherib') for chorus and orchestra (January 1867; performed in St Petersburg, under Balakirev, two months later) belongs to the same circle of ideas. But between 14 September and 9 October 1866 Musorgsky had written three songs: *Svetik Savishna* ('Darling Savishna'), *Akh tï, p'yanaya teterya!* ('You drunken sot!') and *Seminarist* ('The seminarist'), which unmistakably mark the beginning of the full stream of musical naturalism and ironic, realistic comedy in song; the flow of songs in this vein continued throughout 1867. In that year two of them, *Darling Savishna* and *Hopak*, together with *Otchevo, skazhi* ('Tell me why') of nine years earlier, were published by Johansen: these were the first of Musorgsky's works to appear in print since the *Porte-enseigne polka*. Freed from government service and living in the country at his brother's house at Minkino during the summer of 1867, Musorgsky occupied himself with orchestral composition and the piano transcription of movements from Beethoven's quartets; the orchestral works were a piece based on the early *Witch* music, *Ivanova noch' na Lïsoy gore* ('St John's Night on the Bare Mountain'), an orchestral version of the *Intermezzo in modo classico*, with an additional trio, and an unfinished symphonic poem *Podibrad Cheshskiy* ('Poděbrad of Bohemia'), inspired by the Pan-Slav Congress held earlier in the summer.

Returning to St Petersburg in the autumn, Musorgsky, like the other members of the Balakirev–Stasov circle (who had just been ironically dubbed the

'Moguchaya Kuchka', or 'Mighty Handful') became especially interested in Dargomïzhsky, then engaged on his most extreme experiment in operatic naturalism, *Kamenniy gost'* ('The stone guest'). Musorgsky found his own tendencies strongly reinforced, and on 23 June 1868 embarked on his own most daring essay, a setting of Gogol's prose comedy *Zhenit'ba* ('The marriage'); the first act was completed by 20 July, but the work was carried no farther. The completed act was privately performed at Cui's on 6 October, the composer himself singing the part of the hero; but even Dargomïzhsky and his other friends felt that experimentalism had been carried too far. Stasov alone was roused to closer interest in Musorgsky's work and from that time onwards became his adviser and champion. Musorgsky was by this time interested in a fresh project, in which he was able to blend realism with his older strain of romantic lyricism, an opera on the subject of *Boris Godunov*, to his own libretto based partly on Pushkin's play. The first scene was completed in vocal score on 12 November. On 2 January 1869 Musorgsky re-entered the government service as assistant head clerk in the third section of the forestry department of the Ministry of State Property. He was able to live with old friends, the brother and sister A. P. and N. P. Opochinin, and in these settled conditions the original version of *Boris*, in seven scenes, was completed in vocal score by the end of July 1869 and in full score on 27 December. A fortnight before the completion of the full score Musorgsky was promoted to the rank of collegiate assessor.

In July 1870 Musorgsky began negotiations for a production of *Boris* and embarked on the composition of a new opera, *Bobïl'*, the music of one completed scene of which was later transferred to *Khovanshchina*. In the autumn he wrote four naturalistic studies of child life. These songs to his own words were published, together with one earlier piece in the same vein, as a cycle, *Detskaya* ('The nursery'); two more were added in the second edition. But Musorgsky was soon obliged to return to *Boris*. On 22 February 1871 the opera committee of the Mariinsky Theatre rejected his score and, very easily offended though he was, he began with unusual meekness to recast his work, introducing the present third act and the final scene of riot and anarchy, eliminating the scene before St Basil's Cathedral and making other drastic changes. This second version, consisting of a prologue and four acts, was completed in full score on 5 July 1872. During the latter part of the work (autumn 1871 onwards) Musorgsky shared an apartment with another composer of the Balakirev group, Rimsky-Korsakov, then engaged on his opera *The Maid of Pskov*, and in the spring of 1872 both composers interrupted their operas to collaborate with two others of their circle (Borodin and Cui) in a projected opera-ballet, *Mlada*, which was never completed. For part of his contribution to *Mlada* Musorgsky again drew on his old *Oedipus* music and his *St John's Night on the Bare Mountain*; *Mlada* in turn yielded material for later compositions. From that period the Balakirev circle tended to disintegrate.

On 17 February 1872 the finale of the first act of *Boris* was performed at a Russian Musical Society concert in St Petersburg, under Nápravník, and on 15 April Balakirev conducted the polonaise at a concert of the Free School of Music. But in the autumn the opera committee of the Imperial Theatres rejected the second version, as it had the first. Nevertheless, on the initiative of some of the singers and in defiance of the committee, three scenes from *Boris* were performed as part of a benefit performance for the stage manager of the Mariinsky Theatre on 17 February 1873, and met with great success. A month or two later the publisher Bessel announced that he had acquired the rights in the opera and opened subscriptions for the vocal score. This was issued in January 1874 (it represents a modification of the second version), and on 8 February 1874 *Boris Godunov* was produced at the Mariinsky Theatre, St Petersburg, for the benefit of the singer Yuliya Platonova. It was repeated a week later, and eight more performances were given in the course of the season.

Since June–July 1872 Musorgsky had on Stasov's suggestion been collecting historical and musical material for another historical opera, *Khovanshchina*, dealing with the political disturbances under the regency which preceded Peter the Great's full accession to the throne. Instead of writing a complete libretto, or at least preparing a scenario, he appears to have confused himself by too much study of historical sources and then to have written fragments of libretto with too little reference to a definite plan. From this period date most of Musorgsky's dicta on the function of art, the value of technique and so on, all expressed in letters to his confidant Stasov. In the summer of 1873 he formed a close friendship with a family connection, Count A. A. Golenishchev-Kutuzov, a poet of some ability, and agreed to share a flat with him. At the same period he began the music of *Khovanshchina*, on which he continued to work intermittently until August 1880, although most of it was written in 1873 and 1875–6. He was no longer capable of sustained effort; under the influence of heavy drinking his character had begun to deteriorate seriously, and he confessed to 'fits of dementia'. Stasov failed to induce him to visit Liszt, who had expressed admiration of *The Nursery*, and his friend's temporary absence in western Europe removed a restraining influence. Nevertheless Musorgsky earned official promotion to the grade of court councillor (13 December 1873) and was made senior head clerk of his department (17 March 1875).

Even the successful production of *Boris* had an unfortunate effect on the composer personally: it inflated his self-esteem and, owing to several unlucky circumstances, wounded it at the same time. Little was done to *Khovanshchina* in 1874, although the familiar 'introduction' dates from September of that year. From June to November Musorgsky composed the song cycle *Bez solntsa* ('Sunless') to poems by Golenishchev-Kutuzov; in June he also wrote the cycle of piano pieces *Kartinki s vïstavki* ('Pictures at an exhibition'), suggested by a memorial exhibition of the architectural drawings, stage designs and watercolours of his friend Victor Hartmann, who had died the year before. A more serious deflection from *Khovanshchina* was the idea of a comic opera based on Gogol's short story *Sorochinskaya yarmarka* ('Sorochintsy fair'), which occurred to him that summer, though he temporarily abandoned the project early in 1875. During the first half of 1875 he wrote the first three numbers of a new song cycle to Golenishchev-Kutuzov's words, *Pesni i plyaski smerti* ('Songs and dances of death'). When the poet, who married a few months later, went off to the country, Musorgsky was given a home by a retired naval officer, P. A. Naumov.

At the same time he had drifted away from his earlier musical friends, Cui and Rimsky-Korsakov, partly because of their pursuit of different musical ideals, partly because of their very different ways of life.

During the spring of 1876 Musorgsky and Lyudmila Shestakova, Glinka's sister, were much concerned in organizing the jubilee celebrations of the bass singer Osip Petrov, the first Varlaam in *Boris*. This event seems to have turned his thoughts back to *Sorochintsy Fair*, which he had conceived from the outset with Petrov in mind, and during the latter part of 1876 he worked at both the Gogol opera and *Khovanshchina*. The next year he thrust *Khovanshchina* aside entirely in favour of *Sorochintsy Fair*, but after Petrov's death (14 March 1878) he cooled towards that in turn. At this period he was experimenting with a type of compromise between lyrical melody and subtly accurate, naturalistic declamation, 'the incorporation of recitative in melody. . . . I should like to call it "intelligently justified" melody'. The results are apparent in some passages of the two operas and, more immediately, in a group of songs to poems by Alexey Tolstoy composed between 17 March and 2 April 1877. On 14 July the same year he completed a short choral piece, *Iisus Navin* ('Jesus Navin'), based on two numbers from *Salammbô*. During the earlier part of 1878 Musorgsky appears to have led a more respectable life. Balakirev, just beginning to show himself again in the musical world after six years of retirement, was 'pleasantly surprised' on meeting him. On 4 June Musorgsky was promoted to collegiate councillor. Later in the summer there was a serious relapse but, thanks to the efforts of Stasov and Balakirev, he was transferred from the forestry department to a temporary post in the Revision Commission of Government Control, whose director, the folksong enthusiast T. I Filippov, proved exceedingly lenient.

The following year Filippov was even so complaisant as to allow Musorgsky leave for a three-months concert tour in the Ukraine, Crimea and towns along the Don and the Volga. An old acquaintance, the contralto Darya Leonova, invited him to' make this provincial tour as her accompanist, and between 11 August and 29 October they gave concerts at Poltava, Elizavetgrad, Nikolayev, Kherson, Odessa, Sevastopol, Yalta, Rostov-na-Donu, Novocherkassk, Voronezh, Tambov and Tver (see Keldïsh and Yakovlev, 1932, for full programmes). Besides accompanying Leonova, who naturally included some of his songs in her programmes, Musorgsky appeared as soloist in transcriptions of excerpts from his operas, including the Coronation Scene from *Boris*, the March of the Preobrazhensky Guards from *Khovanshchina* and the *Bare Mountain* music (now described as 'a musical picture from a new comic opera, *Sorochintsy Fair*'). At the later concerts he also played a 'grand musical picture', *Burya na Chernom more* ('Storm on the Black Sea'), which was never written down. Two slighter travel impressions for piano, *Na yuzhnom beregu Krïma* ('On the southern shore of the Crimea'), were published the following year.

On 13 January 1880 Musorgsky was at last obliged to leave the government service, but Filippov and other friends guaranteed him a monthly pension of 100 rubles on condition that he finish *Khovanshchina*. Unfortunately, shortly afterwards another group of well-wishers offered him a sum of 80 rubles on condition that he

9. Musorgsky's 'Boris Godunov', first production (St Petersburg, Mariinsky Theatre, 1874), the inn near the Lithuanian border (Act 2 scene i): engraving by K. Veyrman after N. Negadayev's painting of the design by I. P. Andreyev (from Vsemirnaya illyustratsiya', 9 March 1874)

finish *Sorochintsy Fair* within a year. (They also pressed him to make piano arrangements of excerpts from it for the publisher Bernard, and the popular *Hopak* first appeared in this form.) In consequence both operas remained unfinished. During this last year of his life Musorgsky made further appearances as Leonova's accompanist. She also took him with her to her summer villa at Oranienbaum and employed him as accompanist, theory teacher and factotum in the music school which she instituted in St Petersburg; he composed a number of folksong arrangements and vocalises for the pupils there. Besides working at his two operas he contemplated writing an orchestral suite on oriental themes and composed (January or February 1880) a trio *alla turca* for a processional march on a Russian folksong, originally part of the *Mlada* music. This 'new' march, intended to accompany one of a series of *tableaux vivants* of the reign of Alexander II, was performed under the title *Vzyatiye Karsa* ('The capture of Kars') by Nápravníl at a concert of the Russian Musical Society in St Petersburg on 30 October.

On 15 February 1881 Musorgsky made his last public appearance, when Rimsky-Korsakov conducted *The Destruction of Sennacherib* at a concert of the Free School of Music, and he acknowledged the applause. Eight days later he went to Leonova (according to her own account) 'in a state of great nervous excitement', saying 'that there was nothing left for him but to go and beg in the streets'. That evening he had a fit of alcoholic epilepsy. He spent the night at Leonova's house and the next day (24 February) had three more fits. On 26 February he was removed by his friends to the Nikolayevsky Military Hospital. There was a temporary improvement (14–17 March) during which Repin painted his famous portrait, but on 28 March he died. He was buried in the Nevsky Cemetery two days later.

CHAPTER TWO

Posthumous completion of works

Comparatively few of Musorgsky's works were published
during his lifetime, and the editing of the posthumous
publications was mainly – at first solely – carried out
by Rimsky-Korsakov; these were issued by Bessel. In
Rimsky-Korsakov's opinion Musorgsky, though 'so
talented, original, full of so much that was new and
vital', revealed in his manuscripts technical clumsiness,
'absurd, disconnected harmony, ugly part-writing,
sometimes strikingly illogical modulation, sometimes a
depressing lack of it, unsuccessful scoring of the orchestral things. . . . Publication without some setting in
order by a skilled hand would have had no sense, except
a biographical–historical one'. If an 'archaeologically
exact edition' was called for after 50 years, one could
always be produced; 'what was needed at the moment
was an edition for performance, for practical artistic
aims, for familiarization with his enormous talent, not for
the study of his personality and artistic transgressions'.

Accordingly every composition that passed through
Rimsky-Korsakov's hands was to a greater or lesser
degree 'corrected' by him. In the case of the *Bare
Mountain* music he entirely rejected the completed
orchestral version of 1867 (which was not published
until 1968) and composed what was virtually a new
orchestral piece on Musorgsky's various materials, most
nearly approximating to the version with chorus that

Musorgsky had prepared for *Sorochintsy Fair*. The most important, and most necessary, of Rimsky-Korsakov's immediate tasks was the completion and orchestration of *Khovanshchina*, produced by an amateur group in St Petersburg on 21 February 1886; the vocal score of the Rimsky-Korsakov version was published by Bessel in 1883. Passages omitted by Rimsky-Korsakov were orchestrated by Ravel and Stravinsky and inserted for the first Paris production (5 June 1913); Stravinsky composed the final chorus afresh from Musorgsky's themes, and this was published by Bessel in 1913. These insertions in the Rimsky-Korsakov version were balanced by drastic cuts. Rimsky-Korsakov later turned his attention to the compositions published in Musorgsky's lifetime and produced editions which for a number of years supplanted the authentic texts. When in 1898 Belyayev reissued the seven songs originally published by Johansen 30 years earlier, they were anonymously edited by Rimsky-Korsakov. He also edited for Bessel in 1908 new editions of the songs originally published by that firm, making few changes but producing a 'free paraphrase' of the first number of *The Nursery*.

All these re-editions are of minor importance compared with Rimsky-Korsakov's versions of *Boris Godunov*. As early as 1888 he rescored the polonaise, in 1891–2 the Coronation Scene; in 1896 he produced a completely new version of the opera with drastic cuts, wholesale rewriting and complete rescoring of the surviving text, insertion of a certain amount of new music composed by himself and transposition of the order of the last two scenes. This version was produced privately in the Great Hall of the St Petersburg Conservatory on

10 December 1896, by the Mamontov Opera Company with Shalyapin (Moscow, 19 December 1898; St Petersburg, 19 March 1899), and by the Imperial Theatres, again with Shalyapin (Moscow, 26 April 1901; St Petersburg, 22 November 1904). The vocal score was published by Bessel. During 1906–8 Rimsky-Korsakov prepared a fresh version, also published in vocal score by Bessel, in which he restored the cuts but not the original text and left in his own additions. For the Paris production of *Boris* (19 May 1908), the first in western Europe, he composed two new passages for the Coronation Scene.

Rimsky-Korsakov left the fragmentary *Salammbô* untouched, but a year or two before his death he decided on the publication of the single act of *The Marriage*; the vocal score, edited by him with the relatively few changes mentioned in the preface to the score, was published by Bessel in 1908. He also began the orchestration, but completed only a few pages; the single act was subsequently orchestrated by the Soviet conductor Alexander Gauk (and supposedly by Ravel, but the matter is controversial). In 1931 Ippolitov-Ivanov composed and orchestrated the three remaining acts of Gogol's comedy. Rimsky-Korsakov made no attempt to edit *Sorochintsy Fair* (apart from the *Bare Mountain* music inserted in it); on his suggestion the completion of the libretto was entrusted to Golenishchev-Kutuzov, that of the music to A. K. Lyadov. Little was done, but in 1886 Bessel published Khivrya's song and Parasya's *dumka* with piano, and the *hopak* for piano solo (all three in practically pure texts), and during the period 1904–14 a series of further numbers: (*a*) the *parobok*'s *dumka*, edited and orchestrated by Lyadov, with a vocal score (1904); (*b*) Lyadov's orchestration of the *hopak* with a 'piano arrangement', essentially identical with the 1886 edition (1904); (*c*) Lyadov's rewritten version of the introduction, in full score and piano arrangements; (*d*) Introduction and Fair Scene, edited by V. G. Karatïgin in vocal score (1912); (*e*) the scene between Cherevik and the *kum*, edited by Karatïgin in vocal score (1912); (*f*) the comic scene from Act 2, edited by Karatïgin in vocal score (1912); (*g*) Parasya's *dumka*, orchestrated by V. A. Senilov (1912); and (*h*) Khivrya's song, orchestrated by Lyadov, with vocal score essentially identical with the 1886 edition (1914). Karatïgin's edition and completion of the finale of Act 2 was engraved but never published. Of the Lyadov–Karatïgin numbers (*c*), (*d*) (Fair Scene only) and (*f*) were first performed as illustrations to a lecture on *Sorochintsy Fair* by Karatïgin, given privately at Count Osten-Drizen's in St Petersburg, with piano and without chorus, on 29 March 1911; they were repeated in public and with costumes and scenery, with the addition of the finale of Act 2, in the Comedia Theatre, St Petersburg, on 30 December of the same year. On 21 October 1913, a pastiche of all the available numbers in the Lyadov and Karatïgin editions, with Rimsky-Korsakov's version of the *Bare Mountain*, was produced at the Moscow Free Theatre, the lacunae in the action being filled with spoken dialogue by K. A. Mardzhanov; the numbers edited by Karatïgin were orchestrated by Yu. S. Sakhnovsky, who also composed a few additional passages. This production caused legal action by Bessel on a point of copyright, and Sakhnovsky's score was suppressed. In 1915 César Cui prepared a complete musical version, using all the available numbers and in some cases Lyadov's orchestration, and composing additional music, partly on Musorgsky's themes, as required; the vocal score of Cui's version was published by Bessel in 1916, and on 26 October 1917 it was produced at the Theatre of Musical Drama, Petrograd. Another complete version was prepared by N. N. Tcherepnin in Paris after the Russian Revolution. This was based on the existing editions by Lyadov, Karatïgin and Cui, but Cui's additions were not used; Tcherepnin filled the lacunae with music borrowed from *Salammbô*, songs and other works by Musorgsky. Tcherepnin's version, the one usually performed outside Russia, was produced at Monte Carlo on 17 March 1923 and published in vocal score by Bessel in 1924.

One other garbled text must be mentioned: that of the collection of songs from the years 1857–66 entitled by Musorgsky *Yunïye godï* ('Years of youth'). It was acquired by Charles Malherbe, archivist of the Paris Opéra, in 1909. The collection consists partly of songs hitherto unknown, partly of variants of published songs. Four of the former were published as a supplement to the *Bulletin français de la S.I.M.* (1909) and, in an edition by Karatïgin, by Bessel's firm in 1911. In 1923 Bessel issued in Paris the whole collection except for the last number (a duet arrangement of Gordigiani's *Ogni sabato*), four songs being reprinted from Karatïgin's edition, 12 inaccurately copied from the Paris autograph and one (*Kalistrat*) reprinted from the Rimsky-Korsakov edition of the variant not in the Paris collection.

From about 1908 onwards growing dissatisfaction with the Rimsky-Korsakov versions of Musorgsky's music, particularly that of *Boris*, was felt both in Russia and in western Europe, and a vigorous campaign for the publication and performance of the true texts was carried on by Russian and Western critics, led in England and France by M. D. Calvocoressi. In 1928 the Russian State Music Publishing Corporation at last embarked on a 'complete collected edition' of Musorgsky's music in accordance with the composer's manuscripts, embodying all textual variants and provided with elaborate critical apparatus. This edition, of which Pavel Lamm was editor-in-chief, was interrupted in 1939 by the outbreak of war. At the same time *Khovanshchina* was completed by Lamm and Asaf'yev and orchestrated by Asaf'yev in a version faithfully embodying all the material left by Musorgsky; *Sorochintsy Fair* was completed in the same spirit in 1930 by Vissarion Shebalin. Musorgsky's 1869 version of *Boris* was produced in Leningrad on 16 February 1928 and in London (at Sadler's Wells) on 30 September 1935. Lamm's edition of the full score of *Boris*, a conflation of sources, was superseded in 1975 by David Lloyd-Jones's, which restores Musorgsky's own full score as the basic text while printing other sources separately.

CHAPTER THREE

Style and aesthetic

During the last year of his life Musorgsky wrote an
autobiographical sketch, inaccurate in many respects
but concluding with a statement of his artistic position
that could hardly be bettered:

Musorgsky cannot be classed with any existing group of musicians,
either by the character of his compositions or by his musical views. The
formula of his artistic *profession de foi* may be explained by his view of
the function of art: art is a means of communicating with people, not an
aim in itself. This guiding principle has defined the whole of his creative
activity. Proceeding from the conviction that human speech is strictly
controlled by musical laws (Virchow, Gervinus), he considers the function of art to be the reproduction in musical sounds not merely of
feelings, but first and foremost of human speech. Acknowledging that in
the realm of art only artist–reformers such as Palestrina, Bach, Gluck,
Beethoven, Berlioz and Liszt have created the laws of art, he considers
these laws as not immutable but liable to change and progress, like
everything else in man's inner world.

But if Musorgsky could not class himself with any
existing group of musicians, he could very easily have
placed himself beside other artists, the great Russian
novelists of his day and such painters as Kramskoy,
Surikov, Gey and Repin. He shared with these (particularly with the painters): a disdain for formal beauty
and technical polish and every other manifestation of
'art for art's sake'; the desire to relate his art as closely
as possible to life, especially to that of the Russian
masses; to nourish his art on events and in turn to
employ it as a medium for communicating human ex-

131

perience; and a somewhat selfconscious and aggressive Russianness and an intense sympathy with the Russian peasant, newly freed from serfdom. The philosophical basis of their outlook was stated most satisfactorily by Chernïshevsky in his dissertation *Esteticheskiye otnosheniya iskusstva k deystvitel'nosti* ('The aesthetic relationship of art and reality', St Petersburg, 1855) and his own criticism of it in the journal *Sovremennik*.

Musorgsky's earlier, lyrical and romantic compositions, written before he had arrived at this viewpoint, reveal the influences of Glinka, Balakirev and (in the case of *Salammbô*) Serov, of Schumann and (a little later) Liszt and Meyerbeer. The harmonic language of these works is limited and conventional, their workmanship amateurish; the instrumental pieces reveal the structural weaknesses that mark even his mature essays in instrumental music: squareness, primitiveness, lack of organic cohesion. Yet more personal traits soon begin to show themselves. The main theme of the *Intermezzo in modo classico* (1861) is doubly characteristic in that its origin was pantomimic (it was suggested by the sight of peasants plunging heavily through deep snowdrifts on a sunny winter day) and that, although the composer himself described it as 'in modo classico' and 'à la Bach', its separate motifs show an affinity with Russian folk melody. In the song *Kalistratushka* (1864), of which the first version is called 'study in folk style', the voice part, already fully typical of Musorgsky's mature type of free, asymmetrical lyrical melody, is very close to folk melody, while the cadential dissolution of the harmony into bare octaves (e.g. at the end of the first vocal phrase) is also typical of the Russian folk polyphony recorded by Melgunov, Kastal'sky and others; an actual folktune appears in the piano part in the *tranquillo* section.

This predominantly lyrical strain in Musorgsky's style was never completely submerged at any period; but, side by side with the lyrical songs of 1866–8, *Evreyskaya pesnya* ('Hebrew song'), *Po nad Donom sad tsvetet* ('The garden by the Don'), *Detskaya pesenka* ('Child's song') and others, sharply opposed tendencies appear. Instead of lyrical melody the voice parts of such songs as *Darling Savishna, The Seminarist* and *You Drunken Sot!* (all 1866) are attempts at 'quasi-phonographic' representation of human speech, not of speech in general but the peculiar speech of sharply realized individuals: a village idiot babbling out his amorous plea to the village beauty, a theological student allowing erotic thoughts to creep into his memorizing of Latin nouns of the third declension, a woman scolding a drunken husband. Some degree of stylization is inevitable in the musical representation of speech, but Musorgsky aimed at the minimum possible; when, from time to time, he abandoned represented speech, he naturally lapsed into his lyrical folksong-like idiom or, as in *The Seminarist,* deliberately imitated the music of the Orthodox Church. At the same time the piano parts are contrived to underline the characterization of the vocal line with pantomimically inspired motifs and unorthodox and empirical, but often strikingly evocative, harmony. In his songs of this type Musorgsky showed not so much a subjective sympathy for his characters as an ability to put himself in their place: *Darling Savishna, Ozornik* ('The ragamuffin'), *Sirotka* ('The orphan') and *The Nursery.* Even a comic character, as in *The Seminarist,* is rendered with only slight exaggeration, as a good actor might play the

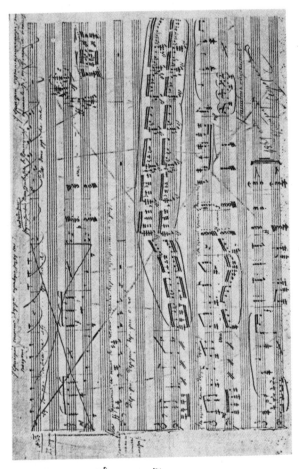

10. Autograph
MS from the
vocal score of
Musorgsky's
opera 'Boris
Godunov', 2nd
version, 1871–2,
rev. 1873),
showing the
original ending
of Act 1 scene ii

part. But a little later, perhaps under the influence of Dargomïzhsky's songs, this ironic-comic element became exaggerated into less objective and thus less effective satire, as in *Kozyol* ('The he-goat'), *Klassik* ('The classicist') and *Rayok* ('The peepshow'), the last two being lampoons of the composer's musical enemies. These tendencies – 'recorded' speech with the minimum of stylization, pantomimic instrumental motifs and empirical, expressionistic harmony, satirical comedy – are manifested in their most extreme forms and without lyrical relief in *The Marriage*.

In *Boris Godunov* these two tendencies, the lyrical and the naturalistic, exist side by side in nearly perfect equilibrium. In *Khovanshchina* and the later songs they tend to be fused rather than opposed, and the lyrical element tends to gain the upper hand. In the *Sunless* cycle a new element of subjective pessimism makes its appearance, though in no work of Musorgsky is his empirical harmony more subtly effective. The *Pictures at an Exhibition*, dating from the same year as *Sunless* (1874), reveal the characteristic juxtaposition of lyrical and pantomimic (and comic) elements. After 1874 a gradual falling-off in quality is perceptible in all Musorgsky's work, though even the fragments of *Sorochintsy Fair* show him still striving to learn from folk music and the intonations of folk speech (in both cases, those of the Ukraine), still mingling pure lyricism with satirical comedy.

Boris Godunov and *Khovanshchina* are, like all the Russian historical operas of that period, offshoots of Meyerbeerian grand opera, however much they may differ from the prototypes in musical language, in musical and dramatic technique and in aesthetic point of view. Musorgsky's originality as a dramatic composer is most easily gauged by reference to that standard. In place of well-made theatrical plots there are cross-sections of the life of a whole people; instead of conventionalized characters in *Boris* (though hardly in *Khovanshchina*), sharply realized individuals. The personal tragedy of Boris is heightened, not weakened, by being set against a wholly living background not only of the court circle (his children, the treacherous boyar Shuysky) but of the Russian people generally, represented by individuals such as the various monks, the police officers, the idiot, the innkeeper, even the anonymous members of the crowd; as a result Boris himself comes to stand for the entire suffering nation. In *Khovanshchina* the same thing is attempted much less successfully; neither the elder Khovansky nor Dosifey is presented in the round, as Boris is; the forces opposed to them are shown only in the person of the lay figure Shaklovity, while the forces opposed to Boris are personified in the very human Pretender. Even 'the people' in *Khovanshchina* have less vital representatives. The score of *Khovanshchina* contains some of Musorgsky's best lyrical writing (for example, the introduction and Golitsïn's departure into exile), one of his finest strokes of musical irony (the snatch of folksong sung by Shaklovity over the elder Khovansky's dead body) and some typical pantomimic effects (such as the scribe's 'writing' figure); but it lacks the dramatic incisiveness of the earlier work. Few operas contain so little dead matter as *Boris*, particularly in its original version of 1869; apart from the grandeur and depth of the treatment as a whole, episodic as that whole is, the score is full of singularly effective subtleties of every kind.

Musorgsky did not use leitmotifs as Wagner did, but in the more limited way common in the third quarter of the 19th century; however, he used the device in a quite peculiar manner, to make points that could hardly be made by other means. A single theme serves in *Boris* both for the real, murdered Tsarevich and for the Pretender, the false Dmitry, and so reflects the superstitious doubt and confusion in Boris's mind; in *Khovanshchina* the theme of Marfa's conjuration scene is later linked in turn with the fates of the elder Khovansky, Golitsïn and Andrey Khovansky – all Tsar Peter's enemies are doomed. Of the innumerable very different subtleties of harmony and orchestration in *Boris* it must suffice to mention the simple, solemn trombone chords in the second scene of the Prologue, just before Boris's call to 'pay a solemn tribute to the tombs of Russia's rulers', the grating harmonies of the high string tremolo of the hallucination scene, the bare open 5ths on the second syllable of the word 'Siberia' in the map scene, the harmonic setting of the treacherous Shuysky's account to the Duma of the tsar's hallucinations. Musorgsky's orchestration is seldom beautiful for its own sake; his harmony would often be nonsensical as absolute music; but he used both with infallible instinct as instruments of dramatic expression. As a musical translator of words and all that can be expressed in words, of psychological states and even physical movements he is unsurpassed; as an absolute musician he was hopelessly limited, with remarkably little ability to construct pure music or even a purely musical texture.

WORKS

Edition: *M. P. Musorgsky: Polnoye sobraniye sochineniy* [Complete collection of works], ed. P. Lamm, with B. V. Asaf'yev (Moscow, 1928–34/*R*1969, 1939 [addl vol.viii]) [L]

Numbers in right-hand margins denote references in the text.

STAGE

Han d'Islande (opera, after Hugo), projected 1856 — 110

Edip v Afinakh [Oedipus in Athens] (opera, after Ozerov), projected 1858–60 — 110, 111–12, 117

Salammbô (opera, after Flaubert), 1863–6, inc. — 112, 113, 115, 120, 127, 129, 132

Zhenit'ba [The marriage] (comic opera, after Gogol), 1868, Act 1 only, St Petersburg, Suvorin Theatre School, 1 April 1909, L iv/2 — 116, 127, 133

Boris Godunov (opera, Musorgsky, after Pushkin and Karamzin): 1st version, 7 scenes, 1868–9, Leningrad, 16 Feb 1928: 2nd version, prol and 4 acts, 1871–2, rev. 1873, vocal score (1874), St Petersburg, Mariinsky Theatre, 8 Feb 1874; ed. D. Lloyd-Jones (London, 1975) — 31, 54, 112, 116, 117–18, 119, 120, 121, 122, 126–7, 129, 130, 134, 135–7, 195

Bobil' [The landless peasant] (opera, after Spielhagen: Hans und Crete), projected 1870 — 116–17

Mlada (opera-ballet, V. A. Krïlov), collab. Rimsky-Korsakov, Borodin, Cui, projected 1872, L iv/3, viii/1 — 51, 117, 123

Khovanshchina (opera, Musorgsky), 1872–80, completed and orchd Rimsky-Korsakov, St Petersburg, 21 Feb 1886, L ii, vii/2 — 117, 118, 119, 120, 121, 123, 126, 130, 135–7

Sorochinskaya yarmarka [Sorochintsy fair] (comic opera, after Gogol), 1874–80, completed and orchd Lyadov, V. G. Karatïgin and others, Moscow, Free Theatre, 21 Oct 1913 and St Petersburg, Comedia Theatre, 30 Dec 1913, L iii — 119, 120, 121, 123, 126, 127–9, 130, 135

Pugachovshchina (opera, after Pushkin), projected 1877

CHORAL

Marsh Shamilya [Shamil's march], T, B, chorus, orch. 1859 — 111

Porazheniye Sennakheriba [The destruction of Sennacherib], 1866–7 (1871), rev. 1874 — 115, 123

Iisus Navin [Jesus Navin], A, B, chorus, pf, 1874–7 — 120

3 vocalises, 3 female vv, 1880 — 123

5 Russian folksongs, arr. 4 male vv, 1880: Skazhi, devitsa milaya; Ti vzoydi, solntse krasnoye; U vorot, vorot batyshkinïkh; Uzh ti, volya, moya volya, with 2 solo T: no.5, inc.

ORCHESTRAL

Scherzo, B♭, 1858, orig. for pf, L vii/4 — 110, 111

Alla marcia notturna, 1861 — 111

Symphony, D, projected 1861–2 — 81, 111, 112

Ivanova noch' na Lïsoy gore [St John's Night on the Bare Mountain], 1867; orig. version ed. S. Kirkov (Moscow, 1968) — 111, 115, 117, 121, 125–6, 127, 128

Intermezzo symphonique in modo classico, b, 1867, orig. for pf, with new trio, L vii/5 — 112, 115

Podibrad Cheshskiy [Podébrad of Bohemia], sym. poem, projected 1867 — 115

Vzyatiye Karsa [The capture of Kars], march, 1880 — 123

PIANO
(in L viii unless otherwise stated)

Porte-enseigne polka, 1852 (1852); Souvenir d'enfance, 1857; 2 sonatas, E♭, [♯, 1858, no.1 inc., both lost; Scherzo, c♯, 1858: Scherzo, B♭, 1858, orchd; Impromptu passionné, 1859: Ein Kinderscherz, 1859, rev. 1860 (1873); Preludio in modo classico, 1860, lost; Intermezzo in modo classico, 1860–61 (1873), orchd 1867, rearr. pf, 1867; Menuet monstre, 1861, lost — 109, 110, 115, 110, 111, 111, 112, 132, 113

Iz vospominaniy detstva [From memories of childhood], 1865: 1 Nyanya i ya [Nurse and I], 2 Pervoye nakazaniye: Nyanya zapirayet menya v temnuyu komnatu [First punishment: Nurse shuts me in a dark room]; Duma [Rêverie], on a theme of V. A. Loginov, 1865; La capriceuse, on a theme of L. Heyden, 1865; Shveya [The seamstress], scherzino, 1871 (1872) — 113, 113

Kartinki s vïstavki [Pictures at an exhibition], suite, 1874, L vii/2; — 31, 119, 135, 166

Burya na Chernom more [Storm on the Black Sea], 1879, lost; Na yuzhnom beregu Krïma [On the southern shore of the Crimea], 1880 (1880); Méditation, albumleaf, 1880 (1880); Une larme, 1880: Na village (Quasi fantasia), ?1880: arr. of Fair Scene and Hopak from Sorochintsy Fair — 121

For pf 4 hands: Allegro and scherzo for a sonata, C, 1860 [scherzo based on Scherzo, c♯, pf solo]; 4-hand arrs, L vii/1, 3, 4 — 111

138

(for 1v, pf, and in L v unless otherwise stated)   32, 110, 115, 121, 126, 129

Gde tï, zvezdochka? [Where art thou, little star?] (N. Grekov), 1857, rev. with orch, 1858

Meines Herzens Sehnsucht, 1858

Otchevo, skazhi [Tell me why], 1858 (1867)   110

Vesyolïy chas [Hour of jollity] (A. Kol'tsov), 1858, 2nd version 1859   115

List'ya shumeli unïlo [Sadly rustled the leaves] (after Pleshcheyev), 1859

Chto vam slova lyubvi? [What are words of love to you?] (A. Amosov), 1860

Mnogo est' u menya teremov i sadov [I have many palaces and gardens] (Kol'tsov), 1863

Pesn' startsa: Stanu skromno u poroga [Old man's song] (Goethe, trans.), 1863   112

Tsar' Saul [King Saul] (Byron, trans. P. Kozlov), 1863, 2nd version 1863 (1870–71)   112

No esli bï s toboyu ya vstretit'sya mogla [But if I could meet thee again] (V. Kurochkin), 1863

Duyut vetri, vetri buynïye [The wild winds blow] (Kol'tsov), 1864   113, 129, 132–3

Kalistratushka (Nekrasov), 1864, 2nd version as Kalistrat, 1864

Noch' [Night] (after Pushkin), 1868, orchd 1868, 2nd version 1864 (1870–71), L vii/3

Molitva [Prayer] (Lermontov), 1865

Otverzhennaya: opït rechitativa [The outcast: essay in recitative] (I. Holz-Miller), 1865

Kolïbel'naya pesnya [Lullaby] (Ostrovsky, from Voyevoda), 1865, 2nd version as Spi, uspï krest'yanskiy sïn [Sleep, sleep, peasant son], 1865

Malyutka: Akh, zachem tvoy glazki poroyu? [Dear one, why are thine eyes sometimes so cold?] (Pleshcheyev), 1866

Ich wollt' meine Schmerzen ergössen (Heine), 1866

Iz slyoz moikh [From my tears] (Heine, trans. M. Mikhaylov), 1866

Svetik Savishna [Darling Savishna] (Musorgsky), 1866 (1867)   115, 133

Akh, tï, p'yanaya teterya! [You drunken sot!] (Musorgsky), 1866   115, 133

Seminarist [The seminarist] (Musorgsky), 1866   115, 133

Hopak (Shevchenko, trans. Mey), 1866 (1867), rev. with orch, 1868, L vii/6   115

Pesn' Yaremï 'Na Dnepre' [Yarema's song 'On the Dnieper'] (Shevchenko, trans. Mey), 1866, lost, 2nd version 1879

Evreyskaya pesnya [Hebrew song] (Mey), 1867 (1868)

Strekotun'ya beloboka [The magpie] (Pushkin), 1867 (1870–77)   133

Po gribï [Gathering mushrooms] (Mey), 1867 (1868)   133

Pirushka [The feast] (Kol'tsov), 1867 (1868)

Ozornïk [The ragamuffin] (Musorgsky), 1867 (1870–71)   133

Kozyol: svetskaya skazochka [The he-goat: a worldly story] (Musorgsky), 1867 (1868)   133

Klassik [The classicist] (Musorgsky), 1867 (1870)   133

Po nad Donom sad tsvetet [The garden by the Don] (Kol'tsov), 1867   133

Sïrotka [The orphan] (Musorgsky), 1868 (1870–71)   133

Kolïbel'naya Eryomushki [Eryomushka's lullaby] (Nekrasov), 1868 (1870–71)

Detskaya pesenka [Child's song] (Mey), 1868 (1870–71)   133

Detskaya [The nursery] (Musorgsky) (1870): 1 S nyaney [With nurse], 1868; 2 V uglu [In the corner], 1870; 3 Zhuk [The cockchafer], 1870; 4 S kukloy [With the doll], 1870; 5 Na son gryadushchiy [Going to sleep], 1870; 6 Poyekhal na palochke [On the hobbyhorse], 1872; 7 Kot Matros [The cat Sailor], 1872 [6 and 7 in 2/1873]   117, 119, 126, 133

Rayok [The peepshow] (Musorgsky), 1870 (1870–71)   133

Vechernyaya pesenka [Evening song] (?Pleshcheyev), 1871

Bez solntsa [Sunless] (Golenishchev-Kutuzov), 1874 (1874): 1 V chetïryokh stenakh [Between four walls]; 2 Menya tï v tolpe ne uznala [Thou didst not know me in the crowd]; 3 Okonchen prazdnïy, shumnïy den' [The idle, noisy day is ended]; 4 Skuchay [Boredom]; 5 Elegiya [Elegy]; 6 Nad rekoy [On the river]   119, 135

Zabïtïy [Forgotten] (Golenishchev-Kutuzov), 1874

Nadgrabnoye pis'mo [Epitaph] (Musorgsky), 1874, inc.

Krapivnaya gora [The nettle mountain] (Musorgsky), 1874, inc.

Pesni i plyaski smerti [Songs and dances of death] (Golenishchev-Kutuzov): 1 Kolïbel'naya [Lullaby], 1875; 2 Serenada [Serenade], 1875; 3 Trepak, 1875; 4 Polkovodets [The field-marshal], 1877   119

Neponyatnaya [The sphinx] (Musorgsky), 1875

Ne bozhnïim gromom udarilo [Not like thunder, trouble struck] (A. K. Tolstoy), 1877   120

Gornïim tikho letela dusha nebesami [Softly the spirit flew up to heaven] (Tolstoy), 1877   120

Spes' [Pride] (Tolstoy), 1877

Oy, chest' li to molodtsu ien pryasti? [Is spinning man's work?] (Tolstoy), 1877   120

Rassevayetsya, rasstupayetsya [It scatters and breaks] (Tolstoy), 1877   120

Videniye [The vision] (Golenishchev-Kutuzov), 1877

Strannik [The wanderer] (Rückert, trans. Pleshcheyev), 1878

Pesnya Mefistofelya o blokhe [Mephistopheles' song of the flea] (Goethe, trans. A. Strugovshchikov), 1879   120

BIBLIOGRAPHY

V. V. Stasov: 'Modest Petrovich Musorgsky: biografichesky ocherk', [Biographical essay], *Vestnik Evropï* (1881), no.5, pp.285–316; no.6, pp.506–45

P. d'Alheim: *Moussorgski* (Paris, 1896)

M. D. Calvocoressi: *Moussorgsky* (Paris, 1908, rev. 2/1911; Eng. trans., 1919)

M. Olenina d'Alheim: *Le legs de Moussorgski* (Paris, 1908)

MS (1917), Jan–Feb [special issue, incl. Musorgsky's autobiographical note]

V. Karatïgin: *Musorgskiy* (Petrograd, 1922)

J. Handschin: *Mussorgski: Versuch einer Einführung* (Zurich, 1924)

R. Godet: *En marge de Boris Godounof* (Paris and London, 1926)

O. von Reisemann: 'Modest Petrowitsch Mussorgski', *Monographien zur russischen Musik*, ii (Munich, 1926)

V. Belyayev: *'Boris Godounov' in its Genuine Version* (London, 1928)

I. Glebov [B. V. Asaf'yev]: *K vosstanovleniyu Borisa Godunova Musorgskovo* [On the restoration of Musorgsky's Boris Godunov] (Moscow, 1928)

S. Lopashev and others: *Musorgskiy i evo 'Khovanshchina': sbornik statey* [Musorgsky and his *Khovanshchina*: a collection of essays] (Moscow, 1928)

I. Glebov: 'Die ästhetischen Anschauungen Mussorgskijs', *Die Musik*, xxi (1929), 561

V. Belyayev and others: *Boris Godunov: stat'i i issledovaniya* [*Boris Godunov*: essays and papers] (Moscow, 1930)

V. Fédorov: 'Sur un manuscrit de Moussorgskii: les différentes éditions de ses lieder', *RdM*, xiii (1932), 10

Yu. Keldïsh and V. Yakovlev, eds.: *M. P. Musorgskiy k pyatid'esyatoletiyu so dnya smerti: stat'i i materialï* [On the 50th anniversary of Musorgsky's death: essays and material] (Moscow, 1932)

A. N. Rimsky-Korsakov, ed.: *M. P. Musorgskiy: pis'ma i dokumentï* [Letters and documents] (Moscow and Leningrad, 1932)

Yu. Keldïsh: *Romansovaya lirika Musorgskovo* [Musorgsky's lyrical songs] (Moscow, 1933)

V. Fédorov: *Moussorgsky* (Paris, 1935)

A. A. Golenishchev-Kutuzov: 'Vospominaniya o M. P. Musorgskom' [Memories of Musorgsky], *Muzikal'noe nasledstvo*, ed. M. V. Ivanov-Boretsky, i (Moscow, 1935)

K. Nilsson: *Die Rimskij-Korsakoffsche Bearbeitung des 'Boris Godunoff' von Mussorgskij als Objekt der vergleichenden Musikwissenschaft* (Münster, 1937)

G. Abraham: *'The Fair of Sorochintsy* and Cherepnin's Completion of it', *On Russian Music* (London, 1939), 216

Bibliography

A. Frankenstein: 'Victor Hartmann and Modeste Musorgsky', *MQ*, xxv (1939), 268

Yu. Keldïsh, ed.: *M. P. Musorgskiy: pis'ma k A. A. Golenishchevu-Kutuzovu* [Letters to A. A. Golenishchev-Kutuzov] (Moscow and Leningrad, 1939)

SovM (1939), April [special issue, incl. Musorgsky's autobiographical note]

N. Tumanina: *M. P. Musorgskiy: zhizn i tvorchestvo* [Life and works] (Moscow and Leningrad, 1939)

M. D. Calvocoressi: *Mussorgsky* (London, 1946, rev. 2/1974)

J. Leyda and S. Bertensson, eds.: *The Musorgsky Reader: a Life of M. P. Musorgsky in Letters and Documents* (New York, 1947/R1970)

A. S. Ogolevets, ed.: *V. Stasov: izbrannïye stat'i o M. P. Musorgskom* [Selected articles on Musorgsky] (Moscow, 1952)

T. N. Livanova and others, eds.: *B. V. Asaf'yev: Izbrannïy trudï* [Collected works], iii (Moscow, 1954)

M. D. Calvocoressi: *Modest Mussorgsky: his Life and Works* (London, 1956/R1967)

V. A. Vasina-Grossman: 'Vokal'noe tvorchestvo Musorgskovo', *Russkiy klassicheskiy romans XIX veka* (Moscow, 1956)

A. Orlova: *Trudï i dni M. P. Musorgskovo: letopis' zhizni i tvorchestva* [Works and days of Musorgsky: a chronicle of his life and work] (Moscow, 1963)

A. Ogolevets: *Vokal'naya dramaturgiya Musorgskovo* (Moscow, 1966)

G. Abraham: *Slavonic and Romantic Music* (London, 1968) [incl. 'Mussorgsky's *Boris* and Pushkin's', p.178; 'The Mediterranean Element in *Boris Godunov*', p.188]

V. I. Serov: *Modest Musorgsky* (New York, 1968)

A. A. Orlova and M. S. Pekelis, eds.: *M. P. Musorgskiy: literaturnoye naslediye* (Moscow, 1971)

D. Lloyd-Jones: *Boris Godunov: Critical Commentary* (London, 1975)

S. I. Shlifshteyn: *Musorgskiy: khudozhnik, vremya, sud'ba* [Musorgsky: artist, time, fate] (Moscow, 1975)

L. Hübsch: *Modest Mussorgsky: Bilder einer Ausstellung*, Meisterwerke der Musik, xv (Munich, 1978)

R. W. Oldani: *New Perspectives on Mussorgsky's Boris Godunov* (diss., U. of Michigan, 1978)

——: 'Boris Godunov and the Censor', *19th Century Music*, ii (1978–9), 245

M. Schandert: *Das Problem der originalen Instrumentation des Boris Godunow von M. P. Mussorgski* (Hamburg, 1979)

E. R. Reilly: *A Guide to Mussorgsky: a Scorography* (New York, 1980) [rev., enlarged edn. of essays on *Boris Godunov* etc pubd in *Musical Newsletter*]

R. C. Ridenour: *Nationalism, Modernism, and Personal Rivalry in Nineteenth-century Russian Music* (Ann Arbor, Mich., 1981)

R. Taruskin: *Opera and Drama in Russia as Practiced and Preached in the 1860s* (Ann Arbor, Mich., 1981)

J. Walker: 'Mussorgsky's *Sunless* Cycle in Russian Criticism: Focus of Controversy', *MQ*, lxvii (1981), 382

M. H. Brown, ed.: *Musorgsky: In Memoriam 1881–1981* (Ann Arbor, 1982)

P. Weber-Bockholdt: *Die Lieder Mussorgskijs: Herkunft und Erscheinungsform* (Munich, 1982)

A. A. Orlova: *Musorgsky's Days and Works: a Biography in Documents* (Ann Arbor, 1983)

R. Taruskin: 'Musorgsky vs. Musorgsky: the versions of *Boris Godunov*', *19th Century Music*, viii/2 (1984–5), 91

——: 'Serov and Musorgsky', *Slavonic and Western Music: Essays for Gerald Abraham* (Ann Arbor and Oxford, 1985), 139

142

PYOTR IL'YICH TCHAIKOVSKY

David Brown

CHAPTER ONE

1840–70

Standing outside the nationalist circle of composers around Balakirev, Tchaikovsky nevertheless dominates 19th-century Russian music as its greatest talent. His formal conservatory training instilled in him Western-orientated attitudes and techniques, but his essential nature, as he always insisted, was Russian, both in his actual use of folksong and in his deep absorption in Russian life and ways of thought. His natural gifts, especially his genius for what he called the 'lyrical idea', the beautiful, self-contained melody, have given his music an enduring appeal; it was his hard-won but secure and professional technique, his seemingly instinctive structural resourcefulness, and his ability to use these for the expression of his emotional life, which enabled him to realize his potential more fully than any of his major Russian contemporaries.

I Early years

Pyotr Il'yich Tchaikovsky was born in Kamsko-Votkinsk, Vyatka province, on 7 May 1840. He was the second son of Il'ya Petrovich Tchaikovsky, who was a mining engineer and manager of the metal works at Kamsko-Votkinsk; his second wife and the composer's mother, Alexandra Andreyevna (née Assier), was the grand-daughter of a French émigré, Michel d'Assier, a fact that may have some relevance to Tchaikovsky's strong attraction to French music. Her father had been an epileptic, and she herself was of a nervous disposition: it was from his mother's side that Tchaikovsky inherited his morbid sensitivity. According to his brother Modest there is no evidence of any previous member of the family having been a professional musician.

What may be the first record of Tchaikovsky attempting composition dates from September 1844, when his father reported to his wife, who was in St Petersburg, that 'Sasha [the composer's two and a half-year-old sister, Alexandra] and Pyotr have composed a song, *Our mama in Petersburg*'. Certainly Tchaikovsky's musical interests and aptitudes revealed themselves clearly in the following year, when he started taking piano lessons with a local teacher, Mariya Palchikova, whose abilities he quickly outstripped. His musical experiences were supplemented by the family's orchestrion, which played excerpts from Mozart's *Don Giovanni* (a work that always retained a special aura for Tchaikovsky), as well as pieces by Bellini, Rossini and Donizetti. He also became familiar with some Chopin mazurkas. Between 1844 and 1848 he benefited greatly from the attention and kindness of Fanny Dürbach, a French governess engaged for his elder brother Nikolay and a cousin. Under her guidance he wrote some sentimental French verses, including a poem on Joan of Arc, and started to learn German.

In February 1848 Tchaikovsky's father retired from his post, and in November the family arrived in St Petersburg, where Tchaikovsky entered a miserable phase at the fashionable Schmelling School; he also started piano lessons with a teacher named Filippov, though these were curtailed in December when

Tchaikovsky had a bad attack of measles and was ordered to rest for six months. In May 1849 the family moved to Alapayevsk where Il'ya had a new appointment. Tchaikovsky and his mother returned to St Petersburg in summer 1850, and in September he was enrolled in the preparatory class of the School of Jurisprudence. His mother also took him to a performance of Glinka's *A Life for the Tsar*, which made a deep and permanent impression on him. The parting from his mother when she returned to Alapayevsk was remembered by Tchaikovsky as 'one of the most terrible days' of his life. Since Fanny Dürbach had left two years earlier he had been exceedingly moody and easily reduced to tears. His life had become unsettled, and this parting from a parent to whom he was emotionally very close was a shock he never forgot and whose effects were profoundly disturbing to his whole disposition. His distress was exacerbated by a sense of guilt at the death from scarlet fever of the eldest son of Modest Vakar, a family friend who had undertaken to lodge and look after him during an epidemic of the disease at Tchaikovsky's school. Despite all Vakar's assurances, he remained convinced that, since he had introduced the disease into the family, he was responsible for the boy's death.

Nevertheless, the nine years spent at the School of Jurisprudence did serve to introduce some stability into his existence, though the homosexual practices common in the school may well have served to reveal or to confirm his own tendencies. In 1852 his father resigned again, and in May the family returned to St Petersburg; Tchaikovsky's happiness was augmented by success in the entrance examination to the School of Jurisprudence itself. But in June 1854 there came a shattering blow in the death of his mother. For relief he turned to music. He had for some years found emotional release in improvisation; he now wrote down a piano waltz, and even thought of attempting an opera on Viktor Olkhovsky's *Hyperbole*. He went for singing lessons to Gavriil Lomakin, and in 1855 began three years of piano tuition with Rudolf Kündinger, a good teacher (whose brother gave Tchaikovsky some lessons in thoroughbass) but one who discouraged him from placing any hopes on a professional career. In 1856 Tchaikovsky met an Italian singing teacher, Luigi Piccioli, who widened his knowledge of Italian opera, and led him to compose a pallid Italianate canzonetta, *Mezza notte*; this was to become Tchaikovsky's first published work.

In May 1859 Tchaikovsky completed his course at the School of Jurisprudence and took a post as clerk in the Ministry of Justice, engaging in a lively social life in which music figured prominently. His father was no longer able to support him, and his idea of becoming a professional musician had to be shelved. Nevertheless, in autumn 1861 he began studying thoroughbass in Nikolay Zaremba's class at the recently founded Russian Musical Society, which in 1862 was transformed into the St Petersburg Conservatory. During summer 1861 he travelled in western Europe, acting as interpreter to a friend of his father and visiting Germany, Belgium, England and France. On his return he engaged in technical studies with Zaremba twice weekly, and at the end of 1862 also joined the composition class of the conservatory's director, Anton Rubinstein, who gave him considerable encouragement. Finally, in 1863, he resigned from the Ministry of

Justice and entered the conservatory as a full-time student, attending Zaremba's class in form and Rubinstein's in instrumentation. Although Tchaikovsky's father had already given moral support to his decision, his circumstances remained straitened; but Rubinstein was able to help by finding him piano and theory pupils. Modest recollected that, despite the privations of this new student life, Tchaikovsky was profoundly contented now that he had at last taken the step of devoting himself to music.

The next two and a half years were spent at the conservatory, where, having been excused the compulsory piano class, Tchaikovsky took up the flute and the organ. For summer 1864 he went to Alexey Golitsïn's estate near Khar'kov. In 1865 his father remarried, and Tchaikovsky and his younger twin brothers Modest and Anatoly, to whom he was devoted, spent a happy summer on the estate of their brother-in-law Lev Davïdov at Kamenka, near Kiev, where Tchaikovsky busied himself with translating Gevaert's *Traité général d'instrumentation* from the French. Rubinstein, who had set him this task, proved well pleased with the completed work. Tchaikovsky had hoped to familiarize himself with Ukrainian folksongs while at Kamenka, so as to gather material that he might use later in his own works; but his disenchantment with those that he heard grew with the feeling that they had been contaminated by contact with 'Western' music. In the end he noted down only one song, which he used first in the quartet movement in B♭, composed later that year, and then in the *Scherzo à la russe* for piano, published as his op.1 no.1. That September Johann Strauss conducted a public performance at Pavlovsk of the Characteristic Dances which

Tchaikovsky had composed earlier that year. In November he made his own début as a conductor, directing the conservatory orchestra in a performance of his Overture in F.

Only one of Tchaikovsky's student compositions is of any permanent value: his overture to Ostrovsky's play *Groza* ('The storm'). Originally Tchaikovsky had thought of using the play for an opera, but he decided to channel his enthusiasm for it into the holiday task required of him by Rubinstein in 1864. He sketched out a programme, and composed the piece while staying on the Golitsïn estate. On completing it, he sent it to Hermann Laroche (a fellow student at the conservatory, who was the first critic to champion his music and who remained a lifelong friend), with instructions to hand it over to Rubinstein. The latter's tastes were idiosyncratic and highly conservative, and he condemned the piece which, though it incorporates a Russian folksong, reflects Tchaikovsky's growing command of Western musical techniques. There is a little influence from Liszt, and the admirable scoring is indebted to Berlioz. Yet most remarkable of all is the degree to which Tchaikovsky's own musical personality is already apparent in the attractive and sometimes striking invention. Nor did Rubinstein give any warmer approval to the setting of Schiller's *An die Freude* which Tchaikovsky presented as his graduation exercise. Tchaikovsky could not face the strain of the official public performance of the piece, and, to Rubinstein's further annoyance, absented himself. Nevertheless, despite the generally adverse critical comment on the cantata (including in due course a vitriolic review from Cui, the spokesman of The Five), the final report on

11. Pyotr Il'yich Tchaikovsky, c1864

151

Tchaikovsky as a student was very favourable, and he graduated with not only a diploma but also a silver medal.

II Progress to maturity

In September 1865, even before his graduation from the St Petersburg Conservatory, Tchaikovsky had been approached by Anton Rubinstein's brother Nikolay with an offer of a post as teacher of harmony at the classes of the Russian Musical Society's Moscow branch (which in September 1866 was to become, under Nikolay's direction, the Moscow Conservatory). Despite the low salary Tchaikovsky accepted and moved to Moscow in January 1866. Initially his awareness of his lack of qualification for teaching made these duties a strain, and he found the constant social attentions of Nikolay Rubinstein, who took him into his own home and pressed upon him his own convivial style of living, somewhat overpowering. Yet the transfer to Moscow was beneficial, despite his longing for St Petersburg, for here he met a whole range of new friends that included his future publisher, Pyotr Jürgenson. Nikolay himself, moreover, was to be a powerful advocate for Tchaikovsky's compositions, conducting or playing in the first performances of many of them over the next 15 years. Above all, Moscow provided a more liberal environment in which he could develop himself as a composer; furthermore Nikolay, unlike his brother Anton, was favourable towards the new group of Russian composers that was forming in St Petersburg under the despotic guidance of Balakirev. In this freer environment Tchaikovsky completed the orchestration of a Concert Overture in C minor, which both Rubinsteins condemned and which remained unperformed. In March, however, Nikolay Rubinstein directed a successful performance of the revised Overture in F, and in consequence and at Nikolay's prompting Tchaikovsky embarked on a symphony.

The composition of the First Symphony proved a severe labour; no previous composition of his had demanded such sustained effort, and his confidence in his creative powers had been devastated by Cui's newly published review of his graduation cantata. The work proceeded sluggishly, though apparently the symphony was at least fully sketched by early June, when Tchaikovsky began its orchestration. By early August, however, overwork brought him to the verge of a breakdown, and the symphony's completion was delayed. Hoping to have it performed in St Petersburg, he showed the unfinished work to Zaremba and Anton Rubinstein, but they censured it heavily. During the autumn Tchaikovsky revised the piece, and in December Nikolay Rubinstein conducted the scherzo in Moscow. For this movement Tchaikovsky had adapted the Mendelssohnian scherzo of his Piano Sonata in C♯ minor, composed in 1865 while he was still a student, adding as a trio an orchestral waltz that was to be the first of a whole line of such compositions. The scherzo was coolly received, though it fared better in St Petersburg in February 1867 when it was coupled with the slow movement, in which a flow of most attractive melody is shaped into a kind of rondo structure, flanked by a string passage salvaged from *The Storm*. This slow movement was particularly successful with the audience; both it and the first movement bear descriptive titles. The symphony was given its first complete performance in February 1868, when it was well received.

The continuing influence of conservatory habits is less evident in the symphony's first movement than in the finale, with its selfconscious demonstrations of contrapuntal techniques. The theme of the introduction (also used as the second subject) is a Russian folktune, but this is the only national element in the music. Though Tchaikovsky could fabricate efficiently contrapuntal passages that are sometimes quite complex, he was incapable of the sort of contrapuntal thinking needed to generate a substantial and living musical organism. Nevertheless, he found that if short contrapuntal passages were repeated sequentially in different keys, with or without modification, or if a new passage followed abruptly in a new key, an illusion of progress resulted. Thus in this finale Tchaikovsky paraded his contrapuntal expertise in modulatory contexts (the transitions and development). Inevitably such passages create a feeling of fabrication which is not dispelled by the extended chromatic lead to the coda, an undeniably original passage that must have displeased Zaremba and Anton Rubinstein. In the first movement even more remained to give them offence, such as Tchaikovsky's penchant for harmonic pungency. Nor are they likely to have approved of the tonal balance of this first movement, with its heavy gravitation to sharp keys, nor of the proportions of the exposition. Despite Tchaikovsky's modulatory facility, he had no more capacity for the organic tonal evolution of Classical symphonic practice than for the organic counterpoint of Baroque precedents, and the two subjects are gigantic, tonally enclosed paragraphs, joined by the briefest of transitions. Yet the exposition is acceptable, for what Tchaikovsky lacked in ability to evolve he made up for in capacity for straightforward statement. The fundamental contour of the opening phrase and its subsequent repetitiveness have a marked affinity with Russian folk music, but the spaciousness and generous emotion of the second subject are already unmistakably Tchaikovsky's own. Despite his lifelong deficiencies as an organic contrapuntist, Tchaikovsky had an innate flair for decorative counterpoint and for devising felicitous contrapuntal combinations; this is already evident in the development, while his gift for combining themes contrapuntally and for neat, if shortwinded, imitative passages is demonstrated in the coda.

Between September and November 1866 Tchaikovsky was also occupied with a Festival Overture on the Danish national hymn, composed in connection with the wedding of the tsarevich to a Danish princess. Royal gratitude was expressed in the form of a pair of cufflinks, which Tchaikovsky promptly sold. At the same time his thoughts were turning towards an opera. He had been contemplating one within a month of his arrival in Moscow, but had dropped the idea when he became engrossed in his First Symphony; now he began to consider an opera, *Voyevoda* ('The voyevoda'), based on Ostrovsky's melodrama *Son na Volge*. Tchaikovsky persuaded the playwright to provide the libretto and started work in March 1867. However, Ostrovsky abandoned the project when Tchaikovsky lost what had been sent him, and the composer himself wrote the libretto of most of Act 2 and the whole of Act 3. The orchestration was completed while he was on a visit to Paris in summer 1868, and the first performance was early in 1869. Despite Tchaikovsky's own report of a great public success, the critics (including his friend Laroche) were unenthusiastic, and the work survived only five performances. Some years later Tchaikovsky came to agree with his critics, and destroyed the score after incorporating some material from it into *Oprichnik* ('The oprichnik'), though virtually the whole opera has been reconstructed from the surviving orchestral parts and other material. At the time he felt in a sufficiently buoyant mood to embark on another opera, and between January and July 1869 he composed a romantic fairy-tale opera, *Undina* ('Undine'). However, the theatre postponed production, and in the end the work never reached the stage. Like *The Voyevoda*, it was later destroyed by Tchaikovsky after some of its best music had been incorporated in other compositions. Work on a third opera, *Mandragora*, begun early in 1870, proceeded no further than a Chorus of Flowers and Insects, which won some approval in concert performances.

In 1866 Tchaikovsky's family organized a holiday in the company of Vera and Elizaveta Davïdova, the sisters-in-law of his own sister, Alexandra. The following year, after a holiday in Finland had had to be abandoned through lack of money, he and Modest again spent some six weeks with the Davïdovs at Hapsal; there Tchaikovsky composed three slight piano pieces, *Souvenir de Hapsal*, of which the third, *Chant sans paroles*, achieved much popularity. By now Vera Davïdova was strongly drawn to Tchaikovsky, but he did not return her feelings. The only woman who seems to have interested him at all was the singer Désirée Artôt, whom he met in September the following year, and in whose company

he spent much time. For Artôt's benefit performance of Auber's *Le domino noir* he provided special
choruses and recitatives. He wrote to his father that they
wished to marry; but his own friends and Artôt's
mother all opposed the match, and the affair was con-
cluded when she suddenly married a Spanish baritone,
Mario Padilla, early in 1869. Thereafter, until the desperate venture of his marriage in 1877, Tchaikovsky
seems to have had no further direct emotional involvement with any woman.

The musical contacts of this period were far more
fruitful. In January 1868 Tchaikovsky met Berlioz,
then visiting Moscow to conduct some concerts.
Balakirev was in Moscow to attend them and three
months later, on a visit to St Petersburg, Tchaikovsky
met other members of Balakirev's circle. The contact
with Balakirev was to have a profound effect on him.
His dances from *The Voyevoda* had already been successfully performed in Moscow, and Balakirev requested
them from Tchaikovsky, intending to give them in St
Petersburg. The performance did not materialize, but on
29 March 1869 Balakirev conducted the first St
Petersburg performance of Tchaikovsky's symphonic
fantasia *Fatum* ('Fate'), composed in the last months of
1868. Balakirev, to whom the work was dedicated, had
strong reservations about it, and subsequently commun-
icated these to Tchaikovsky. Later Tchaikovsky destroyed the piece (though it has been reconstructed from
the surviving orchestral parts). The relationship between
the two men was always uneasy; clearly Balakirev,
though suspicious of anyone with a formal conservatory
training, recognized Tchaikovsky's great talents, and
wanted him for his own circle. As for Tchaikovsky, he

obviously wished passionately for acceptance and recognition by Balakirev and his group, recognizing the force of Balakirev's criticisms while deeply resenting their bluntness. In fact, Balakirev was the only man who ever persuaded Tchaikovsky to rewrite a work several times, and his quite extraordinary catalytic power is forcefully demonstrated in *Romeo and Juliet*. It proved to be Tchaikovsky's first masterpiece.

The idea of a work on this Shakespeare subject was probably first discussed between Balakirev and Tchaikovsky in summer 1869. When Tchaikovsky's creativity failed to stir, Balakirev wrote to him (16 October), outlining his own method of composition from a literary groundplan, and even including the four bars of music with which he would begin. The letter was productive, for within six weeks Tchaikovsky had completed the first version of the piece, which Nikolay Rubinstein conducted in March 1870. Even before this Balakirev had commented on Tchaikovsky's material, approving the first subject, judging the second part of the second subject to be a little overripe, but unreservedly endorsing the first theme. The introduction he found completely inadequate, recommending Tchaikovsky to compose something on the lines of a Lisztian chorale. After the first performance Tchaikovsky took this advice, not merely launching the piece with a modal hymn-like theme, but following Liszt's practice of repeating the whole introduction, starting in another key. This new material necessitated further revisions in the development and coda. A second revision, made in 1880, provided a still better climax to the recapitulation and reordered the coda.

Balakirev's curious obsession with keys of two sharps

and five flats dictated to Tchaikovsky his choice
of tonal relationships in the exposition (B minor and D♭
– in fact C♯). The prominent use of the harp is redolent
of Liszt, while the influence of Glinka is unmistakable
in the alternating, chromatically related chords
suspended on a held note in the violins; this occurs twice
in the development, and obviously derives from
Chernomor's music in *Ruslan and Lyudmila*. Otherwise, *Romeo and Juliet* is thoroughly characteristic.
Quite apart from the powerful stimulus of the play itself,
the adaptation of sonata structure to the demands of the
story created a situation that suited Tchaikovsky ideally,
for it fully justified those very procedures that he had
used with more questionable success in his First
Symphony. There he had been driven, through his deficiencies in organic transition, to make each subject a
self-contained unit, with only the smallest of links between them; now, by using each subject and the
introduction as an embodiment of three separate characters or elements from Shakespeare's play, he made the
construction of such an exposition inevitable, and rendered strong contrasts between the subjects desirable.
The shifting keys within the first subject and the canonic
treatment it receives already foreshadow Tchaikovsky's
tendency to become obsessed with his material in quasi-
developmental manner, though as yet there is no question of it getting out of hand. Likewise, in the development and coda, where the drama itself is played out and
fulfilled, it suited Tchaikovsky ideally to realize the
clash between the chief characters either by simultan-
eous confrontation or by sharp juxtaposition of
representative musical materials, and the sense of dutiful
contrivance from which the developments of the First

159

Symphony do not escape is avoided in this piece. While being as vivid and emotionally powerful as any of Tchaikovsky's works, *Romeo and Juliet* has no excesses.

High nationalism, 1870–74

From the beginning Tchaikovsky's interest in Russian folk music had been quite as strong as that of any member of The Five. Examples of his use or imitation of it have already been cited; to these may be added the national idiom (and the actual use of folksong) in parts of the opera *The Voyevoda*, which Tchaikovsky had composed before he met Balakirev. After finishing this work he had started on the piano duet arrangements of 50 Russian folksongs (1868–9), further confirmation of his preoccupation with indigenous material, though he had no hesitation in 'improving' his material if he thought he could. What principally distinguished Tchaikovsky from The Five was his formal conservatory grounding in Western musical techniques, which entrenched in him concepts of harmonic propriety often inimical to folksong. He rarely succeeded in purging completely the manner in which he treated national material of elements that compromised its essential character. Each member of The Five, on the other hand, had acquired his technique empirically, and contact with such men and attitudes was bound to have a certain broadening, even liberating effect on Tchaikovsky's own technique. He was certainly delighted to have their interest and approval, and in the next few years his music often drew close to theirs in its ideals and procedures. Yet he had to apply such things in his own way, and he knew that Balakirev's direct guidance had to be shed. So when Balakirev proposed in October 1871 a plan for a cantata, *Night*, to absorb the Chorus of Flowers and Insects from the abortive opera *Mandragora*, Tchaikovsky tactfully evaded the suggestion. With the withdrawal of Balakirev from Russian concert life in 1872, contact between the two men was broken for some ten years.

Though Tchaikovsky had found himself in *Romeo and Juliet*, his subsequent creative career was certainly not a consistent further revelation of his own personality; for alongside works which are unmistakably his are others that mark out parallel but less individual lines. One such line is represented by his songs, many of which are hardly more than drawing-room pieces, sometimes almost indistinguishable from those that Glinka was purveying nearly half a century before Tchaikovsky composed his first set. These were the Six Songs op.6, written immediately after the first version of *Romeo and Juliet* in 1869. The melodies of such songs are too often saturated in a sentimentality that thwarts any moment of truly passionate or dramatic utterance, and there is nothing remotely connected with folksong in the majority of them. Of these first songs the last is the best; in its English version, *None but the lonely heart*, it has remained one of his most popular short pieces.

Like this set of songs, Tchaikovsky's next extended composition, his First String Quartet, initiated a line of works in which his personality stands less than fully revealed. In February 1870, shortly after the completion of *Romeo and Juliet* and the op.6 songs, he set to work on a new tragic opera, *The Oprichnik*, drawing his

own libretto from Lazhechnikov's drama. Work proceeded slowly and was interrupted in May by an urgent
summons to Paris to visit a sick friend, Vladimir
Shilovsky. June was spent in Germany, and after six
weeks in Switzerland, where the first revision of *Romeo
and Juliet* was made, he returned to Russia. By the end
of the year he had resumed work on *The Oprichnik*, but
in February 1871 it was again interrupted, this time by
the composition of a string quartet which he planned to
include in a concert of his own works from which he
hoped to make some money. The concert took place
successfully in March; in the audience was Turgenev.
As a medium the string quartet offered Tchaikovsky no
scope for the dramatic contrasts or grand rhetoric possible with the orchestra, and in his First Quartet he
showed himself concerned to compose as absolute a
piece as he could, attempting to think, in the sonata
structures of the outer movements and in the scherzo,
through the mind of a Classical composer. Individuality
is inevitably sacrificed, and the opening of the quartet,
for instance, might be taken for Schubert; the reward of
this self-negation is a notable structural equilibrium and
expressive poise. Only in the second movement, the
famous Andante cantabile based on a folksong collected
at Kamenka, is Tchaikovsky unmistakably himself.

In May Tchaikovsky was again hard at work on *The
Oprichnik*, and after visits to Kamenka and to the estate
of his friend Nikolay Kondrat'yev at Nizy near
Khar'kov, during which he completed his textbook on
harmony, he visited Shilovsky on his estate at Usovo,
not far from Kiev, where he resumed the composition of
his opera, actually permitting his host to compose and
score the prelude to Act 2. On returning to Moscow he

163

moved for the first time into his own flat. Because of the extra expense this involved, he had to supplement his earnings by undertaking some work as a music critic; he continued this part-time occupation until 1876. A holiday in Nice (at Shilovsky's expense) and a lucrative commission for a festival cantata again held up *The Oprichnik*, which was not completed until April 1872.

Abraham has described *The Oprichnik* as 'Meyerbeer translated into Russian', adding, however, that the translation is done thoroughly. The plot is a melodrama of love and conspiracy in which a crucial role is played by the oprichniks, the notorious bodyguard of Ivan the Terrible. A sizable portion of the music was transferred bodily from *The Voyevoda*, and the work was composed, following the precedent set by Glinka's *A Life for the Tsar*, as a succession of self-contained movements linked by a species of accompanied recitative or arioso. A certain musical integration is achieved by the modest use of leitmotifs. Much of the music with which Tchaikovsky supplemented his material from *The Voyevoda* is filled with the same kind of national flavour, and the opera uses a number of real folksongs. The score also has an element arising from the idiom of Slavonic church music. All this is supplemented by a liberal amount of that lyricism which, at its feeblest, is related to the manner of the drawing-room song, and at its best transmutes itself into the full-blooded cantilena which is unmistakably Tchaikovsky's. The work was successful when it reached the stage in April 1874; but Tchaikovsky himself turned against it, and it might have suffered the same fate as his first two operas had he not already sold the rights to Bessel.

Having completed *The Oprichnik*, Tchaikovsky spent

summer 1872 in his customary round of the estates of his family and friends, starting work on his Second Symphony in June while at Kamenka. This work, together with the opera *Kuznets Vakula* ('Vakula the smith'), represents Tchaikovsky's nationalism at its strongest; it received its nickname 'Little Russian' after Tchaikovsky's death because of its incorporation of Ukrainian folktunes. It was completed in November, and when he visited St Petersburg at the end of the year, he played the finale to Rimsky-Korsakov and some friends: all were enraptured by it. Similar enthusiasm greeted the first performance in Moscow in February 1873. Yet Tchaikovsky was immediately dissatisfied with it, and in 1879–80 he provided a virtually new first movement, revised the scherzo, and made a substantial cut in the finale.

The authorized version of the first movement is notable for its economy. As in *Romeo and Juliet*, the theme of the slow introduction (the first of the Ukrainian folktunes) is drawn into the development; but the structure of the introduction itself is quite different, with the single Lisztian repetition of a large section in another key being replaced by a section built around the statement and three repetitions of the folktune, set against different backgrounds after the practice of Glinka. In the exposition, too, instead of a tonally closed first subject as in the First Symphony, Tchaikovsky devised a terser utterance that moves quickly to the dominant of the second subject, an extended paragraph. The theme of the introduction recurs to close the movement. The second movement had originally been the Bridal March in the opera *Undine*; here, again, the influence of Glinka is apparent in the changing backgrounds to which the central theme (another Ukrainian folksong) is treated. The scherzo is clearly conditioned by that of Borodin's First Symphony. It is the finale that is the most fully Russian. Here the third of Tchaikovsky's folksongs, *The Crane*, is first heard in a portentous introduction not unlike the 'promenade' sections of Musorgsky's *Pictures at an Exhibition*, and then in a swift series of repetitions against changing backgrounds to form the first subject, into which is incorporated a passage built over a whole-tone scale. To initiate the development Tchaikovsky, with scant regard for consonance, flung his folktune against a wide-stepping bass, furnished the second subject with an unstable chromatic support which slips it out of key in mid-phrase, and then led a mixture of these two elements through an orgy of modulation to fashion one of the most striking passages anywhere in his work. Nowhere did Tchaikovsky draw closer to Musorgsky at his most boldly imaginative.

At the end of 1872 Tchaikovsky composed a second set of six songs, op.16, which continued the stylistic line of op.6 and was as far removed from any folk tradition; the last is an interesting experiment incorporating the *Dies irae* theme throughout as a kind of cantus firmus. During March and April 1873 he applied himself to the composition of incidental music for Ostrovsky's fairy-tale drama, *Snegurochka* ('The snow maiden'), providing a prelude and 18 separate pieces that incorporate 12 folksongs. As with his later music to *Hamlet*, he relied on some material from earlier works. The attractiveness of the music won it a considerable success with the public when the play was produced in May. Visits to Nizy and Kamenka, and a trip to the

West, intervened before Tchaikovsky settled down at Usovo in August to compose a symphonic fantasia, *Burya* ('The tempest'), based on a plan that Vladimir Stasov had provided for him earlier in the year. Work went easily, and the composition was completed in 11 days. The orchestration was finished on his return to Moscow, and when the work was performed in December it enjoyed a success as great as that of the Second Symphony. *The Tempest* is not, however, one of Tchaikovsky's best orchestral pieces. It is a five-section mirror structure, with musical portrayals of Ariel and Caliban at the centre, flanked by love music for Ferdinand and Miranda, with the sea and Prospero surrounding all. Virtually no effort is made to engage musical material from the various sections, but this would scarcely have mattered if Tchaikovsky's material had been of sufficient quality. The heaving of the sea, depicted by undulating divided strings deployed on massive, slow-moving harmonies, was (according to Rimsky-Korsakov) modelled on the opening of Wagner's *Das Rheingold.* It is an effective enough formula, and the love music has much appeal, though it is not really a match for that of *Romeo and Juliet.* Nevertheless, in his portrayal of Caliban (though hardly Shakespearean and completely lacking the grotesque richness that Musorgsky might have bestowed on it) Tchaikovsky did not succumb to the rather facile creative attitude revealed in the rest of the piece.

Nor was the rapturous reception accorded the Second String Quartet justified by the quality of the piece itself. It was written in January 1874, and Tchaikovsky recorded that none of his works had ever been composed so effortlessly. Here lies a clue to the trouble, for, as with *The Tempest*, the piece has fluency, showing skilled craftsmanship but little of the freshness of invention that had marked the First Quartet. The chromaticism of the first movement's introduction promises well, but the ensuing movement has a blandness that Tchaikovsky's refined textural resourcefulness cannot conceal. The scherzo is the most interesting movement, with its free alternation of bars of two and three beats, and the slow movement contains some characteristic music, though a slender idea is repeated at excessive length. The material of the finale is second rate, too, and its cordiality culminates in a fugato that is as sterile expressively as it is skilful technically.

Tchaikovsky's next major work contained some of the best music he wrote. This was the opera *Vakula the Smith*, set to a libretto based on Gogol's *Christmas Eve*. Polonsky had originally provided this for Serov, but on the latter's death in 1871 the Grand Duchess Helena Pavlovna had made it into a competition piece, offering two prizes and a guarantee of performance at the Mariinsky Theatre for the winning work. Helena Pavlovna's own death in 1873 left the competition in the hands of the Russian Musical Society, who fixed the closing date as August 1875. Immediately after the première of *The Oprichnik* in April 1874, Tchaikovsky left for Italy in his capacity as music critic to review the first performance of *A Life for the Tsar* in Milan. Thoroughly riled that the Glinka première had been postponed so that adjustments could be made to suit Italian taste, he decided not to visit Milan. Late in May he arrived back in Russia. Under the impression that the closing date for the opera competition was January 1875 he withdrew to Nizy; only two and a half months later at Usovo he completed the scoring of his entry. Having submitted it under a pseudonym as required, he learnt of his mistake and forthwith negotiated to withdraw from the competition, hoping to get *Vakula* staged earlier. This request was summarily rejected, but it had revealed his identity to the committee, and the opera's overture was actually publicly performed. Despite these and other improprieties Tchaikovsky was subsequently awarded the prize, and in December 1876 the work was staged. It was not a great success, and nine years later Tchaikovsky revised it, renaming it *Cherevichki* ('The slippers'; in the West it became generally known as *Les caprices d'Oxane*). Even with these later additions that Tchaikovsky made when his most nationalist period was far behind him, the opera remains a thoroughly Russian work.

Unlike Lazhechnikov's *The Oprichnik*, Gogol's delightful fairy tale did not afford melodramatic situations that might all too easily have tempted Tchaikovsky into an exaggerated response in *Vakula the Smith*. Instead it offered a liberal measure of the fantastic which required (and drew) from him a matching musical fantasy that he never surpassed. It is not surprising that this work remained one of his own favourites. Of purely non-Russian music there is surprisingly little, really only the couplets and the minuet in Act 3: the latter is the first of a line of Rococo stylizations that were to appear in his work. Elsewhere in the opera the influence of Glinka is strong; the model for the polonaise in Act 3, and the style of the whole choral scene at the beginning of Act 2 scene ii, can be traced to *A Life for the Tsar*, while the influence of *Ruslan and Lyudmila* is even stronger. This is perhaps surprising, for while *Ruslan* held the greater attraction for Balakirev and his circle, it was Glinka's first opera that had the firmer hold on Tchaikovsky. In *Ruslan* Glinka had worked out his particular idiom for the treatment of magical and fantastic happenings, and this proved a rich source of suggestion to Tchaikovsky for his own handling of the supernatural and unearthly in this opera. There is a good deal that is indebted to *Ruslan* in the opening scene with the Devil (including one passage built on a whole-tone bass), and even more perhaps in the scene of Vakula with the *rusalki* at the beginning of Act 3. In addition to the Russianness arising from Glinka, there is that which came from folksong (especially Ukrainian), most obviously revealed in the number of gopak tunes in the opera. The intonations of folk music also infiltrate the music relating to human emotions rather than to supernatural happenings. On the whole the weakest passages are the more lyrical ones involving Vakula and Oxana. It is when the lyrical vein is subjected to high dramatic pressure that there is a danger of Tchaikovsky's invention taking refuge in routine operatic gestures. Nevertheless, such moments are minor blemishes in one of Tchaikovsky's most inventive and imaginative scores; it is worth observing the marked gift for comedy that he was beginning to develop in his handling of the succession of little scenes between Solokha and her lovers at the beginning of Act 2.

CHAPTER THREE

Increasing problems, 1874–7

Although there was to be a strong resurgence of a national character in parts of *Evgeny Onegin* ('Eugene Onegin'), *Mazepa* ('Mazeppa') and *Charodeyka* ('The sorceress'), Tchaikovsky's period of high nationalism ended with *Vakula the Smith*. Hitherto his music, however impassioned, full-blooded and dramatic, had been free of that emotional excess which spills over into morbidity or hysteria. Yet within three years these characteristics were to affect some works, revealing themselves forcefully in the Fourth Symphony. However, during these same years certain other lines that resist all overstatement become clearer in his output. What might, with some reservation, be called his neo-classical manner, begun in the First Quartet and confirmed in the first movement and finale of the Second, even manifests itself in parts of the Third Symphony; it must be added, however, that by this time the influence of Schumann had made itself evident above that of generalized Classical practice. Meanwhile a far more deliberate foraging into the past ushers in Tchaikovsky's line of Rococo pastiches, presaged in the minuet in *Vakula the Smith*, and firmly instituted by the Rococo Variations for cello and orchestra. In his neo-classical works Tchaikovsky had clearly been drawn to past styles because he thought he might solve certain structural problems more easily within them. In his Rococo pastiches, however, he

171

sought refuge in a musical world that he felt to be purer than that into which his own personal style was being irresistibly drawn. The ballet, too, offered him escape by taking him into an elegant fairy-tale realm arising from a French tradition, where he could exercise freely his splendid gifts for composing memorable dance music.

During these three years there also appeared Tchaikovsky's first essays in composing for a solo instrument and orchestra. In September 1874 he set about the Six Songs op.25, writing an overtly Russian piece in the last, *Kak naladili: Durak* ('As they reiterated: Fool'), and in the fourth, *Kanareyka* ('The canary'), making one of his rare excursions into a pseudo-oriental idiom. Then, in November, he started work on his First Piano Concerto. At the beginning of 1875 he played it over to Nikolay Rubinstein who in a notorious incident summarily condemned it as ill-composed and unplayable. Tchaikovsky was badly hurt but completed the score as planned, ultimately dedicating it to Hans von Bülow, who greatly admired it and gave the first performance in October in Boston. Later Rubinstein recanted his opinion. The dramatic possibilities in the confrontation of heroic soloist and eloquent orchestra obviously fired Tchaikovsky. Structurally the concerto has been faulted for the huge tune which launches the first movement in the wrong key and never returns; yet one of the most admirable features of the first movement is a structural one, namely, Tchaikovsky's enterprising exploitation of tonal instability to enhance the tensions and restlessness that are such essential ingredients in the high drama of the late 19th-century concerto. His resourcefulness is maintained in the other two movements, the finale being an effective type of sonata rondo with a Ukrainian folksong providing the first theme; in the second movement a flow of simple melody is supported by a characteristically Russian semitonal key relationship (D major against a D♭ tonic). The swift waltz theme in D in the middle of the movement is said to be based on a song from Désirée Artôt's repertory, *Il faut s'amuser et rire*.

During April Tchaikovsky completed two further sets of six songs, opp.27 and 28, of which *Korolki* ('The corals' op.28 no.2) is a notable dramatic ballad. Summer 1875 was spent at Usovo, Nizy and Verbovka (another of the Davïdov estates near Kamenka). Here he worked on his Third Symphony, a piece which in its first and last movements is far closer in nature to the Second String Quartet than to the Second Symphony. In the first movement Tchaikovsky was clearly deepening his preoccupations with the basic problems of sonata structure, taking his decisions on what he considered to be the grounds of good technique, unmolested by any imaginative impulse or powerful emotional pressure. Schumann is the prime influence. Though some of Schumann's harmonic practices provided enrichment of Tchaikovsky's resources, the influence of his more forceful and bluff utterances rarely proved beneficial; for what might possess dignity in Schumann too often degenerates into a foursquare sterility when processed by Tchaikovsky. The first subject of the Third Symphony demonstrates this cogently, and Tchaikovsky's endeavour to pare down his material to what he believed to be the bare essentials required for future development permits only a ghost of his real self to remain. The simple counterpoints of the second movement, Alla tedesca, are incomparably more attrac-

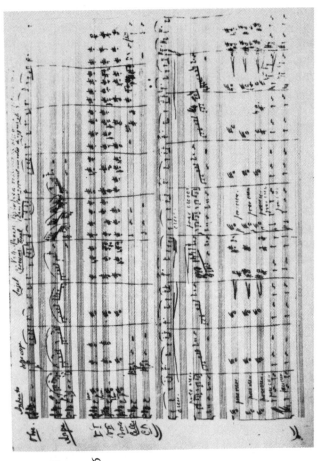

12. Autograph
MS of the
opening of the
Act 1 finale from
Tchaikovsky's
'Swan Lake',
composed 1875–6

tive. Even the Tempo di polacca finale (from which the conductor August Manns later gave the symphony its irrelevant nickname 'Polish') does not escape a demonstration of academic expertise in a lengthy fugato. The delicate scherzo shows Tchaikovsky's fascination with light and varied orchestral textures which he was to exploit with greater mastery in the scherzo of the *Manfred* symphony; the trio of this movement was drawn from music composed for the cantata of 1872.

Despite the charm of the middle three movements, the Third Symphony is the dullest of the series; nevertheless, it was warmly received at its first performance in November. The same was not true of Tchaikovsky's next major work, his first ballet, *Lebedinoye ozero* ('Swan lake'), commissioned by the Imperial Theatres in Moscow. Tchaikovsky began work on the score in August 1875, using some music from a little domestic ballet of the same title composed for his sister Alexandra's children, evidently in 1871. The new work was not finished until the following April and was first performed in March 1877. The performance was poor, and Tchaikovsky's score, already heavily cut, was adulterated by the interpolation of some pieces by Pugni to make it more palatable to the impoverished taste of the audience and easier for the dancers. *Swan Lake* is, however, among the more satisfactory of Tchaikovsky's works. He admitted that he could write well in an opera only when he became personally involved with his characters, and all too often they remained puppet figures of little or no credibility, who drew from him music that was at best efficient. In ballet, however, characterization was of less significance: what was required was music that could establish atmosphere when necessary, and provide at all times a characteristic accompaniment to the movement on stage. With his rich gifts for melody and special flair for writing memorable dance-tunes, with his ready response to the atmosphere of a theatrical situation and his masterly orchestration, Tchaikovsky was ideally equipped as a ballet composer.

Not that *Swan Lake* is a consistently successful piece. In those passages where Tchaikovsky was concerned with dramatic action he showed his aptitude for producing music which, if rarely revealing that vivid pantomimic quality in which Musorgsky excelled, nevertheless felicitously supports the stage action in movements of considerable musical substance and scale, far weightier than anything in earlier Russian ballet. Yet the expectations of the Russian public for decorative spectacle had to be satisfied; thus Act 1 contains a lengthy divertissement quite unrelated to the main plot, and though Act 3 initially contrives to combine such formal dancing with dramatic movement as various characters or groups enter in turn, it subsequently slides into decorative dancing, culminating in five charmingly characterful but irrelevant national stylizations. However, the suite of dances for the swans and the *pas d'action* for the lovers in Act 2 are dramatically justifiable, and the final act is purged of all extraneous matter to grow from its briefly relaxed opening into an organism as purposefully dramatic as it is concise. Warrack has drawn attention to Tchaikovsky's use of key structure as an agent of dramatic articulation, the music for Siegfried and Odette being set mainly in sharper keys, that of Rotbart and the force of evil gravitating towards flat keys. It was with the revival of *Swan Lake* in 1895, with choreography by Petipa and Ivanov, that it received the appreciation that it merited and that has subsequently endured.

At the end of 1875 Tchaikovsky began what was to prove his best-known piano work, the set of 12 pieces, *Les saisons*, composed for publication in the monthly parts of a periodical during 1876. All his piano music is of only minor importance, and despite the popularity subsequently achieved by some of *Les saisons*, this set of salon pieces is of slender value. It was also towards the end of 1875 that Tchaikovsky made the acquaintance of Saint-Saëns, who was visiting Moscow. Then, at the beginning of 1876, cheered by the successful Russian performances of the Third Symphony and First Piano Concerto and by the welcome news of his success with *Vakula the Smith* in the opera competition, he left for Paris. There he attended a performance of Bizet's *Carmen*, a work that made a profound and lasting impression on him, and also started his Third String Quartet. He completed it on his return to Russia, and it was well received at its first performance in March. It is strange that Tchaikovsky, who nine months after the first hearing of his Second Quartet could still judge it to be his best work, should have had immediate reservations about the new piece, fearing that he was repeating himself; for the Third Quartet is far more characteristic than its predecessor. Dedicated to the memory of his violinist friend Ferdinand Laub, the work makes its elegiac function explicit in the third movement, Andante funebre e doloroso. It may be that in the earlier part of this movement the intensity of feeling is stronger than its musical material, but the music's relative austerity provides a splendid foil for the G♭ cantilena that follows. Neither the scherzo nor the finale is as weighty or as consistently characteristic; nevertheless, the former has some effervescent wit, the latter a vigour of the kind displayed in the finale of the First Piano Concerto.

The impact of *Carmen* impelled Tchaikovsky to seek an opera libretto on a similar subject for himself, and in February Laroche sent him one by Zvantsev based on the tale of Francesca da Rimini from Dante's *Inferno*. The need to complete *Swan Lake* prevented Tchaikovsky from undertaking anything else for the moment, and a subsequent recurring ailment drove him to seek a cure in Vichy. There, in early July, he received from Modest some suggestions for an orchestral work. Besides Hamlet, Othello and Lermontov's Tamar, Modest proposed Francesca da Rimini, and a subsequent reading of Dante persuaded Tchaikovsky that he would compose an orchestral piece and not an opera. In August he visited Bayreuth to attend, as a critic, the first complete cycle of the *Ring*; he was warmly received by Liszt, though he failed to meet Wagner. The *Ring* proved not at all to Tchaikovsky's taste, despite his recognition of some remarkably beautiful and striking moments in it. Returning to Russia in late August he composed, at Nikolay Rubinstein's request, his Slavonic March, which provoked a storm of patriotic feeling at its first performance in November; then he settled down to *Francesca da Rimini*, sketching it in full in less than three weeks, and completing it in November. Its first performance in Moscow in March 1877 was warmly greeted by both the public and the critics.

In *Francesca da Rimini* there are already signs of those excesses that were to mark many of Tchaikovsky's works from the Fourth Symphony onwards. Here, however, they arise not so much from an almost hysterical need to find a personal emotional outlet as from a straining after effects to compensate for the work's lack of organic development. The subject of *Francesca da Rimini* did not offer a variety of characters locked in drama, as did *Romeo and Juliet*, but a single individual narrating a sad tale. The evolving conflict of sonata procedures was therefore inappropriate, and Tchaikovsky chose instead a simple ternary scheme whose sections are built through literal or decorated repetition. Francesca's pathetic narration forms the centre of the work, flanked by an Allegro vivo that graphically depicts the buffeting winds of the Second Circle of the Inferno, all of which is preceded by an introduction saturated with plangent diminished 7ths and wailing chromaticism that owe a good deal to Liszt. The absence of any genuine thematic development is matched by the restricted tonal range, most of the piece centring on E or A. The virtuosity of the craftsmanship is more conspicuous than in *Romeo and Juliet*, but *Francesca da Rimini* lacks that work's cogent sense of evolution. The winds of Hell tempt Tchaikovsky into a vivid but facile chromaticism; too many bars are spent in preparing great climaxes that do not match expectations. As for Francesca herself, she is prolix almost to the point of tedium. Set beside the intense subjectivity of the Fourth Symphony's first movement, *Francesca da Rimini* comes to seem an objective piece; yet there is already, in the seemingly interminable alternation of two themes in the central section, a foretaste of the obsessiveness that was to mark some of Tchaikovsky's later music.

There could hardly be a greater contrast between the fervent dramatic expression of *Francesca da Rimini* and

179

the poised elegance of the Variations on a Rococo Theme for cello and orchestra, which followed immediately in December 1876. The former had been an emotional torrent; the latter revealed a world of order and calm in beautifully wrought music, as gracious and as modest as an 18th-century divertimento. In turning to such music of the past as a basis for his own compositions, Tchaikovsky had a purpose the very opposite of that which later impelled Stravinsky; for whereas the latter, in his neo-classical works, subjected styles from the past to his Russian flair for creative caricature as a means of further self-discovery, Tchaikovsky turned to the 18th century as a means of escape from himself. It is highly significant that in his own life he was already preparing desperately for the ultimate step through which he hoped he would gain release from his homosexuality. In his self-loathing, and in order to escape the shame he felt at any public suspicion of his abnormality, he decided on marriage. In the West earlier in the year he had declared his intention of marrying, and before the year was out he had resolved to go through with it.

CHAPTER FOUR

Marriage: crisis and aftermath, 1877–8

In December 1876 Tchaikovsky met Tolstoy who, having been reduced to tears by the Andante cantabile of the First Quartet, furnished him with some folksongs that Tchaikovsky promised to use. Of greater consequence, however, was his first contact at much the same time with the wealthy widow Nadezhda von Meck. Her interest in him had been first aroused by his orchestral piece *The Tempest*, and was stimulated further when the violinist Yosif Kotek, one of Tchaikovsky's former pupils, was engaged by her as resident violinist. Small but handsomely rewarded commissions for violin and piano arrangements of some of Tchaikovsky's own smaller pieces initiated an extraordinary relationship that was to last for 14 years. It was maintained entirely by correspondence, and all personal contact was deliberately avoided; on the occasion when they accidentally met, they hurried past each other without speaking. For each the other thus remained a fantasy figure, unspoilt by the disenchantment of reality. The root of the relationship for Mme von Meck, as for Tchaikovsky, appears to have been a revulsion against physical relations with the opposite sex. The death of her husband in 1876 had released her from sexual demands, and, now evidently frigid, she could idealize Tchaikovsky as revealed in his music, find emotional

181

nourishment and fulfilment in responding to that music, and in correspondence pour out to him her thoughts and feelings without risking the pressures of a more personal relationship. The growing confirmation of his homosexuality was already leaving its marks on Tchaikovsky's music. From the beginning his musical language had been generous in its emotional power, but the element of overstatement, shown both in the inflated gestures of *Francesca da Rimini* and in the heightened emotional temperature of the Fourth Symphony, must surely arise from the need to find an outlet for emotional drives that could not be channelled into a full physical relationship. The advent of Mme von Meck could hardly have been more timely: for him she remained a depersonalized woman, making no physical demands, but longing for the confidences of his most personal thoughts and feelings. When, after the stunning blow of his attempted marriage, an emotional blockage came between Tchaikovsky and his own music (perhaps because his music would have too publicly revealed the feelings of which, after the humiliation of his disastrous marriage, he felt ashamed) the privacy of his written confidences with Mme von Meck became of even more crucial importance. The intensity of feeling within this curious relationship is confirmed by the vicarious physical union which Mme von Meck and Tchaikovsky eagerly sought and finally achieved when, on 23 January 1884, Mme von Meck's son Nikolay married Tchaikovsky's niece Anna Davïdova.

Tchaikovsky's marriage was the rash and hasty act of a desperate man. Sometime in early May 1877, while working on his Fourth Symphony, he received a written declaration of love from a certain Antonina Milyukova, who claimed she had met him at the conservatory, though Tchaikovsky himself could not recollect her. Further letters followed, including a threat of suicide if he would not see her. On 1 June Tchaikovsky visited her and told her firmly but not unkindly that he could not love her. There the matter might have rested, had not a coincidence in his creative life at that moment impelled him to reconsider his attitude. A week before their meeting, with the first three movements of the Fourth Symphony now sketched in full, his attention had been drawn to Pushkin's *Eugene Onegin* as a possible opera subject. He was quickly fired by it and set about working out his own scenario, abandoning plans for an opera on *Othello* or De Vigny's *Cinq-mars*. With Onegin's heartless spurning of Tatyana now firmly in his mind, Tchaikovsky was driven to reconsider his own rejection of Antonina. As a result, within a week of their first meeting he had proposed and, though he tried to make it clear that there could be no physical relationship between them, been accepted. With the last movement of the Fourth Symphony now also finished, he departed for Shilovsky's home at Glebovo, where he settled down to composing *Eugene Onegin* (he had started with Tatyana's Letter Scene which, he perceived, had a remarkable parallel with Antonina's first declaration to him). Before returning to Moscow to prepare for the wedding he had already sketched about two-thirds of the opera. Now at last he informed his family and Mme von Meck of his intention. He married Antonina on 18 July. His nightmare began immediately. After making some family visits he escaped from his wife to Kamenka, pretending that he was taking a cure in the Caucasus. During August he scored some of the Fourth Symphony and worked a little on *Eugene Onegin*. The beginning of the conservatory term on 24 September forced him to return to Moscow and his wife. Unable to stand the strain, he had within days made a pathetic attempt at suicide. When it failed he engineered an urgent summons to St Petersburg, where he arrived on 7 October in a state of complete nervous collapse. A specialist was consulted who, pronouncing his reason to be threatened, ordered a complete change; he was further recommended never to see his wife again. His brother Anatoly promptly left for Moscow to arrange a separation from Antonina, returning to St Petersburg to bear his brother off to western Europe.

With the worst horrors of this most critical event in his life now behind him, Tchaikovsky began to recover. After nearly a month at Clarens in Switzerland, he briefly visited Paris and then moved on to Italy. His personal condition, though still not normal, had further improved, and his financial worries had been removed by news from Nikolay Rubinstein that his conservatory stipend would be paid in full for the session. Moreover, Mme von Meck, from whom he had already requested loans, declared that she would settle on him an annuity of 6000 rubles. Thus, when he was nominated Russian delegate to the Paris Exhibition of 1878, he felt able to decline this appointment which earlier he had agreed to accept. During a visit to Vienna he saw Delibes' ballet *Sylvia*, which he admired greatly, declaring that his own *Swan Lake* was not fit to hold a candle to it. In January 1878 he completed the scoring of his Fourth Symphony, and in February *Eugene Onegin* was completed.

Both the symphony and the opera bear unmistakable marks of the events in Tchaikovsky's private life at the

13. Part of Tchaikovsky's autograph letter (15 July 1877, old style) to Madame von Meck describing his return to Moscow after his wedding, and asking for a loan of money to allow him to escape time of their creation. In 1878, after the symphony was completed, Mme von Meck, the work's dedicatee, elicited from him the programme on which he alleged the work to be based. While it is impossible to take the whole programme seriously, it is certainly easy to believe that the opening theme does symbolize fate, for although it engages briefly with the main material during the first movement's development and coda, its chief function is to intrude peremptorily and inexorably, sweeping aside all other material. On a purely musical level it provides some powerful dramatic moments, while its strategic insertion, first between the exposition and development, then between the recapitulation and coda, aids structural clarity. Its return before the coda of the finale tightens the whole four-movement structure. The first movement, with its enormous expressive range and ruthless climaxes, is one of the most fascinating in all Tchaikovsky's works, generated as it is by the inter-action of a normal sonata structure and a thoroughly unorthodox key scheme founded on a circle of minor 3rds (F, A♭, C♭ (= B), D, F). The first subject, a melancholy waltz with a constant hesitant cross-rhythm, is, like that of *Romeo and Juliet*, a tonally enclosed section encompassing a development, here expanded to substantial proportions. The use in the exposition of the first three keys in the cycle creates a problem that Tchaikovsky solved by treating A♭, the conventional key centre for the second subject, as a transitional key. Thus, having reached A♭ minor and introduced a new clarinet theme, he quickly probed a minor 3rd higher, devised a simple counter-melody to this clarinet tune, and then quickly settled into C♭ for the main second subject, in which he combined material from the preceding A♭ and F minor (first subject) sections. The recapitulation resumes the circle of keys, entering in D minor, a key that is retained for the restatement of the former clarinet tune, thus ensuring that the main part of the second subject will recur in the tonic, F. A hectic coda confirms this as the most nakedly emotional movement that Tchaikovsky had yet composed.

Taneyev censured Tchaikovsky for adopting a style reminiscent of ballet for his middle two movements. This stylistic perception is hardly valid as an objection, for they provide a much needed relief after the first movement, functioning as they do as intermezzos. In the second, the scherzo, Tchaikovsky deliberately exploited the colour contrasts between groups of instruments, scoring the flanks of the ternary structure for pizzicato strings, and allotting the trio first to woodwind, then to brass and timpani, before combining them. All three sections are used in the coda. The finale cannot match the first movement. It uses a folktune as its second theme, badly compromising its national character by expanding its natural three-bar phrases (written by Tchaikovsky as one and a half bars) into ones of four bars; much of the movement is built around this tune, which is either repeated with changing backgrounds after the example of Glinka, or else used for quasi-developmental passages.

The secret of Tchaikovsky's success in *Eugene Onegin* lies in the passionate sympathy he conceived for Tatyana, heightened obviously by the analogies of the tale to current events in his own life. He drew his libretto from Pushkin's verse novel, using the poet's own lines as far as possible. From the beginning he was aware of the problem of translating this story into oper-

14. *Autograph MS of the opening of Tchaikovsky's 'Eugene Onegin', composed 1877–8; Tchaikovsky's own piano reduction for the vocal score can be seen at the foot of the page.*

atic form, realizing that, while it ran deep in feeling, it offered few opportunities for conventional scenic effects. He can have been little surprised, therefore, that at its first performance by students of the Moscow Conservatory in March 1879 it made little impression. Nevertheless, these 'lyrical scenes' comprise his finest opera. Their thematic integration is striking. The short orchestral prelude is founded on a four-note germ (probably conditioned by the fate motif from Bizet's *Carmen*) which haunts much of the first two scenes, permeating the opening ensemble, playing a large part in the exchanges between the women, tinging the first encounter between Tatyana and Onegin, and figuring prominently in the beautifully sensitive scene between Tatyana and the Nurse. In contrast to the highly charged feelings associated with this phrase is the fresh, unsophisticated music of the peasants' chorus and dance. The four-note motif persists in the first part of the Letter Scene, and is rhythmically echoed in the horn answer to the descending oboe phrase of the Andante, which itself generates further motifs in the opera, and which here distils the very essence of Tatyana's feelings. Strangely, however, both elements of this theme seem to have a clear relationship with the duet 'Tu l'as dit' from Meyerbeer's *Les Huguenots*.

Tatyana's long agitated monologue in the Letter Scene is Tchaikovsky's finest operatic scene. Little of the rest of the work quite matches the best that Tchaikovsky put into the first act. The balls at the Larins' and Gremins', which open Acts 2 and 3 respectively, gave Tchaikovsky opportunities both to compensate for the lack of scenic effect elsewhere and also to indulge his gift for ballet music. There can be a certain bitter irony in the unfolding of catastrophic events against the background of cheerful dance music, but there is perhaps too much decorative music, and the incorporation into the Gremin scene of a trivial écossaise, composed for the Bol'shoy Theatre's production in 1885, only exacerbates the situation. Tchaikovsky was uncertain how to complete the opera, and the ending of the definitive version is certainly different from that heard at the first student performance.

Before returning to Russia, Tchaikovsky composed his Violin Concerto. On 9 March he had settled down in Clarens again; stimulated by the arrival of Kotek, and especially by their playing of Lalo's *Symphonie espagnole*, Tchaikovsky launched himself into the concerto, sketching it in 11 days and completing the scoring within a fortnight. At the same time he replaced the original slow movement with another (immediately using the first piece as the *Méditation* for violin and piano op.42 no.1). Despite Kotek's collaboration, Tchaikovsky offered the dedication to Leopold Auer; Kotek was recompensed by the dedication of the *Valse-scherzo* for violin and orchestra, composed the previous year. But, to Tchaikovsky's dismay, Auer refused to give the concerto its first performance on the grounds that the violin writing was impracticable. Consequently its première was delayed until 1881, when it was performed in Vienna by Adolf Brodsky (who in 1876 had also given the first performance of another work intended for Auer, the *Sérénade mélancolique* for violin and orchestra). The concerto was not well received, drawing from Hanslick a damning review which hurt the composer deeply. Yet it is one of the least pretentious and freshest of Tchaikovsky's works, in which a simple concerto pattern is filled with appealing melody that might have spilt over from one of his ballets. The melodic flow and sense of creative delight emanating from it reflect, unusually in a large-scale work, the degree to which he was able for the moment to detach himself from his emotional problems.

CHAPTER FIVE

Creative trough, 1878–84

On returning to Kamenka on 23 April 1878, Tchaikovsky found himself embroiled in troubles (concerning his marriage) which continued for three years. Antonina tormented him by alternately accepting and refusing a divorce, at one stage making life intolerable by moving into the flat above his own. At last, in 1881, it was discovered that she had given birth to an illegitimate child, and Tchaikovsky had the grounds he needed to divorce her. Yet this did not remove the misery of knowing that his abnormality must now be common knowledge, or that Antonina could at any time choose to publicize it. It is not surprising, then, that from this time he seems as far as possible to have avoided contact with anyone except his family and a few close friends, spending as much time as he could in the country or abroad. On returning to Russia, he spent four months at Kamenka and other estates (including two visits to Braïlov, one of Mme von Meck's estates, in her absence). In September he had to return to Moscow; in October he resigned from the conservatory.

In these circumstances his work suffered in quality. His sterility is painfully demonstrated in the Piano Sonata, started just before the Violin Concerto but not completed until August. In this piece, as arid as the concerto is fresh, Tchaikovsky's neo-classical manner sinks to its most inglorious level. In May and June he escaped from larger compositional tasks by compiling a collection of children's pieces for piano, by making his first attempt at church music in setting the Liturgy of St John Chrysostom, and by working on the Six Songs op.38, which he had started in Switzerland and which include *Serenada Don-Zhuana* ('Don Juan's serenade'), one of his most appealing songs. During August he worked on the first of his orchestral suites.

Tchaikovsky's three original orchestral suites are one of the most explicit reflections of his state in these difficult years. It seems that the experience of his marriage had raised a barrier between him and his own music, and his best work of this period is to be found in those genres that did not depend upon too much in the way of personal expression. In the ten years from 1877 it was only in the Piano Trio (1881–2), where an event outside his inner life (the death of Nikolay Rubinstein) stimulated him to a formal expression of grief, and in the *Manfred* symphony (1885), where he could pour out his feelings vicariously through a musical projection of Byron's hero, that he achieved something of the emotional fullness of the Fourth Symphony. In this inhibited condition the suite suited him ideally, for here he could relax in a series of amiable movements without the expressive or structural responsibilities of the symphony. The result is mostly second-rate Tchaikovsky, which sometimes dips towards the level of the salon piece (as in the intermezzo of the First Suite), sometimes raises the level of musical respectability, if not of interest, with a fugue (as in the first movement), and at best enchants the listener with orchestral piquancy (as in the Miniature March) or with a flow of that facile melody which it seems Tchaikovsky could always command (as in the Divertimento). For some of these reasons the suites enjoyed a ready success in Tchaikovsky's lifetime.

The personal void is even more evident in Tchaikovsky's next opera, *Orleanskaya deva* ('The maid of Orleans'), which he began in December 1878 in Florence during an extended visit to the West. The composition went easily, and was completed less than three months later in Paris. Tchaikovsky had compiled his own libretto, planning situations which would allow for crowd spectacle, dramatic climaxes and a large ballet; he even invented a romantic interlude between the main character, Joan of Arc, and a Burgundian knight, Lionel, to afford an opportunity for some love music and to transform Joan into a tragic romantic heroine. In providing these ingredients he produced an unworthy plot which deprived his characters of any real life that might have sparked off his musical imagination. As in *The Oprichnik*, the influence of Meyerbeer and French grand opera is evident, but without the leaven of any significant Russian character. Perhaps there is a hint in the Minstrels' Chorus that opens Act 2, and there is more in the opening Chorus of Maidens; but this latter is merely a dilution of its obvious model, the women's choruses in Glinka's *Ruslan and Lyudmila*. Tchaikovsky had started composition with the scene of Joan's recognition in the latter part of Act 2, and this contains some of the best music in the opera; but even here attractive and sometimes touching passages are embedded in other music of patchy invention. When Joan really engaged his sympathy, Tchaikovsky's inspiration was roused at least a little, though neither the hymn nor Joan's farewell (the latter unmistakably Slavonic in complexion) in Act 1 represents Tchaikovsky at his best; nor does the love-duet in Act 4, though it does offer a more distinctive melodic fund. The faceless music with which the other characters are provided fails to raise them above the level of mere ciphers. Only in the ballet of Act 2, where Tchaikovsky could exercise his natural gift for dance music, did he succeed in producing an extensive stretch of music that rises above the efficiently routine. For the rest, the opera unfolds mostly in vast vistas of undistinguished music, with a liberal amount of pallid and sometimes shortwinded melody supported by conventional harmonic progressions, often artificially animated by mechanical accompaniment patterns. The large solo–choral ensembles that erupt on any pretext are adequately handled, but, compared with the models set in Musorgsky's *Boris Godunov*, are at best glib, at worst banal. With such flatulence and limp lyricism it is not surprising that *The Maid of Orleans* was not successful when it reached the stage in 1881, though it was the first of Tchaikovsky's operas ever to be produced abroad.

Back in Russia in March 1879 Tchaikovsky spent as much as he could of the next eight months on estates in the country. The scoring of *The Maid of Orleans* and the completion of the First Suite occupied him until late summer, and at Kamenka in October he started on his Second Piano Concerto. He undertook the task out of boredom from creative inactivity, working at it deliberately and without hurrying, and pronouncing himself well satisfied with it when he had worked on it in Paris during December (it was completed in Russia the following May). Immediately afterwards he left for Rome, where he spent three months and began his *Italian*

Capriccio. This was a conscious attempt to emulate Glinka's evocation of a Mediterranean world in his Spanish Overtures, and its debt to the second of these, *Recollection of a Summer Night in Madrid,* is patent in its succession of independent sections loosely patched together, each conjuring up some unspecified aspect of Italian life or scenery. The orchestration, too, shows a good deal of Glinka's fastidious ear for clean and well-contrasted sonorities. Nevertheless, Tchaikovsky's material is inferior to Glinka's, and his fantasy less rich. However, the capriccio does have a more consistent creative vitality than the Second Piano Concerto. Whereas Tchaikovsky could relax in the untroubled, kaleidoscopic world of the *Italian Capriccio,* the heavy hand of duty seems to have rested on the concerto. As in the Third Symphony and the Piano Sonata, the ghost of Schumann looms large in the squarely chordal first subject, while the second is a trivial little tune. The most interesting section of the movement is the development, which unfolds as two orchestral ritornello/solo cadenza sections. Though the opening theme of the slow movement, in which solo violin and cello collaborate with the pianist, is admirable, the central melody is not; aware that the movement was too long for the material, Tchaikovsky authorized some cuts, and others are occasionally made in performances. The finale, though far from the best of Tchaikovsky's last movements, is the most consistently satisfactory part of the concerto.

Returning to St Petersburg in March 1880, Tchaikovsky met the young Grand Duke Konstantin Romanov, a great admirer of his music. (Subsequently the two men corresponded, and in 1887 Tchaikovsky set some of the grand duke's verses.) He did not stay

long in St Petersburg or Moscow, however, but escaped
to the country for the rest of the year. During the
summer the Six Duets op.46 and the Seven Songs op.47
were written, and in the autumn at Kamenka the overture *1812* was composed for the Moscow Exhibition.
Tchaikovsky felt no enthusiasm for the work while composing it, and reasonably enough doubted its value when
it was completed. But the Serenade for strings, composed at exactly the same time, was written from inner
compulsion. Here at last Tchaikovsky composed a piece
to which Anton Rubinstein found himself able to give
wholehearted approval. It is Tchaikovsky's equivalent of
an 18th-century divertimento, inhabiting a world not so
far removed from that of his Rococo pastiches.

Tchaikovsky remained in Russia until the première of
The Maid of Orleans in February 1881; the next day,
26 February, he left for the West. At Nice he heard of
the sudden death on 23 March in Paris of Nikolay
Rubinstein. After attending Rubinstein's funeral he
returned to Kamenka on 11 May, making this his head-
quarters until November. As his sister and her husband
were away, he found himself in charge of their children,
whom he adored. Some progress was made on his Vesper
Service, but his main effort was directed into editing the
complete church music of Bortnyansky for Jürgenson.
With his poor opinion of Bortnyansky he found this an
uncongenial task. By August he had already started
work on a new opera, *Mazeppa*, which was to occupy
him off and on for the next two years. In November he
was back in the West, staying in Rome where he began
work on his Piano Trio in December. The medium was
not one he liked, but he wished to write a memorial
work for Rubinstein incorporating an elaborate piano

part, and Mme von Meck had been pressing for such a piece for her resident piano trio, whose current pianist was the young Debussy. The trio is in two movements, of which the second is a long set of variations on a simple tune which had some particular association with Rubinstein, though Tchaikovsky denied each variation was a portrayal of some incident in his life. Like the corresponding movement of the Fourth Symphony, this first movement sets some of the thematic events of a sonata structure against an unorthodox tonal background, thus drastically modifying their functions within the movement. Though not equalling the achievement of the Fourth Symphony, this 'Pezzo elegiaco', as Tchaikovsky labelled it, displays a musical quality and personal voice that remained unmatched in his music of 1878–85.

In April 1882 Tchaikovsky returned to Russia, soon resuming work on *Mazeppa*, which he finished composing in September. After the faceless music of *The Maid of Orleans*, that of *Mazeppa* sounds distinctly Russian, and there are passages in which there is a marked resurgence of a national idiom, notably in the first scene with its admirable and Glinka-like opening chorus in 5/4, and in the last scene of Act 2, actually described as a 'folk scene'. This tale, drawn from Pushkin, of an elderly hetman who is capable of tender love, yet who can be utterly ruthless in the pursuit of that love and of his personal ambition, offered better material than *The Maid of Orleans*. Tchaikovsky began composition with the love scene for Mazeppa and Mariya in Act 2, and this drew from him some fine music. The execution scene has plenty of conventional theatrical power, but the finest scene comes at the end, when the deserted and

15. Nadezhda von Meck

demented Mariya sings a lullaby over the body of Andrey, the young man who, if fate had allowed, might have brought her happiness. Yet Tchaikovsky remained little stirred by Mazeppa himself, and the opera remains a sadly uneven work. Just before Tchaikovsky returned to Russia the scoring of *Mazeppa* was completed in Paris, where he had spent the first four months of 1883; during this period he fulfilled three commissions in connection with the coronation of Alexander III. Back in Russia, he started working on his Second Suite in July, completing it in October. This five-movement work is notable chiefly for its use of accordions ad lib in the third movement, and for its alleged imitation of Dargomïzhsky in the kazachok finale. During October and November he composed 15 of the 16 Children's Songs op.54. This set includes the famous *Legenda* ('Legend'), whose popularity later caused Tchaikovsky both to orchestrate it and arrange it for unaccompanied mixed chorus.

By this time Tchaikovsky's reputation and the enthusiasm of the tsar for his music were such that *Mazeppa* was given concurrent productions in St Petersburg and Moscow. Tchaikovsky attended the one in Moscow on 15 February 1884, but left for the West the next day, neither waiting for the première of his Second Suite that evening, nor passing through St Petersburg to attend the first performance there of the opera three days later. His absence occasioned an expression of surprise from the tsar, who nevertheless did not withhold the Order of St Vladimir (fourth class); Tchaikovsky was obliged to return from Paris to receive the decoration in March. The early summer of 1884 saw the completion of the four-movement Third Suite. The last movement, theme and variations, is the one movement in all Tchaikovsky's suites that has found a place in the repertory. Having abandoned his original idea of making the work a symphony, Tchaikovsky used the first movement as the second movement of the Concert Fantasia for piano and orchestra, which dates from about the same time. To 1884 also belong the Six Songs op.57.

CHAPTER SIX

Creative renewal, 1884–90

With the exception of the Piano Trio, none of the compositions since the Violin Concerto can be ranked among Tchaikovsky's better works. During 1884, however, he began to shed the unsociability and restlessness which had driven him to retreat to country estates or to wander over Europe. The tsar's decoration was a visible seal of official approval that helped his social rehabilitation, and the great popular success of *Eugene Onegin* in St Petersburg later in the year bolstered his social confidence. In addition he was elected head of the Moscow branch of the Russian Musical Society. When in November he was urgently summoned to Switzerland to visit Kotek, who was dying of tuberculosis, he suffered acutely from homesickness and from the longing for a real home of his own. In February 1885 he settled just outside Moscow, at Maidanovo near Klin; this house, and others nearby, were to be his homes for the rest of his life.

At this period, too, his contact with Balakirev was renewed, with fruitful consequences. Early in 1878 he had written to Mme von Meck an unsparing verdict on members of The Five, condemning Balakirev especially for what he considered to be his musical misguidance of the group. For some years Tchaikovsky had had no contact with his former mentor, but in 1882 Balakirev wrote to him and elicited a warm response. Balakirev's suggestion that Tchaikovsky should compose a work on Byron's *Manfred* was firmly rejected at that stage, but when two years later Balakirev sent him a modified plan for the piece, he agreed to compose it. Quite apart from the older man's extraordinary powers of musical persuasion, it is obvious that Tchaikovsky hoped Balakirev's strong Christian convictions might also provide for him an escape from earthly guilt. Certainly the two men drew close together for a while. In October 1885 the *Manfred* symphony was finished.

The original plan for this work had been devised in the 1860s by Vladimir Stasov for Balakirev who, feeling that it was not congenial to him, proposed it to the ailing Berlioz in 1868. When Balakirev presented it to Tchaikovsky, he drew his attention to Berlioz's *Symphonie fantastique* and *Harold en Italie*, and even specified various works that might provide 'helpful materials' for Tchaikovsky's separate movements. Among those Balakirev suggested for the first and last movements were the 'Orgie de brigands' from Berlioz's *Harold en Italie*, and Tchaikovsky's own *Francesca da Rimini* (which Balakirev considered Tchaikovsky's best work); for the scherzo he proposed the Queen Mab scherzo from Berlioz's *Roméo et Juliette* and the scherzo from Tchaikovsky's Third Symphony. For the slow movement he suggested the 'Scène aux champs' from Berlioz's *Symphonie fantastique*. Tchaikovsky's music in his middle two movements shows how respectfully he heeded Balakirev's suggestions, though the Berlioz models are transmuted into two of Tchaikovsky's most delightful creations, the one bewitching, the other of a charming freshness. Berlioz's practice of an *idée fixe* was accepted, too, the symphony's opening theme intruding (as in *Harold en Italie*) rather than integrating with the scene in each of the middle movements, and confronting new material in the finale. The first movement, a musical picture of Manfred haunted by memories of his beloved Astarte, is a unique organism, though features both of sonata practice and of the explicitly ternary structure of *Francesca da Rimini* are detectable in it. The endless chromatic swirls of the earlier piece are here replaced by sturdier harmonic language, abounding in 7th chords and strong dissonance presented with a particularly dark orchestral palette. The gloomy, rugged blocks that embody Manfred contain some of Tchaikovsky's toughest music, just as his personification of Astarte's shade elicits some of his tenderest invention. In the finale liberal quotations from this movement are pitted against the Bacchanalian forces of Arimanes. While the wholesale parading of familiar material from the first movement certainly binds the ends of the symphony together, this is achieved at the cost of musical integrity within the finale itself. The burden of the programme lies too heavily upon this movement, marring a symphony that is otherwise one of Tchaikovsky's most characteristic and fully realized conceptions.

While finishing the scoring of the *Manfred* symphony, Tchaikovsky embarked on another opera, *Charodeyka* ('The sorceress'). In his more settled life and regular daily routine at Maidanovo he worked steadily on the opera until early April 1886; he then set out to join Anatoly for a month at Tbilisi, where he was fêted by the local musicians. In May he visited Paris, travelling by sea from Batum to Marseilles. The whole expedition proved very pleasant, and back at Maidanovo

in June he resumed work on *The Sorceress*, completing
the composition in August (though the orchestration
was not finished for another nine months). The next day
he set to work on the 12 Songs op.60. In January
1887 he conducted *The Slippers* (the revision of *Vakula
the Smith*, made two years earlier), and in March directed an entire concert of his own works. After these
hard-won victories over his nerves he felt able to embark on concert tours abroad, conducting mostly his
own compositions. With the scoring of *The Sorceress*
finished, June was spent with Modest and Anatoly at
Borzhom in the Caucasus, where he scored the four
pieces by Mozart which make up his Fourth Suite,
'Mozartiana'. In July a sudden summons took him to
Aachen to visit the dying Kondrat'yev. During this visit,
in August, he composed the *Pezzo capriccioso* for cello
and orchestra. Back in Russia in September, he conducted the première of *The Sorceress* in November, and
before the year was out had composed the Six Songs
op.63, to words by the Grand Duke Konstantin.

The Sorceress proved a failure, and one that hurt
Tchaikovsky deeply, though the adverse verdict was not
undeserved. Shpazhinsky's tale of an innkeeper's daughter who is courted by two princes (father and son), with
melodramatic consequences, is poor stuff, and far too
involved to provide a satisfactory scenario. Realizing
this, Tchaikovsky cut both Shpazhinsky's libretto and,
subsequently, his own music. But the real trouble was
that yet again his characters had failed to engross his
sympathy, and only the first act, in which there is a
strong national flavour, is of any real quality. This is
largely concerned with setting the scene, placing
Nastasya, the heroine, in a rustic world, and prompting

16. The Tchaikovsky brothers (left to right): Anatoly, Nikolay, Ippolit, Pyotr and Modest

Tchaikovsky to reopen that national vein that he had so profitably mined in the earlier 1870s. The result is an abundance of racy music, the repetitiveness of many of the folky melodies eliciting from him a variety of felicitous accompaniments. But with Act 2, where the conventional passions and contrived melodramatic happenings begin, the invention loses character, and the treatment becomes, characteristically, no more than efficient. Occasionally the level rises, as in the earlier part of the love scene between the heroine and Prince Yuri at the end of Act 3. Nastasya was the one character who really engaged Tchaikovsky's interest, and in this scene her urgent wish to convince Yuri of her innocence and detain him is substantiated by some appealing and tender phrases. But at the end, when the conventional expressions of mutual love are reached, the defined musical character slips away into a generalized amorous aura that prompted no more than a routine response from Tchaikovsky. As in *The Maid of Orleans*, the more melodramatic incidents are served with a generous allowance of hectic sequential tumults, laden with diminished 7ths. In spite of its first act *The Sorceress* must rank among the weaker of Tchaikovsky's works.

Tchaikovsky himself conducted the first four performances of *The Sorceress*, as well as a further concert of his own works in November, and in December set out on his first foreign tour as a conductor. In Germany he met Brahms, Grieg, Ethel Smyth and – a reunion that seems to have touched them both – Désirée Artôt. In December 1877 he had made the acquaintance of Brahms's First Symphony, and had disliked it. When the two men now met face to face there was at first some constraint between them, though Brahms did his best to

be friendly and succeeded in breaking down his somewhat embarrassed colleague's reserve. Tchaikovsky conducted in Leipzig, Hamburg, Berlin and Prague, where
he was rapturously received. Concerts in Paris and
London followed. On his return to Russia in April 1888
he revisited Tbilisi, and then moved into a new house at
Frolovskoye. Though at this time he evidently felt more
pleasure in his garden than in composition, he set about
his Fifth Symphony in May, finding that inspiration
came as the work progressed. Before completing it in
August he had started the fantasy overture *Hamlet*
which was finished in October. Three days later the last
of the Six Songs op.65, composed to French texts, was
completed.

Though Tchaikovsky did jot down an embryonic
programme for his Fifth Symphony, he reverted to a
more traditional structure with little evidence of the
influence of external factors; the exception is that the
principle of a motto theme, established in the Fourth
Symphony, is here extended to all four movements, as in
the *Manfred* symphony. The only irregular feature of
the first movement is the three-stage exposition, somewhat similar to that of the Fourth Symphony, in which
the string theme of the second stage (in B minor)
becomes the accelerated answering phrase to the new
two-bar woodwind motif ushering in the third stage,
which is the true second subject set in D major. Thus
Tchaikovsky established the same tonal relationship between his subjects as in the First Piano Concerto's first
movement. The waltz-conditioning of much of the
thematic material of this movement prepares for the
explicit waltz which does duty as the scherzo. Between
these two movements is one of the composer's most

personal utterances, an extended flow of yearning melody that is quintessential Tchaikovsky. As in the two preceding symphonies, it is the finale that is the weakest part, especially the peroration from which almost all trace of tonal tension is gone, and which brazenly restates the motto theme in a blatant attempt to synthesize extra power. The motto theme, as Abraham has pointed out, is derived from the trio in Act 1 of Glinka's *A Life for the Tsar*, where it had set the words 'Turn not into sorrow'. In a notebook Tchaikovsky had specified the motto theme as signifying 'complete resignation before fate', and the emphatic reiterations that it receives at the conclusion of this finale might be interpreted as a firm riposte to the inexorable, peremptorily intrusive fate as embodied in the motto theme of the Fourth Symphony. However, Tchaikovsky himself later sensed the musical insincerity of such overstatement as that at the end of the Fifth Symphony. Certainly it provides a crude end to a work which, if not Tchaikovsky's most enterprising, resounds in every bar with his individual voice, speaking in those heightened emotional accents already heard in the Fourth Symphony and *Manfred* symphony.

Hamlet differs from *Romeo and Juliet* in that Tchaikovsky was not concerned with diverse characters and the musical realization of dramatic tensions; instead, like *Francesca da Rimini*, it centres on one person. Not requiring dramatic clashes, Tchaikovsky dispensed with a development section, articulating instead a series of psychological or emotional states, though presumably the march section which concludes both the exposition and recapitulation conveniently signals Fortinbras's two arrivals. Despite the absence of

17. Principals in the first production of 'The Sleeping Beauty', first performed at the Mariinsky Theatre, St Petersburg, on 15 January 1890, with Carlotta Brianza (centre) as Aurora

dramatic confrontations, *Hamlet* is a more complex piece than *Francesca da Rimini*, not least because Shakespeare's hero provides a diversity of traits which Tchaikovsky's invention builds into a figure as Byronic as Manfred.

Tchaikovsky himself conducted the first performances of both the Fifth Symphony and *Hamlet*, also directing the former in Prague during a visit in November to conduct *Eugene Onegin*. Back home in December he continued to work on a new three-act ballet, *Spyashchaya krasavitsa* ('The sleeping beauty'), completing sketches of the prologue and first two acts by the end of January 1889. A further concert tour followed when Tchaikovsky conducted in Cologne, Frankfurt, Dresden, Berlin, Geneva and Hamburg. In Hamburg he had a second meeting with Brahms who delayed his own departure for a day to hear Tchaikovsky's Fifth Symphony: he approved of all of it except the finale. Tchaikovsky invited Brahms to conduct a concert of the Russian Musical Society, but without success. During the last part of the tour, which took him to Paris and London, he worked on the third act of *The Sleeping Beauty*. After returning to Russia by sea to Batum he visited Anatoly at Tbilisi, and at Frolovskoye started orchestrating the ballet. This task, which caused him a good deal of trouble, occupied much of the summer.

Tchaikovsky rightly rated *The Sleeping Beauty* as one of his best works. The scenario was precisely designed by Petipa from Perrault's fairy tale, and its structure proved far more satisfactory than that of *Swan Lake*, for while the prologue and first two acts, in which the main plot unfolds, contain a certain number of set dances, they are well scaled; they are not merely gratuitous choreographic decoration, but have some marginal relevance to the drama itself. The formal divertissement element is reserved for the last act, in which set decorative dances could be dramatically excused as part of the wedding entertainment. In any case these dances are far more striking than most such pieces in *Swan Lake*, for a number of them are character-pieces for figures from fairy stories (Puss-in-Boots, Little Red Riding Hood etc), and this elicited from Tchaikovsky a far more individual type of invention, and some display of his pantomimic gift. Likewise in the prologue and first two acts the musical ideas are more striking and pointed, the characterization more precise, and the music excellently paced to the sequence of dramatic events. Tchaikovsky's gift for evoking atmosphere is even more splendidly revealed in this score than in *Swan Lake*, whether he was required to suggest bustling activity, as at the beginning of Act 1, or the magically haunted world of the forest and the night, as in Act 2. This conjunction of characterful musical invention, structural fluency and sure sense of atmosphere, all framed within an admirably structured plot, makes *The Sleeping Beauty* his most consistently successful theatre piece, and one of the peaks of the ballet repertory.

Tchaikovsky's next stage work, also one of his best known, was less satisfactory, though it enjoyed a far greater initial success. Soon after the first performance of *The Sleeping Beauty* in January 1890 he left for Florence, where he settled down to a new opera, *Pikovaya dama* ('The queen of spades'), commissioned for the famous tenor Nikolay Figner and his wife Medea. Tchaikovsky became so bound up in the work that the whole was sketched in six weeks. Three weeks later he left for Rome, where he stayed about a fortnight, returning to St Petersburg on 4 May. During the next six weeks the scoring of the opera was completed at Frolovskoye.

Pushkin's original story of *The Queen of Spades* has a spare simplicity which gives its ghoulishness and wry humour a particular edge. Modest, however, turned it into a romantic melodrama, adding a fair amount of love interest, and inflaming the end by making Liza throw herself into a canal (a scene added at his brother's request) and Hermann die at the gaming table. Though the general level of musical invention is not his best, *The Queen of Spades* is Tchaikovsky's most conventionally effective opera. He responded strongly to the character of Hermann (recording that he actually wept while composing the last scene), and especially to any opportunity for underlining the macabre or chilling, or simply for conjuring up some sort of musical atmosphere. His style had evolved to a condition that particularly suited it to such purposes, as is most powerfully demonstrated in the great scene in the Countess's bedroom (scene iv), the most consistent in the whole opera. To offset – or enhance – the emotional tension or morbidity of a good part of the music, Tchaikovsky incorporated into the opera the largest amount of Rococo material to appear in any of his works, as part of his evocation of the bygone Russia of Catherine the Great; there is not only a complete pastoral cantata in scene iii, but also a setting of some words by 18th-century poets and the quotation of an aria from Grétry's *Richard Coeur de Lion* in scene iv. A tiny echo of national music is heard in the Russian Song with Chorus in scene ii. Tchaikovsky himself devised the effective idea of ending the ballroom scene by building up towards a grand entry of the Empress

18. *Tchaikovsky* (*centre*) *with Nikolay and Medea Figner, who created the roles of Hermann and Liza in 'The Queen of Spades' in 1890*

herself with all awaiting her as the curtain falls. As part of the supernatural vocabulary in the later scenes Tchaikovsky followed Glinka's example in using the whole-tone scale. It is not surprising that such a skilfully theatrical opera was an immediate success.

In June, immediately after finishing *The Queen of Spades*, Tchaikovsky composed the string sextet, *Souvenir de Florence*, whose untroubled world is in complete contrast to that of the opera. In this sextet his neo-classical line reaches its end. During its 19 years this succession of works had changed its character much. The First Quartet is the closest to true Classical precedents, the line later developing a strong bias towards Schumann which sapped its life and drew it into the earnest banality of the Piano Sonata. Subsequently it found renewal in the Serenade for Strings, whose more relaxed world (which owes something to that of Tchaikovsky's Rococo pastiches) is also inhabited by the pleasantly urbane *Souvenir de Florence*. Tchaikovsky's next large work, the symphonic ballad *Voyevoda* ('The voyevoda'), was sketched during the early autumn while he was visiting Anatoly at Tbilisi for six weeks (the piece has no connection with the earlier opera of the same title). At Tbilisi also, on 6 October, he suddenly received from Mme von Meck a letter announcing that she was bankrupt, and that his allowance would have to be discontinued. By now Tchaikovsky was no longer dependent upon her financially, for in addition to his royalties he had the life pension of 3000 rubles a year granted to him by the tsar in 1888. His increased income in the next three years in fact more than made up the loss. He might have been relatively unaffected by the news, had she been prepared to continue the correspondence and had her story of bankruptcy been true; but, as Tchaikovsky soon discovered, it was false, and when he wrote to her she made no reply. In fact it seems that his last letter never reached her and that the complete rift between them was the result of misunderstanding. According to Galina von Meck, a month or so before his death Tchaikovsky endeavoured to heal the breach, and died believing he had done so. Nevertheless, at the time of the rupture his pride was deeply wounded by the conclusion that for 14 years he had been merely a pleasant diversion for her. Disenchanted by the shattering of this image of his fantasy friend, and deprived of a correspondent in whose precious confidences he could find emotional release, he became profoundly embittered.

CHAPTER SEVEN

Last years, 1891–3

The last years of Tchaikovsky's life were marked by
increasing outer success and deepening inner gloom.
The triumph of the opera *The Queen of Spades* led to a
commission from the Imperial Theatre for two one-act
pieces, an opera and a ballet. Before settling down to
these, Tchaikovsky composed incidental music for a
production of *Hamlet*, completing it in three weeks
during January and February 1891. To finish the work
easily he fell back on material from his earlier works,
drawing on *The Snow Maiden*, the Third Symphony,
the string Elegy in honour of Ivan Samarin (1884) and,
of course, his own fantasy overture *Hamlet*, which he
shortened and rescored as the overture. Having finished
this chore he set to work in February on the new ballet,
Shchelkunchik ('The nutcracker'), before leaving in
March for another conducting tour, this time to the
USA. In Paris he was enchanted by a new instrument,
the celesta, and resolved to use it both in *The Voyevoda*
and in the new ballet. After conducting a concert, he
embarked for New York in a thoroughly depressed,
homesick state that was increased by news of his sister
Alexandra's death. His deplorable nervous condition
was relieved by the kindness and respect shown to him
by the Americans, and the tour, which included concerts
in Baltimore and Philadelphia after four in New York
(and also visits to Niagara Falls and Washington), was a

great success with both the public and the press. Leaving the USA on 21 May he returned to Russia via Hamburg. To his dismay the woods at Frolovskoye had been cut down; but he settled back into his old house at Maidanovo, and began work on the one-act opera, *Iolanta* ('Iolanthe'), and *The Nutcracker*.

Although the ballet subject had been prescribed for him, Tchaikovsky had himself chosen that for the opera. Yet the romantic story of a blind princess, set in Provence, obviously failed to stir much of a response in him, and the result is a pretty but rather characterless piece, though there are premonitions of the dark world of the Sixth Symphony. Tchaikovsky did not think highly of the music he wrote for *The Nutcracker*, rightly rating it below that of *The Sleeping Beauty*. Certainly *The Nutcracker* is the least important of Tchaikovsky's three ballets. Nevertheless, the criticisms that are habitually levelled against it should be tempered by consideration of the restrictions it imposed on Tchaikovsky. The rigorous scenario that Petipa devised (and expanded into two acts) from the fairy tale by Dumas *père* from Hoffmann provided no opportunity for the expression of human feelings beyond the most trivial, confining him mostly within a world of tinsel, sweets and fantasy, peopled by wedding-cake fairy figures engaged in inconsequential acts or in mere choreographic divertissement. In view of the lack of real dramatic or human motivation, Tchaikovsky's treatment of the subject is as good as could be expected. It is true that much of the harmonic language is essentially simple, even trite, and some of the melodic material is naive almost to the point of banality. There is no really strong tune anywhere in the work, and what had been characterful in the preceding two ballets has now sometimes become merely cute. Yet at its best the melodic invention is charming and pretty, and by this time Tchaikovsky's virtuosity in devising varied orchestral colours and his mastery of contrapuntal devices, whether sparkling counterpoints or patterned figurations, was such as to ensure endless fascination in the surface attractiveness of the score.

Early in 1892 Tchaikovsky compiled a suite from the ballet, creating what was to become one of his most frequently heard compositions. The suite was a hurriedly devised replacement for the symphonic ballad, *The Voyevoda*, against which he had turned so violently after its first performance in November 1891 that he had destroyed the score. Of all Tchaikovsky's works that have subsequently been restored from the orchestral parts, *The Voyevoda* is perhaps the most valuable. Pushkin's ballad (after Mickiewicz) concerns a voyevoda, or warrior, who returns home to find his wife engaged in a romantic interlude; his servant, told to shoot the unfaithful wife, misses his aim and kills his master instead. Tchaikovsky planned *The Voyevoda*, like *Francesca da Rimini*, as a ternary structure, the voyevoda's appearance and subsequent death forming the flanks, the centre unfolding as a love scene centring on E♭, thus creating the maximum tonal tension with the voyevoda's portrayal in A minor (it is worth noting that Tchaikovsky had used the same tonal tension between the two subjects of the fantasy overture *Hamlet*, and also in *The Nutcracker*, beginning and ending it in B♭, but concluding the first and beginning the second act in E major). The music with which Tchaikovsky filled this scheme in *The Voyevoda* contains some first-rate, if not consistent, invention and a notable range of colour in

219

19. Tchaikovsky in his doctoral robes, Cambridge, 1893

the orchestration, which is less remarkable, perhaps, in the opulent sounds of the love scene than in the sinister portrayal of the voyevoda, and in the dark, deep sounds that signify his death, and that look forward to the world of the Sixth Symphony.

At the beginning of 1892 Tchaikovsky embarked on yet another foreign tour, conducting in Warsaw, hearing a fine performance of *Eugene Onegin* under Mahler in Hamburg, but feeling so homesick in Paris that he cut short the tour and hurried back to Russia. In May, shortly before taking a three-week cure in Vichy, he moved to a new (and his last) home near Klin, where he began work on a Symphony in E♭. It was virtually completed, but in December his dissatisfaction with it led him to convert the first movement into a concert piece for piano and orchestra (the indifferent Piano Concerto no.3), and to start a similar metamorphosis of the Andante and finale. The reception of *Iolanthe* and *The Nutcracker* was disappointing, but the revised *Souvenir de Florence* was warmly received. Meanwhile proof of Tchaikovsky's international reputation came from France, where he was elected a corresponding member of the Académie Française, and from England, where he was nominated for an honorary MusD by Cambridge University. In late December he left for the West, meeting in her home near Basle his old governess, Fanny Dürbach, whom he had not seen for over 40 years; he visited Paris, conducted successfully in Brussels, and on his return to Russia was continuously fêted for nearly a fortnight in Odessa. On his way back to Klin, where he arrived on 15 February 1893, a scheme for a new symphony came to him.

The idea for this new 'Programme Symphony' (as

Tchaikovsky called it at this stage) seems to go back to a document that he evidently scribbled in 1892. 'The ultimate essence of the plan of the symphony is LIFE. First movement – all impulsive passion, confidence, thirst for activity. Must be short. (Finale DEATH – result of collapse.) Second movement love; third disappointments; fourth ends dying away (also short).' By February 1893 the plan was obviously much modified, and Tchaikovsky had decided that among the numerous structural modifications within this symphony the finale would be a long-drawn Adagio. The work was fully sketched by April, but the composition of his last group of songs (op.73) and final set of piano pieces (op.72) intervened before the scoring was undertaken. Furthermore, in May Tchaikovsky had to go to England, where he shared a Philharmonic Society concert with Saint-Saëns, rather eclipsing the Frenchman with a triumphant performance of his own Fourth Symphony. In Cambridge he conducted *Francesca da Rimini*, and received the MusD along with Saint-Saëns, Boito, Bruch (whom he found insufferable) and (*in absentia*) Grieg. Nearly a month of the summer was spent scoring the symphony; as so often in his later works, this caused him a good deal of trouble. In August it was completed, and was first performed on 28 October. The title 'Pathétique' was proposed by Modest on the day after the première.

Tchaikovsky's Sixth Symphony was both his last work and his most profoundly pessimistic. Its expressive extremes are great, the dynamic range stretching from *ffff* to *ppppp*. The first subject emerges from the lowest depths of the introduction, and the opposition of character between the two subjects is the strongest in all

Tchaikovsky's sonata structures. The scale of this exposition is huge, and is compensated by telescoping the development and recapitulation, the latter being gathered up into the ferocious activity of the former (which includes a quotation from the music of the Russian Orthodox Requiem) so that the final catharsis is achieved in the middle of the recapitulation. By shortening the ensuing second subject and concluding with an economical coda, a notable sense of progressive compression is achieved as the movement advances. As in the Fifth Symphony, one of the middle movements is a waltz, this time given a curious but charming limp by being written in 5/4. The trio, *con dolcezza e flebile*, exploits some of the harmonic tensions that also appear in the outer movements. The march grows into a substantial third movement whose fertile ornamentation and sparkling sound provide an ironic background for the agonies of the finale, with its obsessive clinging to two descending melodic ideas supported by some of Tchaikovsky's most plangent harmonies. The result is the most explicit emotional declaration in all Tchaikovsky's works, a mixture of anguish, brooding and sorrow, which finally retreats into the subterranean gloom in which the whole symphony had started, fading into oblivion. It is not surprising that Tchaikovsky rated the Sixth Symphony as among the most sincere of his works.

On 6 November 1893, nine days after the première of the Sixth Symphony, Tchaikovsky died. That he committed suicide can hardly be doubted. In 1978 the Soviet scholar, Alexandra Orlova, revealed a narrative dictated to her in 1966 by the aged Alexander Voitov of the Russian Museum in Leningrad. According to this, a member of the Russian aristocracy had written a letter accusing the composer of a liaison with his nephew, and had entrusted it to Nikolay Jacobi, a high-ranking civil servant, for transmission to the tsar. Jacobi, like Tchaikovsky a former pupil of the School of Jurisprudence, feared the dishonour with which this disclosure would tarnish the 'school uniform', and hastily instituted a court of honour (which included six of Tchaikovsky's contemporaries from the school) to decide how the scandal might be averted. Tchaikovsky was summoned to appear before this court on 31 October which, after more than five hours of deliberations, decreed that the composer should kill himself. Two days later the composer was mortally ill. Though this story lacks firm confirmation, the assertion that he died of cholera from drinking unboiled water cannot be credited. Quite apart from the implausibility that unboiled drinking water would have been set upon a table in a public restaurant during a cholera epidemic, there are gross inconsistencies between the detailed accounts of Tchaikovsky's last days published respectively by Modest Tchaikovsky and Lev Bertenson (one of the doctors who attended the composer) with the aim of silencing rumours. In addition, these accounts are often at variance with the bulletins issued during the composer's illness. It seems it must be accepted that there was an active conspiracy among Tchaikovsky's closest relatives and associates to conceal the true circumstances surrounding his death, and that others who witnessed what had happened tactfully refrained from asking questions. This seems to have been Rimsky-Korsakov's position, though he later freely revealed his bewilderment in his *Memoirs*: 'How odd that, though

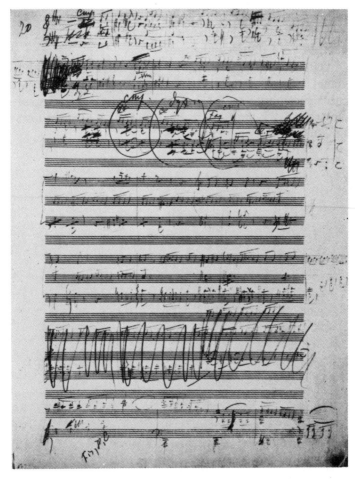

20. *Tchaikovsky's autograph sketches for the opening of the Allegro non troppo from the first movement of his Sixth Symphony ('Pathétique'), composed 1893*

death was the result of cholera, there was free access to the requiems. I remember that Verzhbilovich . . . kissed the body on the face and head.'

Tchaikovsky was buried in the Alexander Nevsky cemetery in St Petersburg. A second performance of the Sixth Symphony on 18 November made a deep impression, the work being seen in retrospect as a premonition of the composer's own end.

CHAPTER EIGHT

Technique and style

In spite of the heavy conditioning of his conservatory training, Tchaikovsky's innate Russianness and his love of Russian folk music ensured that he could never become a mere imitator of Western practices and styles. In consequence, his work shows a remarkable range of character and technique, and this breadth was fostered further by the diverse expressive purposes he sought in his compositions, whether it was to fashion a poised 'Classical' form, simulate the elegance of the 18th-century Rococo, plunge into the bold, emancipated world of the Russian nationalists, or forge a musical language that might be a vehicle for his own overwrought emotions. Thus his fund of melody ranges from efficient, if not first-rate, inventions of a Western cast to folksong stylizations. On occasions he used folksongs themselves, and the influence of modal practices is heard repeatedly, if not very strongly, in his original tunes. Yet Tchaikovsky's most characteristic melodic types are the dance-tunes (especially waltzes) which fill not only his ballets, but spill over in profusion into all his other genres except church music, and the impassioned cantilenas, often of considerable strength of contour, whose full-blooded emotion is often heightened by harmonic support containing complementary expressive tensions. Tchaikovsky knew well and sometimes employed the characteristic repetitive trait of certain Russian folktunes that extend themselves by constant variations on a single motif. Yet the repetitions in his own tunes are normally sequential, thus reflecting Western practices, and may be extended at immense length. Clearly this almost obsessive dwelling on a single phrase was frequently conditioned by Tchaikovsky's emotional identification with the expressive properties of that phrase, and the release it afforded through such repetitions; so, too, the relentless reiteration to which he subjected certain of his tunes fulfilled a similar purpose. At times such repetitions result in expressive surfeit, but they can build into an emotional experience of almost unbearable intensity.

Though Tchaikovsky did experiment in unusual metres, his very Russian sense for dynamic rhythm was usually applied to provide a firm, essentially regular metre, as shown in his innumerable dance-tunes, where it is occasionally used with such elemental vigour that it becomes the main expressive agent. A strong metrical drive may also be used as a means of synthetic propulsion in a large-scale symphonic movement. Tchaikovsky also revealed a wide range of practice in his harmony. His first two quartets in particular show how thoroughly he was grounded in Western harmonic and textural procedures. At the opposite extreme are such unorthodox progressions as fill the centre of the finale to the Second Symphony, a movement that also includes one of the few applications in his work of the whole-tone scale in the bass. These last practices are not typical, however, and show the explicit influence of the Russian nationalists. Tchaikovsky's more normal harmonic language is based on relatively conventional progressions (the first love theme of *Romeo and Juliet*, for instance, is built over a circle of 5ths), though frequently such progressions involve a typically Russian liberality in the use of pedals, and also some sort of decorative chromaticism which gives it its individuality. Tchaikovsky's most favoured chromatic chord is the major triad on the flattened submediant in a major-key context, an elevation to the status of harmonic support of a note which had been, since Glinka, the favoured chromatic degree of the scale for Russian composers. But usually Tchaikovsky's chromaticism, like Glinka's, arises from contrapuntal decoration, ranging from single chromatic passing notes or dissonances to extended scales that may be set quite abrasively against the melody. A rare example of fundamental chromaticism occurs at the opening of the Second Quartet, the effect of which is, nevertheless, less close to that which Wagner was currently exploiting than to that to which Bartók came some 35 years later at the opening of his First Quartet. The harmonic palette of Tchaikovsky's later works is increasingly enriched by 7th chords and trenchant dissonance.

Most of Tchaikovsky's music involves the orchestra, and his textural practices become increasingly conditioned by considerations of orchestral colour. In spite of his grounding in Western orchestral practices, Tchaikovsky from the beginning showed a typically Russian disposition for bright and sharply differentiated orchestral colouring in the tradition initiated by Glinka. The mastery and resourcefulness with which he handled the orchestra is occasionally compromised by an excess and even brashness which disfigures the music as acutely as the overblown emotions that it is sometimes forced to bear. A tendency for the musical fabric itself to be conditioned by the orchestral sound envisaged by Tchaikovsky can be heard in the scherzo of the Third Symphony and in *Francesca da Rimini*, not only in the conventional tempest textures of the outer sections, but more significantly in certain of the accompaniment figurations of the central passage. In the scherzo of the *Manfred* symphony the process is carried much further, the result being a kaleidoscopic web of delicate sound of remarkable virtuosity. Much of the life of *The Nutcracker* ballet stems from the fascination of the orchestral textures and accompaniments. In the pieces mentioned it is primarily the fleet delicacy of the treble instruments that Tchaikovsky exploited, but this is balanced in the later music by a matching exploration of the darker, even gloomy sounds of the bass instruments.

Since his death Tchaikovsky has gained remarkable popularity. Yet the very directness of his utterance, founded primarily on his ability to fashion themes of remarkable eloquence and emotional power supported by matching harmony and rich orchestral resource, has often been interpreted as a sign of essential shallowness. Likewise the way in which his world of strong emotions has been freely plundered by composers of lower intentions has proved detrimental to his reputation. But when popular adulation and critical prejudice are set aside Tchaikovsky can be seen as a composer who toiled unceasingly over creative problems, whose range was wide both in genre and in type of expression, who could bring to the solution of a structural problem a quite notable enterprise, and whose professional competence was of the highest.

WORKS

Edition: *P. I. Tchaikovsky: Polnoye sobraniye sochineniy* [Complete edition of compositions] (Moscow and Leningrad, 1940–71) [T]

(*printed works published in Moscow unless otherwise stated*)

Numbers in the right-hand column denote references in the text.

STAGE

(* – full score; † – vocal score/ballet piano score)

Op.	Title	Libretto	Composed	Published	First performance	T	
.	Boris Godunov, music for Fountain Scene	Pushkin	?1863–4	lost	—	—	172
—	Dmitry Samozvanets i Vasily Shuysky [Dmitry the Pretender and Vasily Shuysky], 2 pieces, small orch: Introduction Mazurka	Ostrovsky	by 11 Feb 1867	— 1955 1962	—	— xiv, 3 xiv, 8	
—	Putanitsa [The tangle], couplets for the vaudeville	P. Fyodorov	Dec 1867	lost	Moscow, Dec 1867	—	
3	Voyevoda [The voyevoda], opera, 3 [destroyed by Tchaikovsky, reconstructed by Pavel Lamm; material used in Characteristic Dances, orch, 1864–5, and Potpourri, pf, 1868]	Ostrovsky and Tchaikovsky, after Ostrovsky: Son na Volge [A dream on the Volga]	20 March 1867–sum. 1868	1953	Moscow, Bol'shoy, 11 Feb 1869	*ia, b, v, †i suppl.	155–6, 157, 161, 164, 215
—	Recitatives and choruses for Auber's Le domino noir	—	Oct 1868	lost	Moscow, 1868	—	157
—	Undina [Undine], opera, 3 [destroyed by Tchaikovsky, 1873; frags. only]: Undine's aria Act 1 finale	V. Sollogub, after Zhukovsky's trans. of F. de la Motte Fouqué	Jan–July 1869	Moscow and Leningrad, 1950	Moscow, 28 March 1870, excerpts only	*ii, 3, †ii, 161 *ii, 44, †ii, 169	156, 165
—	Mandragora, opera, Chorus of Flowers and Insects only, mixed and children's vv, pf; orchd later	S. Rachinsky	8 Jan 1870; orchd by 25 Jan 1870	Moscow and Leningrad, 1950	Moscow, 30 Dec 1870	*ii, 92, †ii, 191	156, 162

231

Op.	Title	Libretto	Composed	Published	First performance	T	
—	Oprichnik [The oprichnik], opera, 4	Tchaikovsky, after I. Lazhechnikov: Oprichniki [The oprichniks]	Feb 1870–April 1872	*St Petersburg, 1896, †St Petersburg, 1874	St Petersburg, Mariinsky, 24 April 1874	*iiia, b, †xxxiv	156, 162–3, 164, 168, 194
—	Le barbier de Séville, couplets 'Vous l'ordonnez' for Almaviva, 1v, 2 vn	Beaumarchais, trans. M. Sadovsky	by 24 Feb 1872	1906	Moscow, Conservatory, 24 Feb 1872	*xiv, 19	
12	Snegurochka [The snow maiden], incidental music, solo vv, chorus, small orch	Ostrovsky	March–April 1873	*1895, †1873	Moscow, Bol'shoy (by Maliy Company), 23 May 1873	*xiv, 23	166, 217
14	Kuznets Vakula [Vakula the smith], opera, 3 [rev. as Cherevichki]	Ya. Polonsky, after Gogol: Noch' pered rozhdestvom [Christmas eve]	June–2 Sept 1874	†1876	St Petersburg, Mariinsky, 6 Dec 1876	—	165, 168, 169–70, 171, 177, 205
—	Recitatives for Mozart's Le nozze di Figaro	—	1875	†1884	Moscow, Conservatory, 17 May 1876	—	
20	Lebedinoye ozero [Swan lake], ballet, 4	V. Begichev and V. Heltser	Aug 1875–22 April 1876	*1895, †1877	Moscow, Bol'shoy, 4 March 1877	*xi, †vi	174, 175–7, 178, 184, 211, 212
24	Yevgeny Onegin [Eugene Onegin], lyric scenes, 3	K. Shilovsky and Tchaikovsky, after Pushkin	May 1877–1 Feb 1878	*1880, †1878	Moscow, Maliy, 29 March 1879	*iv, †xxxvi	171, 183, 184, 187–90, 202, 211, 221
—	Orleanskaya deva [The maid of Orleans], opera, 4	Tchaikovsky, after Zhukovsky's trans. of Schiller: Die Jungfrau von Orleans	17 Dec 1878–4 Sept 1879; rev. 1882	*1902, †1880	St Petersburg, Mariinsky, 25 Feb 1881	*va, b, †xxxvii	194–5, 197, 198, 207
?	La fée, cradle song for the play Montenegrins receiving the news of Russia's declaration of war on Turkey, music for tableau, small orch	—	13 July 1879 8 11 Feb 1880	lost lost	Kamenka	—	
—	Mazepa [Mazeppa], opera, 3	V. Burenin, rev. Tchaikovsky, after Pushkin: Poltava	sum. 1881–28 April 1883	*1899, †1883	Moscow, Bol'shoy, 15 Feb 1884	*viia, b, †xxxviii	171, 197, 198, 200
—	Cherevichki [The slippers] (Les caprices d'Oxane), comic-fantastic opera, 4 [rev. of Kuznets Vakula]	Ya. Polonsky, after Gogol: Noch' pered rozhdestvom [Christmas eve]	Feb–3 April 1885	*1898, †1885	Moscow, Bol'shoy, 31 Jan 1887	*viia, b, †xxxix	169, 205

Op.	Title, forces		Composed	Published/MS	First performance	T	
—	Charodeyka [The sorceress], opera, 4	I. Shpazhinsky	Oct 1885–18 May 1887	*1901, †1887	St Petersburg, Mariinsky, 1 Nov 1887	*viiia, b, †xla, b	204, 205, 207
—	Voyevoda, Domovoy's monologue, melodrama for the play	Ostrovsky	25–9 Jan 1886	1940	Moscow, Malïy, 31 Jan 1886	*xiv, 277	
66	Spyashchaya krasavitsa [The sleeping beauty], ballet, prol, 3	M. Petipa and I. Vsevolozhsky, after C. Perrault: La belle au bois dormant	Oct 1888–1 Sept 1889	*1952, †1889	St Petersburg, Mariinsky, 15 Jan 1890	*xiia, b, v, g, †lvii	210, 211–12, 218
68	Pikovaya dama [The queen of spades], opera, 3	M. and P. Tchaikovsky, after Pushkin	31 Jan–20 June 1890	*1891, †1890	St Petersburg, Mariinsky, 19 Dec 1890	*ixa, b, v, †xii	212–14, 217
67a	Hamlet, incidental music, solo vv, small orch	Shakespeare	13 Jan–3 Feb 1891	*1896	St Petersburg, Mikhaylovsky, 21 Feb 1891	*xiv, 320	166, 217
69	Iolanta [Iolanthe], lyric opera, 1	M. Tchaikovsky, after V. Zotov's trans. of H. Hertz's King René's Daughter	22 July–27 Dec 1891	*1892, †1892	St Petersburg, Mariinsky, 18 Dec 1892	*x, †xlii	218, 221
71	Shchelkunchik [The nutcracker], fairy ballet, 2	M. Petipa, after A. Dumas père's version of E. T. A. Hoffmann's Nussknacker und Mausekönig	Feb 1891–4 April 1892	*1892, †1892	St Petersburg, Mariinsky, 18 Dec 1892	*xiiia, b, †liv	217, 218–19, 221, 230
—	Romeo and Juliet, duet, S, T, orch [partly based on orch fantasy ov.; incomplete, completed by Taneyev]	Shakespeare, trans. A. Sokolovsky	1881 or 1893	1895	—	—	

ORCHESTRAL
(for full orchestra unless otherwise stated)

Op.	Title, forces	Composed	Published/MS	First performance	T
—	Allegro ma non tanto, G, str	1863–4	—	—	—
—	Little Allegro, with introduction, D, 2 fl, str	1863–4	—	—	—
—	Andante ma non troppo, A, small orch	1863–4	—	—	—
—	Agitato and allegro, e, small orch	1863–4	—	—	—
—	Allegro vivo, c	1863–4	—	—	—
—	The Romans in the Coliseum, orch	1863–4	lost	—	—

Op.	Title, forces	Composed	Published/MS	First performance	T	
76	Groza [The storm], ov., e, to Ostrovsky's play	sum. 1864	St Petersburg, 1896	St Petersburg, 7 March 1896	xxi, 3	150, 153
—	Characteristic Dances [rev. as Dances of the Hay Maidens in opera Voyevoda]	wint. 1864–5	—	Pavlovsk, 11 Sept 1865	—	149
—	Overture, F					
	1st version for small orch	begun 27 Aug 1865	1952	St Petersburg, 26 Nov 1865	xxi, 85	150
	2nd version for full orch	Feb 1866	1952	Moscow, 16 March 1866	xxi, 121	153
—	Concert Overture, c	sum. 1865–?31 Jan 1866	1952	Voronezh, 1931	xxi, 213	152–3
13	Symphony no.1, g ('Winter daydreams')					153–5, 159, 160, 165
	1st version	March–Aug 1866	—			
	2nd version	Nov–Dec 1866	—	Moscow, 15 Feb 1868	xva	
	3rd version	1874	1875	Moscow, 1 Dec 1883		
15	Festival Ov., D, on the Danish national hymn [arr. pf 4 hands (1878), T la]	22 Sept–24 Nov 1866	1892	Moscow, 11 Feb 1867	xxii, 1	155
77	Fatum [Fate], sym. poem, c [destroyed by Tchaikovsky, reconstructed 1896]	22 Sept–Dec 1868	St Petersburg, 1896	Moscow, 27 Feb 1869	xxii, 81	157
—	Romeo and Juliet, fantasy ov., b, after Shakespeare					31, 158–60, 162, 163, 165, 167, 179, 186, 209, 228
	1st version	7 Oct–27 Nov 1869	Moscow and Leningrad, 1950	Moscow, 16 March 1870	xxiii, 3	
	2nd version	sum. 1870	Berlin, 1871	St Petersburg, 17 Feb 1872	xxiii, 199, frag. only	
	3rd version	completed 10 Sept 1880	Berlin, 1881	Tbilisi, 1 May 1886	xxiii, 89	
—	Serenade for Nikolay Rubinstein's name day, small orch	13 Dec 1872	1961	Moscow, 18 Dec 1872	xxiv, 3	
17	Symphony no.2, c ('Little Russian')	June–Nov 1872	1954	Moscow, 7 Feb 1873	xvb, 169	31, 165–6, 167, 173, 228
	1st version [arr. pf 4 hands (St Petersburg, 1874), T xlvi]					
	2nd version [arr. pf 4 hands (St Petersburg, 1880), T xlvii]	Dec 1879–Jan 1880	St Petersburg, 1880	St Petersburg, 12 Feb 1881	xvb, 9	165
18	Burya [The tempest], sym. fantasia, f, after Shakespeare	19 Aug–22 Oct 1873	1877	Moscow, 19 Dec 1873	xxiv, 13	167, 168, 181
29	Symphony no.3, D ('Polish')	17 June–13 Aug 1875	1877	Moscow, 19 Nov 1875	xvia	171, 173, 175, 177, 196, 203, 209, 217, 230
31	Slavonic March, Bb [arr. pf 4 hands (1876)]	completed 7 Oct 1876	1880	Moscow, 17 Nov 1876	xxiv, 117	178

No.	Title	Composed	Pubd	First performance	Edn	Pages
32	Francesca da Rimini, sym. fantasia, e, after Dante	7 Oct–17 Nov 1876	1878	Moscow, 9 March 1877	xxiv, 187	178–80, 182, 203, 204, 209, 211, 219, 222, 230
36	Symphony no.4, f	May 1877–7 Jan 1878	1880	Moscow, 22 Feb 1878	xvib	171, 178, 179, 182, 183, 184–6, 193, 198, 208, 209, 222
43	Suite no.1, D [arr. pf 4 hands (1879)]	27 Aug 1878–Aug 1879	1879	Moscow, 23 Nov 1879	xixa	193–4, 200–201
45	Italian Capriccio, A [arr. pf 4 hands (1880), T la, 41]	16 Jan–27 May 1880	1880	Moscow, 18 Dec 1880	xxv, 3	195–6
48	Serenade, C, str [arr. pf 4 hands (1881)]	21 Sept–4 Nov 1880	1881	St Petersburg, 30 Oct 1881	xx, 301	197, 215
49	1812, festival ov., Eb [arr. pf, and pf 4 hands (1882)]	12 Oct–19 Nov 1880	1882	Moscow, 20 Aug 1882	xxv, 97	197
—	Festival Coronation March, D [arr. pf (1883)]	21 March–1 April 1883	1883	Moscow, 4 June 1883	xxv, 187	193–4, 200
53	Suite no.2, C [movts 2–5 arr. pf 4 hands (1884)]	13 June–25 Oct 1883	1884	Moscow, 16 Feb 1884	xixb	193–4, 200–201
55	Suite no.3, G [arr. pf 4 hands (1885)]	April–31 July 1884	1885	St Petersburg, 24 Jan 1885	xx, 3	193–4, 200–201
—	Elegy, G, in honour of Ivan Samarin, str [used as Act 4 entr'acte, Hamlet, 1891]	18 Nov 1884	1890	Moscow, 28 Dec 1884	—	217
58	Manfred, sym., after Byron, b [arr. pf 4 hands, collab. A. Hubert (1886)]	April–4 Oct 1885	1886	Moscow, 23 March 1886	xviii	175, 193, 203–4, 208, 209, 230
—	Jurists' March, D	completed 17 Nov 1885	1894	—	—	
61	Suite no.4, G ('Mozartiana') [based on works by Mozart]	29 June–9 Aug 1887	1887	Moscow, 26 Nov 1887	xx, 225	205
64	Symphony no.5, e	May–26 Aug 1888	1888	St Petersburg, 17 Nov 1888	xviia	208–9, 211, 223
67	Hamlet, fantasy ov., f, after Shakespeare	June–19 Oct 1888	1890	St Petersburg, 24 Nov 1888	xiv, 285	208, 209, 211, 217, 219, 221
78	Voyevoda [The voyevoda], sym. ballad, a, after Mickiewicz	Sept 1890–4 Oct 1891	St Petersburg, 1897	Moscow, 18 Nov 1891	—	215, 217, 218
71a	Shchelkunchik [The nutcracker], suite from the ballet [arr. pf (1897)]	Jan–21 Feb 1892	1892	St Petersburg, 19 March 1892	—	219
—	Symphony no.7, Eb [unfinished; sketches used for Pf Conc. no.3, and for Andante and Finale, pf, orch]	May–Dec 1892	—	—	—	221
74	Symphony no.6, b ('Pathétique') [arr. pf 4 hands (1893)]	16 Feb–31 Aug 1893	1894	St Petersburg, 28 Oct 1893	xviib	218, 221–3, 225, 226
	SOLO INSTRUMENT AND ORCHESTRA					
23	Piano Concerto no.1, bb; arr. 2 pf	Nov 1874–21 Feb 1875; 1875	1879; 1875	Boston, 25 Oct 1875	xxviii, 5; xlvia, 5	172–3, 177, 178, 208

Op.	Title, forces	Composed	Published/MS	First performance	T	
26	Sérénade mélancolique, b, vn, orch	Jan 1875	1879	Moscow, 28 Jan 1876	xxxa, 3	190
	arr. vn, pf		1876			
33	Variations on a Rococo Theme, A, vc, orch	Dec 1876	1889	Moscow, 30 Nov 1877	—	171, 180
	arr. vc, pf		1878		lvb, 5	
34	Valse-scherzo, C, vn, orch	1877	1895	Paris, 20 Sept 1878	xxxa, 19	190
	arr. vn, pf		1878			
35	Violin Concerto, D	17 March–11 April 1878	1888	Vienna, 4 Dec 1881	xxxa, 49	190–91, 192, 202
	arr. vn, pf		1878			
44	Piano Concerto no.2, G	22 Oct 1879–10 May 1880	1881	New York, 12 Nov 1881	xxviii, 167	195, 196
	arr. 2 pf		1880		xlviia, 131	
56	Concert Fantasia, G, pf, orch	June–6 Oct 1884	1893	Moscow, 6 March 1885	xxix, 5	201
	arr. 2 pf		1884		xlvib, 5	
62	Pezzo capriccioso, b, vc, orch	24–31 Aug 1887	1888	Moscow, 7 Dec 1889	lvb, 43	205
	arr. vc, pf		1888		xxix, 161	
75	Piano Concerto no.3, Eb [1 movt; also named Allegro de concert and Konzertstück]	5 July–15 Oct 1893	1888	St Petersburg, 19 Jan 1895		221
	arr. 2 pf		1894		xlvib, 73	
79	Andante, Bb, Finale, Eb, pf, orch [unfinished; completed and orchd Taneyev]	begun after 15 Oct 1893	1894 St Petersburg, 1897	St Petersburg, 20 Feb 1896	lxii, 3	
	arr. 2 pf		St Petersburg, 1897		lxii, 137	

CHORAL

Op.	Title, forces	Composed	Published/MS	First performance	T	
—	[oratorio]	?1863–4	lost	—	—	—
—	Na son gryadushchy [At bedtime] (N. Ogaryov), unacc. chorus [arr. mixed chorus, orch (1960). T xxvii, 455]	1863–4	1941 [unacc.]	—	—	—
—	K radosti [Ode to joy] (Schiller: An die Freude, trans. K. Aksakov and others), cantata, S, A, T, B, chorus, orch	Nov–Dec 1865	1960	St Petersburg Conservatory, 10 Jan 1866	xxvii, 3	150, 153
—	Priroda i lyubov [Nature and love] (Tchaikovsky), SSA, pf	Dec 1870	1894	Moscow, 28 March 1871	—	—
—	Cantata (Ya. Polonsky) in commemoration of the bicentenary of the birth of Peter the Great, T, chorus, orch	Feb–March 1872	1960	Moscow, 12 June 1872	xxvii, 189	164

—	Cantata (hymn) (N. Nekrasov) in celebration of the golden jubilee of Osip Petrov, T, chorus, orch	by 29 Dec 1875	1960	St Petersburg Conservatory, 6 May 1876	xxvii, 341	—
41	Liturgy of St John Chrysostom, unacc. chorus [arr. pf. 1879]	May–July 1878	1879	—	—	193
—	Cantata, unacc. 4-pt. women's chorus	?Dec 1881	lost	—	—	—
—	Vecher [Evening] (?Tchaikovsky), unacc. 3-pt. men's chorus	by 25 Dec 1881	1881	—	—	—
52	Vesper Service, unacc. chorus (17 harmonizations of liturgical songs) [also with pf acc., 1882]	May 1881–7 Dec 1882	1882	—	—	197
—	Couplets on a theme from Glinka's A Life for the Tsar, linked with the Russian National Anthem of A. Lvov	14–16 Feb 1883	after 1897	Moscow, Red Square, 22 May 1883	—	—
—	Moskva [Moscow] (A. Maykov), coronation cantata, Mez, Bar, chorus, orch	21 March–5 April 1883	score 1888; vocal score 1885	Moscow, Kremlin, 27 May 1883	xxvii, 361	—
—	9 sacred pieces, unacc. mixed chorus [also with pf acc., 1885]:		1885		—	
	Kheruvimskaya pesnya [Cherubim's song], F	Nov 1884				
	Kheruvimskaya pesnya, D					
	Kheruvimskaya pesnya, C					
	Tebe poyom [We sing to thee] (tune taken from the Ordinary)	April 1885				
	Dostoyno est' [It is very meet]					
	Otche nash [Our Father]					
	Blazhenni yazhe izbral [I, a blessed one, chose]					
	Da ispravitsya [Let my prayer ascend], 3vv, chorus					
	Nine sili nebesniye [Today the heavenly powers]					
—	Hymn in honour of SS Cyril and Methodius (Tchaikovsky), unacc. chorus, based on a Cz. hymn [arr. pf. 1885]	18–20 March 1885	1885	Moscow Conservatory, 18 April 1885	—	—
—	Song (Tchaikovsky) for the golden jubilee of the Imperial School of Jurisprudence, unacc. chorus	by 9 Oct 1885	1885	—	—	—

Op.	Title, forces	Composed	Published/MS	First performance	T
—	Blazhen, kto ulibayetsya [Blessed is he who smiles] (Grand Duke Konstantin Romanov), unacc. 4-pt. men's chorus	19 Dec 1887	1889	Moscow, 20 March 1892	—
—	Angel vopiyashe [An angel crying], unacc. chorus	2 March 1887	1906	—	—
—	Nochevala tuchka zolotaya [The golden cloud has slept] (Lermontov), unacc. chorus	17 July 1887	1922	—	—
—	A greeting (Ya. Polonsky) to Anton Rubinstein for his golden jubilee as an artist, unacc. chorus	2–12 Oct 1889	1889	St Petersburg, Hall of the Court Assembly, 30 Nov 1889	—
54/5	Legenda [Legend] (Pleshcheyev), unacc. chorus [arr. of solo song]	by 27 Dec 1889	1890	—	200
—	Solovushka [The nightingale] (Tchaikovsky), unacc. chorus	by 27 Dec 1889	1890	Moscow, 25 Dec 1892	—
—	Ne kukushechka vo sirom boru ['Tis not the cuckoo in the damp pinewood] (N. Tsiganov), unacc. chorus	by 26 Feb 1891	1894	—	—
—	Bez pori, da bez vremeni [Without time, without season] (Tsiganov), unacc. 4-pt. women's chorus	by 26 Feb 1891	1894	—	—
—	Shto smolknul veseliya glas [The voice of mirth grew silent] (Pushkin), unacc. 4-pt. male chorus	by 26 Feb 1891	1894	—	—
—	Noch [Night] (Tchaikovsky), SATB, pf [reworking of part of Mozart's Fantasia in c k475]	13–15 March 1893	1893	Moscow Conservatory, 21 Oct 1893	—
—	Vesna [Spring], unacc. women's chorus	—	lost	—	—

CHAMBER MUSIC

op.	Title, forces	Published/MS	T
—	Adagio, C, 4 hn, 1863–4		181
—	Adagio, F, 2 fl, 2 ob, 2 cl, eng hn, b cl, 1863–4		
—	Adagio molto, Eb, str qt, harp, 1863–4		
—	Allegretto, E, str qt, 1863–4		
—	Allegretto moderato, D, str trio, 1863–4		
—	Allegro, c, pf sextet (pf, 2 vn, va, vc, db), 1863–4		149
—	Allegro vivace, Bb, str qt, 1863–4		
—	Andante ma non troppo, e, prelude, str qt, 1863–4		
—	Andante molto, G, str qt, 1863–4		
—	String Quartet, Bb [1 movt only], begun 27 Aug 1865, completed by 11 Nov 1865 (1940), T xxxi, 3		162, 163, 168, 171, 181, 215, 228, 229
11	String Quartet no.1, D [Andante cantabile arr. vc, str orch by Tchaikovsky, ?1886–8], Feb 1871 (1872), T xxxi, 25		167–8, 171, 173, 177, 228, 229
22	String Quartet no.2, F, completed by 30 Jan 1874 (1876), T xxxi, 63		177, 228, 229
30	String Quartet no.3, eb [Andante funebre arr. vn, pf by Tchaikovsky, 1877 (1877)], early Jan–1 March 1876 (1876), T xxxi, 115		177–8

19 Six morceaux, by 8 Nov 1873 (1874), T iib, 91:
1 Rêverie du soir, g
2 Scherzo humoristique, D
3 Feuillet d'album, D
4 Nocturne, c# [transcr. vc, small orch by Tchaikovsky, c1888]
5 Capriccioso, Bb
6 Thème original et variations, F

21 Six morceaux, composés sur un seul thème, by 12 Dec 1873 (St Petersburg, 1873), T iib, 139:
1 Prélude, B
2 Fugue à 4 voix, g#
3 Impromptu, c#
4 Marche funèbre, ab
5 Mazurque, ab
6 Scherzo, Ab   177

37b Les saisons, Dec 1875–Nov 1876 (1876), T liii, 3:
1 Janvier: Au coin du feu, A
2 Février: Carnaval, D
3 Mars: Chant de l'alouette, g
4 Avril: Perce-neige, Bb
5 Mai: Les nuits de mai, G
6 Juin: Barcarolle, g
7 Juillet: Chant du faucheur, Eb
8 Août: La moisson, b
9 Septembre: La chasse, G
10 Octobre: Chant d'automne, d
11 Novembre: Troika, E
12 Décembre: Noël, Ab

— Funeral March on themes from opera The Oprichnik, 19–28 March 1877, lost

— March for the Volunteer Fleet, C, 6 May 1878 (1878) [pubd under pseud. P. Sinopov], T iib, 65

39 Album pour enfants: 24 pièces faciles (à la Schumann), 13–16 May 1878 (1878), T, liii, 139 [Tchaikovsky's orig. sequence; nos. in brackets indicate Jürgenson's pubd order]:   193
1 (1) Prière du matin, G
2 (2) Le matin en hiver, D
3 (4) Maman, G
4 (3) Le petit cavalier, D

---

42 Souvenir d'un lieu cher, vn, pf, March–May 1878 (1879):
1 Méditation, d
2 Scherzo, c
3 Mélodie, Eb   190

50 Piano Trio, a, Dec 1881–9 Feb 1882 (1882), T xxxiia   193, 197–8, 202

70 Souvenir de Florence, str sextet, D, 24 June–Aug 1890 (opening sketched in 1887; rev. Dec 1891–Jan 1892 (1892), T xxxiib   214–15, 221

PIANO

(for solo pf unless otherwise stated)

op.

— Anastasiya valse, 1854 (1913)   177

— Piece on the tune Vozle rechki, vozle mostu [By the river, by the bridge], musical joke after Konstantin Lyadov, Sept–Dec 1862, lost

— Allegro, f, 1863–4, inc.   148

— Theme and variations, a, 1863–4 (1909), T iia, 3   153

80 Sonata, c#, 1865 (1900), T iia, 27

1 Two pieces, March 1867 (1867), T iia, 81:
1 Scherzo à la russe, Bb, on Ukrainian folktune (first called Capriccio)   149
2 Impromptu, eb, 1863–4

2 Souvenir de Hapsal, June–July 1867 (1868), T iia, 105:   156
1 Ruines d'un château, e
2 Scherzo, F
3 Chant sans paroles, F

— Potpourri on themes from the opera Voyevoda, 1868 (1868) [pubd under pseud. Cramer], T iib, 197   156

4 Valse caprice, D, Oct 1868 (1868), T iib, 3

5 Romance, f, Nov 1868 (1868), T iib, 23

7 Valse-scherzo [no.1], A, by 15 Feb 1870 (1870), T iib, 31

8 Capriccio, Gb, by 15 Feb 1870 (1870), T iib, 43

9 Trois morceaux, by 7 Nov 1870 (1871), T iib, 57:
1 Rêverie, D
2 Polka de salon, Bb
3 Mazurka de salon, d

10 Deux morceaux, Dec 1871 (1876), T iib, 81:
1 Nocturne, F, also (1874)
2 Humoresque, e [arr. vn, pf by Tchaikovsky, 1877]

5 (5) Marche des soldats de bois, D
6 (9) La nouvelle poupée, Bb
7 (6) La poupée malade, g
8 (7) Enterrement de la poupée, c
9 (8) Valse, Eb
10 (14) Polka, Bb
11 (10) Mazurka, d
12 (11) Chanson russe, F
13 (12) Le paysan prélude, Bb
14 (13) Chanson populaire (Kamarinskaya), D
15 (15) Chanson italienne, D
16 (16) Mélodie antique française, g
17 (17) Chanson allemande, Eb
18 (18) Chanson napolitaine, Eb
19 (19) Conte de la vieille bonne, C
20 (20) La sorcière (Baba Yaga), e
21 (21) Douce rêverie, C
22 (22) Chant de l'alouette, G
23 (24) A l'église, e
24 (23) L'orgue de barberie, G

40 Douze morceaux (difficulté moyenne), 24 Feb–12 May 1878 (1879), T lii, 73
1 Etude, G
2 Chanson triste, g
3 Marche funèbre, c
4 Mazurka, C
5 Mazurka, D
6 Chant sans paroles, a
7 Au village, a
8 Valse, Ab
9 Valse, f# [1st version, 16 July 1876; rev. 1878]
10 Danse russe, a
11 Scherzo, d
12 Rêverie interrompue, f

37 Sonata, G, 13 March–7 Aug 1878 (1879), T lii, 173   192, 196, 215
51 Six morceaux, Aug–22 Sept 1882 (1882), T lii, 3:
1 Valse de salon, Ab
2 Polka peu dansante, b
3 Menuetto scherzoso, Eb
4 Natha-valse, A [1st version, 17 Aug 1878]
5 Romance, F
6 Valse sentimentale, f

— Impromptu-caprice, G, 2 Oct 1884 (Paris, 1885), T liii, 57
59 Dumka: Russian rustic scene, c, 27 Feb–5 March 1886 (1886). T liii, 63
— Valse-scherzo [no.2], A, by 28 Aug 1889 (1889), T liii, 77
— Impromptu, Ab, 2–21 Oct 1889 (St Petersburg, 1889), T liii, 85
— Aveu passioni, e, ?1892 (Moscow and Leningrad, 1949), T liii, 229 [largely a transcr. of an episode in the sym. ballad The Voyevoda, 1890–91]
— Military march [for the Yurevsky Regiment], Bb, 5 April–17 May 1893 (1894), T liii, 91
72 Dix-huit morceaux, 19 April–4 May 1893 (1893), T liii, 97:   222
1 Impromptu, f
2 Berceuse, Ab
3 Tendres reproches, c#
4 Danse caractéristique, D
5 Méditation, D
6 Mazurque pour danser, Bb
7 Polacca de concert, Eb
8 Dialogue, B
9 Un poco di Schumann, Db
10 Scherzo-fantaisie, Eb
11 Valse bluette, Eb
12 L'espiègle, E
13 Echo rustique, Eb
14 Chant élégiaque, Db
15 Un poco di Chopin, c#
16 Valse à cinq temps, D
17 Passé lointain, Eb
18 Scène dansante (invitation au trépak), C
— Impromptu (Momento lirico), Ab, ?1893 (1894), T lxiii, 295 [inc.: completed by Taneyev]

SONGS AND DUETS
(all in T xliv–xlv)

op.
— Pesnya Zemfiri [Zemfira's song] (Pushkin: Tsïganï) c1855–60, ed. in SovM (1940)   162
— Moy geniy, moy angel, moy drug [My genius, my angel, my friend] (A. Fet: K Oleliy [To Ophelia]), c1855–60, ed. in SovM (1940)
— Mezza notte, c1855–60 (St Petersburg, c1865)   148

6　Six Songs, 27 Nov–29 Dec 1869 (1870): Ne ver, moy drug [Do not believe, my friend] (A. K. Tolstoy); Ni slova, o moy drug [Not a word, O my friend] (A. Pleshcheyev, after M. Hartmann: Molchaniye [Silence]); I bol'no, i sladko [Both painfully and sweetly] (E. Rostopchina: Slova dlya muziki [Words for music]); Slyoza drozhit [A tear trembles] (A. K. Tolstoy); Otchevo? [Why?] (L. Mey, after Heine: Warum sind dann die Rosen so blas? from Lyrisches Intermezzo); Net, tolko tot, kto znal [No, only he who has known] (L. Mey, after Goethe: Nur wer die Sehnsucht kennt, Mignon's song from Wilhelm Meister), usually known in Eng. as None but the lonely heart　162, 166

—　Zabit tak skoro [To forget so soon] (A. Apukhtin), 1870 (1873)　162

16　Six Songs, ?Dec 1872 (St Petersburg, 1873): Kolibel'naya pesnya [Cradle song] (A. Maykov, from cycle Novogrecheskiye pesni [New Greek songs]), arr. pf, 1873; Pogodi [Wait] (N. Grekov); Poymi khot raz [Accept but once] (A. Fet); O, spoy zhe tu pesnyu [O sing that song] (A. Pleshcheyev, after Felicia Hemans: Mother O sing that song we to rest), arr. pf, and vn, pf, 1873; Tvoy obraz svetliy [Thy radiant image] (Tchaikovsky), arr. pf, 1872; Novogrecheskaya pesnya (V tyomnom ade) [In dark Hell] (A. Maykov, from cycle Novogrecheskiye pesni [New Greek songs])　166

—　Unosi moyo serdtse [Take my heart away] (Fet: Pevitse [The singer]), by 11 Oct 1873, ed. in Nouvelliste (1873)

—　Glazki vesni golubiye [Blue eyes of spring] (M. Mikhaylov, after a poem from Heine's Die blauen Frühlingsaugen), by 11 Oct 1873, ed. in Nouvelliste (1874)　166

25　Six Songs, Sept 1874–early 1875 (St Petersburg, 1875): Primireniye [Reconciliation] (N. Shcherbina); Kak nad goryacheyu zoloy [As o'er the burning ashes] (F. Tyutchev); Pesnya Minoni [Mignon's song] (F. Tyutchev, after Goethe's Kennst du das Land, from Wilhelm Meister); Kanareyka [The canary] (L. Mey); Ya s neyu nikogda ne govoril [I never spoke to her] (L. Mey, from cycle Oktavi [Octaves]); Kak naladili: Durak [As they reiterated: 'Fool'] (Mey: Pesnya [Song])　172, 172, 172

27　Six Songs, by 20 April 1875 (1875): Na son gryadushchiy [At bedtime] (N. Ogaryov); Smotri, von oblako [Look, yonder cloud] (Grekov); Ne otkhodi ot menya [Do not leave me] (Fet, from cycle, Melodii [Melodies]); Vecher [Evening] (Mey, after Shevchenko); Ali mat menya sozhala? [Was it the mother who bore me?] (Mey, after Mickiewicz); Moya balovnitsa [My spoilt darling] (Mey, after Mickiewicz); rev. later　173

28　Six Songs, by 23 April 1875 (1875): Net, nikogda ne nazovu [No, I shall never tell] (Grekov, after Musset: Chanson de fortunio); Korolki [The corals] (Mey, after L.-V. Kondratowicz); Zachem? [Why did I dream of you?] (Mey); On tak menya lyubil [He loved me so much] (?A. Apukhtin); Ni otziva, ni slova, ni priveta [No response, or word, or greeting] (Apukhtin); Strashnaya minuta [The fearful minute] (Tchaikovsky)　173

—　Khotel bi v edinoye slovo [I should like in a single word] (Mey, after a poem in Heine's Die Heimkehr), by 10 July 1875, ed. in Nouvelliste (1875)

—　Ne dolgo nam gulyat [We have not far to walk] (Grekov), by 10 July 1875, ed. in Nouvelliste (1875–6)

38　Six Songs, 23 Feb–8 June 1878 (1878): Serenada Don-Zhuana [Don Juan's serenade] (A. K. Tolstoy); To bilo ranneyu vesnoy [It was in the early spring] (A. K. Tolstoy); Sred shumnovo bala [Amid the din of the ball] (A. K. Tolstoy); O, esli b ti mogla [O, if only you could for one moment] (A. K. Tolstoy); Lyubov mertvetsa [The love of a dead man] (Lermontov); Pimpinella (Tchaikovsky, from a Florentine popular song)　193

46　Six Duets, 16 June–5 Sept 1880 (1881): Vecher [Evening] (I. Surikov), S, Mez; Shotlandskaya ballada [Scottish ballad: Edward] (trans. A. K. Tolstoy), S, Bar; Slyozi [Tears] (F. Tyutchev), S, Mez; V ogorode, vozle brodu [In the garden, near the ford] (Surikov, after Shevchenko), S, Mez; Minula strast [Passion spent] (A. K. Tolstoy), S, T; Rassvet [Dawn] (Surikov), S, Mez, orchd, T xxvii　197

47　Seven Songs, July–Aug 1880 (1881): Kabi znala ya [If only I had known] (A. K. Tolstoy); Gornimi tikho letela dusha nebesami [Softly the spirit flew up to heaven] (A. K. Tolstoy); Na zemlyu sumrak pal [Dusk fell on the earth] (N. Berg, after Mickiewicz); Usni, pechalniy drug [Sleep, poor friend] (A. K. Tolstoy); Blagoslavlyayu vas, lesa [I bless you, forests] (A. K. Tolstoy, from John Damascene); Den li tsarit? [Does the day reign?] (Apukhtin), orchd 24 Feb 1888, lost; Ya li v pole da ne travushka bila? [Was I not a little blade of grass?] (Surikov;　197

Malorossyskaya pesnya [Ukrainian song]), orchd by 7 Oct 1884, T xxvii

54 Sixteen Children's Songs, nos.1–15, 28 Oct–15 Nov 1883, no.16,   200
19 Jan 1881: nos.1–16 (1884): Babushka i vnuchek [Granny and grandson] (Pleshcheyev); Ptichka [The little bird] (Pleshcheyev, from a Pol. source); Vesna [Spring] (Pleshcheyev, from a Pol. source); Moy sadik [My little garden] (Pleshcheyev); Legenda [Legend] (When Jesus Christ was but a child) (Pleshcheyev, from an Eng. source), orchd 14 April 1884 (1890), T xxvii, 501, arr. unacc. mixed chorus by 27 Dec 1889; Na beregu [On the bank] (Pleshcheyev, from an Eng. source); Zimniy vecher [Winter evening] (Pleshcheyev); Kukushka [The cuckoo] (Pleshcheyev, after C. Gellert); Vesna [Uzh tayet sneg] [Spring (The snow is already melting)] (Pleshcheyev); Kolibel'naya pesnya v buryu [Lullaby in a storm] (Pleshcheyev); Tsvetok [The flower] (Pleshcheyev, after L. Ratisbonne); Zima [Winter] (Pleshcheyev); Vesennyaya pesnya [Spring song] (Pleshcheyev); Osen [Autumn] (Pleshcheyev); Lastochka [The swallow] (Surikov, after T. Lenartowicz); Detskaya pesnya [Child's song] (K. Axakov) (1881)

57 Six Songs, no.1, ?early 1884; nos.2–6, Nov 1884; nos.1–6   201
(1885): Skazhi, o chom v teni vetvey [Tell me, what in the shade of the branches] (V. Sollogub); Na nivi zhyoltïye [On the golden cornfields] (A. K. Tolstoy); Ne sprashivay [Do not ask] (A. Strugovshchikov, after Goethe's Heiss mich nicht reden, from Wilhelm Meister); Usni [Sleep] (D. Merezhkovsky); Smert' [Death] (Merezhkovsky); Lish tï odin [Only thou alone] (Pleshcheyev, after A. Kristen)

60 Twelve Songs, 31 Aug–20 Sept 1886; nos. 1–6 (1886), nos. 7–12   205
(1887): Vcherashnyaya noch' [Last night] (A. Khomyakov: Nachtstück); Ya tebe nichevo ne skazhu [I'll tell you nothing] (Fet, from cycle Melodiy [Melodies]); O, esli b znali vï [O, if only you knew] (Pleshcheyev); Solovey [The nightingale] (Pushkin, after V. Stefanović Karadzić: Songs of the western Slavs]; Prostïye slova [Simple words] (Tchaikovsky); Nochi bezumniye [Frenzied nights] (Apukhtin); Pesn' tsiganki [Gypsy's song] (Ya. Polonsky); Prosti [Forgive] (N. Nekrasov); Noch' [Night] (Polonsky); Za oknom v teni melkayet [Behind the window in the shadow] (Polonsky): Vïzov [Challenge]; Podvig

[Exploit] (A. Khomyakov); Nam zvezdï krotkiye siyali [The mild stars shone for us] (Pleshcheyev: Slova dlya muziki [Words for music])

63 Six Songs (Grand Duke Konstantin Romanov), Nov–Dec 1887   205
(1888): Ya snachala tebya ne lyubila [I did not love you at first]; Rastvoril ya okno [I opened the window]; Ya vam ne nravlyus [I do not please you]; Pervoye svidaniye [The first meeting]; Uzh gasli v komnatakh ogni [The fires in the rooms were already out]; Serenada (O dïtya, pod okoshkom tvoim) [Serenade (O child, beneath thy window)]

65 Six Songs (Fr. texts, trans. A. Gorchakova), sum.–22 Oct 1888   208
(1889): Sérénade (Où vas-tu, souffle d'aurore) (E. Turquéty: Aurore); Déception (P. Collin); Sérénade (J'aime dans le rayon de la limpide aurore) (Collin); Qu'importe que l'hiver (Collin); Les larmes (A.-M. Blanchecotte); Rondel (Collin)

73 Six Songs (D. Rathaus), 5–17 May 1893 (1893): Mï sideli s toboy   222
[We sat together] (from cycle Romansi [Songs]); Noch' [Night]; V etu lunnuyu noch' [In this moonlight]; Zakatilos solntse [The sun has set]; Sred mrachnïkh dnei ['Mid sombre days] (from cycle Romansi [Songs]); Snova, kak prezhde, odin [Again, as before, alone]

— Kto idyot? [Who goes?] (Apukhtin), lost

ARRANGEMENTS AND EDITIONS
Weber: Scherzo, Pf Sonata, op.39 (J199), orchd 1863
Beethoven: 1st movt, Pf Sonata, op.31 no.2, orchd ?1863; 4 versions
Beethoven: 1st movt, Vn Sonata, op.47 ('Kreutzer'), orchd 1863–4
Gung'l: Valse: Le retour, pf, orchd 1863–4
Schumann: Adagio and Allegro brillante from Etudes symphoniques, op.13, orchd 1864
K. Kral: Triumphal March, pf, orchd May 1867
Dargomïzhsky: Malorossiyskiy kazachok [Little Russian kazachok], fantasia, arr. pf 1868
E. Tarnovskaya: Ya pomnyu vsyo [I remember all], song transcr. pf by Dubuque, arr. pf 4 hands 1868
50 Russ. folksongs, arr. pf 4 hands, 1868 (nos.1–25), and by 7 Oct 1869 (nos.26–50) [1–25 taken mostly from the collection of K. Villebois; 25–50 taken from Balakirev's collection, except no.47, collected by Tchaikovsky], T lxi, 3   161

A. Rubinstein: Ivan Grozniy [Ivan the Terrible], musical picture, orch, arr. pf 4 hands 8 Oct–11 Nov 1869
A. Dubuque: Maria-Dagmar, polka, pf, orchd 1869
Dargomizhsky: Nochevala tuchka zolotaya [The golden cloud has slept], 3vv, pf, pf pt. orchd 1870
A. Rubinstein: Don Quixote, musical picture, orch, arr. pf 4 hands 1870
Stradella: O del mio dolce, aria, 1v, pf, orchd 10 Nov 1870
Cimarosa: Trio Le faccio un inchino from Il matrimonio segreto, orch from vocal score 1870
Weber: Finale (Perpetuum mobile) from Pf Sonata, op.24 (J138), transcr. pf L.H. only 1871
V. Prokunin: 66 Russ. folksongs, ed. 1872, T lxi. 61
M. A. Mamontova: A Collection of Children's Songs on Russ. and Ukrainian Melodies, harmonized by 7 Sept 1872 (1st issue of 24 songs), and by May 1877 (2nd issue of 19 songs), T lxi, 169
Anon.: Gaudeamus igitur, arr. for 4-pt. men's chorus, pf 1874
Haydn: Gott erhalte, Austrian national anthem, orchd by 24 Feb 1874
Schumann: Ballade vom Haideknaben, op.121 no.1, declamation, 1v, pf, orchd 11 March 1874
Liszt: Der König in Thule, 1v, pf, orchd 3 Nov 1874
Bortnyansky: Complete church music, ed. 3 July–8 Nov 1881
Mozart: 4 pieces, usually known as Suite no.4 ('Mozartiana'): Gigue (K574); Minuet (K355); Ave verum corpus (K618); Theme and 10 variations on a theme of Gluck from La rencontre imprévue (K455), orchd 29 June–9 Aug 1887, T xx, 225
H. Laroche: Karmozina: fantasy ov., pf, orchd 27 Aug–27 Sept 1888
S. Menter: Ungarische Zigeunerweisen, pf, arr. pf, orch 1893

WRITINGS

Diaries, 1858–9 (destroyed by accident, 1866), 1873, 1882 (lost), 1884–91 (1885 lost; 1888 pubd as 'Avtobiograficheskoye opisaniye puteshestviya za granitsu v 1888 godu', 1894 [see below])   164, 178
57 reviews or critical articles pubd in journals, 1868–76; first pubd collectively in 1898 [see Bibliography, 'Source material']; full list in Dombayev
Rukovodstvo k prakticheskomu izucheniyu garmoniy [Guide to the practical study of harmony], completed 14 Aug 1871 (1872)   163

Kratkiy uchebnik garmoniy, prisposoblenniy k chteniyu dukhovno-muzikal'nïkh sochineniy v Rossiy [A short manual of harmony, adapted to the study of religious music in Russia], 1874 (1875)
'Avtobiograficheskoye opisaniye puteshestviya za granitsu v 1888 godu' [Autobiographical description of a journey abroad in 1888], Russkiy vestnik (1894), no.2, pp.165–203
Autobiography, 1889, lost
'Vagner i evo muzïka' [Wagner and his music], Morning Journal (New York, 3 May 1891)
'Beseda s Chaykovskim v noyabre 1892 g. v Peterburge' [A conversation with Tchaikovsky in November 1892 in St Petersburg], Peterburgskaya zhizn' (24 Nov 1892)
Editing and correcting of musical terms in Slovar' russkovo yazïka [Dictionary of the Russian language], ii–iii, Oct 1892–3 (1892 and 1895)

TRANSLATIONS   149

F.-A. Gevaert: Traité général d'instrumentation (1863), sum. 1865 (1866)
Meyerbeer: Les Huguenots: Urbain's cavatina 'Une dame noble et sage', by 17 June 1868 (1868)
Schumann: Musikalische Haus- und Lebensregeln (1850), by 1 Aug 1868 (1869)
J. C. Lobe: Katechismus der Musik (1851), completed 20 Nov 1869 (1870)
Trans. from the Ger. of texts used by A. Rubinstein:
12 persische Lieder, op.34 (F. von Bodenstedt, after Mirza Shafi), by 24 Dec 1869 (1870)
4 songs, op.32 nos.1 and 6 and op.33 nos.2 and 4, ?1870–71 (?1871)
6 romances, op.72, ?1870–71 (?1871)
6 romances, op.76, ?1871 (?1872)
3 songs, op.83 nos.1, 5 and 9, ?1871 (?1872)
Mozart: Le nozze di Figaro, trans. of da Ponte's lib, 1875 (1884)
Trans. from the It. of 6 texts used by Glinka, by 27 Dec 1877 (1878): Mio ben, ricordati; Ho perduto il mio tesoro; Mi sento il cor traffigere; Pur nel sonno; Tu sei figlia; Molitva [Prayer] (vocal qt)
Handel: Israel in Egypt, trans. of text (collab. Taneyev), 1886 (1912)

BIBLIOGRAPHY

CATALOGUES AND BIBLIOGRAPHIES

B. Jürgenson, ed.: *Catalogue thématique des oeuvres de P. Tschaikowsky* (Moscow, 1897/*R*1965)

M. Shemanin: 'Literatura o P. I. Chaykovskom za 17 let (1917–34)' [Literature about Tchaikovsky, 1917–34], *Muzïkal'noye nasledstvo* (Moscow, 1935)

Z. V. Korotkova-Leviton and others, eds.: *Avtografï P. I. Chaykovskovo v arkhive Doma-Muzeya v Klinu: spravochnik* [Tchaikovsky: autographs in the House Museum, Klin: a guide] (Moscow and Leningrad, 1950)

V. A. Kiselyov, ed.: *Avtografï P. I. Chaykovskovo v fondakh Gosudarstvennovo tsentralnovo muzeya muzïkal'noy kulturï imeni M. I. Glinki: katalog-spravochnik* [Tchaikovsky's autographs in the State Central Glinka Museum of Musical Culture: catalogue] (Moscow, 1956)

G. S. Dombayev: *Tvorchestvo P. I. Chaykovskovo* [Tchaikovsky's works] (Moscow, 1958)

SOURCE MATERIAL

H. Laroche, ed.: *P. I. Chaykovsky: muzïkal'noye feletonï i zametki* (Moscow, 1898; Ger. trans., 1899, as *Musikalische Erinnerungen und Feuilletons*)

P. I. Tchaikovsky: *Guide to the Practical Study of Harmony* (Leipzig, 1900)

S. M. Lyapunov, ed.: *Perepiska M. A. Balakireva s P. I. Chaykovskim* [Balakirev's correspondence with Tchaikovsky] (St Petersburg, 1912); repr. in *M. A. Balakirev: vospominaniya i pis'ma*, ed. A. A. Orlova (Leningrad, 1962), 115–203

M. Tchaikovsky, ed.: *Pis'ma P. I. Chaykovskovo i S. I. Taneyeva* [Letters of Tchaikovsky and Taneyev] (Moscow, 1916); ed. V. A. Zhdanov (Moscow, 1951)

I. I. Tchaikovsky, ed.: *P. Chaykovsky: dnevniki (1873–1891)* [Diaries 1873–91] (Moscow and Petrograd, 1923; Eng. trans., 1945)

V. A. Zhdanov and N. T. Zhegin, eds.: *P. Chaykovsky: perepiska s N. F. von Meck* [Correspondence with Nadezhda von Meck] (Moscow and Leningrad, 1934–6)

——: *P. Chaykovsky: perepiska s P. I. Yurgensonom* [Correspondence with Jürgenson] (Moscow, 1938–52)

V. Yakovlev, ed.: *Dni i godï P. I. Chaykovskovo* [The days and years of Tchaikovsky] (Moscow and Leningrad, 1940)

V. A. Zhdanov, ed.: *P. I. Chaykovsky: pis'ma k rodnïm, 1850–1879* [Letters to his family], (Moscow, 1940)

Bibliography

T. Sokolova, ed.: *P. Chaykovsky: muzïkal'no-kriticheskiye stat'i* (Moscow, 1953)

P. *Chaykovsky: literaturnïye proizvedeniya i perepiska* [Literary works and correspondence] (Moscow, 1953–81)

V. A. Zhdanov, ed.: *P. Chaykovsky: pis'ma k blizkim* [Letters to relatives] (Moscow, 1955)

K. Klindworth: 'Unveröffentlichte Briefe an Tschaikowsky', *Musik und Geschichte*, xv (1965), 547

L. Atanova, ed.: 'Pis'ma k P. I. Chaykovskomu' [Letters to Tchaikovsky], *SovM* (1966), no.5, p.112

G. von Meck, ed.: *Piotr Ilyich Tchaikovsky, Letters to his Family: an Autobiography* (London, 1981)

BIOGRAPHIES AND STUDIES

H. A. Laroche: *Na pamyat' o P. I. Chaykovskom* [In memory of Tchaikovsky] (St Petersburg, 1894)

——: *Pamyati Chaykovskovo* [Memories of Tchaikovsky] (St Petersburg, 1894)

V. V. Stasov: *Sobraniye sochineny* [Collected works], iii (St Petersburg, 1894)

V. S. Baskin: *P. I. Chaykovsky* (St Petersburg, 1895)

H. A. Laroche: *Chaykovsky kak dramaticheskiy kompozitor* [Tchaikovsky as a dramatic composer] (St Petersburg, 1895); orig. in *EIT 1893–4*

N. D. Kashkin: *Vospominaniya o P. I. Chaykovskom* [Reminiscences of Tchaikovsky] (Moscow, 1896, 2/1954)

I. Pryashnikov: 'P. I. Chaykovsky kak dirizhor', *RMG* (1896), 1001

V. V. Bessel: 'Moi vospominaniya o P. I. Chaykovskom' [My reminiscences of Tchaikovsky], *EIT 1896–7*

G. Timofeyev: *P. I. Chaykovsky v role muzïkal'novo kritika* [Tchaikovsky in the role of music critic] (St Petersburg, 1899)

I. Knorr: *Peter Jljitsch Tschaikowsky* (Berlin, 1900)

K. de-Lazari: 'Vospominaniya o P. I. Chaykovskom' [Reminiscences of Tchaikovsky], *Rossiya* (1900), nos.388, 393, 405, 441

R. Newmarch: *Tchaikovsky: his Life and Works* (London, 1900)

M. I. Tchaikovsky: *Zhizn' P. I. Chaykovskovo* [Tchaikovsky's life] (Moscow, 1900–02; Eng. trans., abridged, 1906)

E. Newman: 'The Essential Tchaikovsky', *Contemporary Review*, lxxix (1901), 887

D. G. Mason: *From Grieg to Brahms: Studies in some Modern Composers* (New York, 1902)

E. Evans: *Tchaikovsky* (London, 1906, rev. 2/1935)

R. Genik: 'Fortepiannoye tvorchestvo Chaykovskovo' [Tchaikovsky's piano works], *RMG* (1908)

I. A. Klimenko: *Moi vospominaniya o P. I. Chaykovskom* [My reminiscences of Tchaikovsky] (Ryazan, 1908)

N. A. Rimsky-Korsakov: *Letopis' moyey muzïkal'noy zhizni* (St Petersburg, 1909; Eng. trans., 1942)

A. Tchaikovskaya: 'Vospominaniya vdovï P. I. Chaykovskovo' [Reminiscences of Tchaikovsky's widow], *RMG* (1913)

R. Newmarch: 'Tchaikovsky', *The Russian Opera* (London, 1914), 334

I. Glebov and V. Yakovlev: *Proshloye russkoy muzïki . . . 1. P. I. Chaykovsky* [The past of Russian music: 1. Tchaikovsky] (Petrograd, 1920)

I. Glebov: *P. I. Chaykovsky: evo zhizn' i tvorchestvo* [Life and works] (Petrograd, 1922)

——: *Instrumental'noye tvorchestvo Chaykovskovo* [Tchaikovsky's instrumental works] (Petrograd, 1922)

H. A. Laroche: *Sobraniye muzïkal'no-kriticheskikh statey* [Collected critical articles on music] (Moscow, 1922–4)

I. Glebov: *Chaykovsky: opït kharakteristiki* [An attempt at a description] (Petrograd and Berlin, 1923)

E. Blom: 'The Early Tchaikovsky Symphonies', *The Stepchildren of Music* (London, 1925), 153

——: *Tchaikovsky: Orchestral Works* (London, 1927)

N. F. Findeizen: *Kamernaya muzïka Chaykovskovo* [Tchaikovsky's chamber music] (Moscow, 1930)

R. Felber: 'Tchaikovsky and Tolstoy', *The Chesterian*, xci (1931), 65

G. Abraham: 'Tchaikovsky Revalued', *Studies in Russian Music* (London, 1935), 334

A. Budyakovsky: *P. I. Chaykovsky: simfonicheskaya muzïka* [Symphonic music] (Leningrad, 1935)

D. F. Tovey: *Essays in Musical Analysis* (London, 1935–9) [vols.ii and vi incl. studies of Tchaikovsky's Syms. nos.5 and 6]

G. Abraham and M. D. Calvocoressi: *Masters of Russian Music* (London, 1936) [incl. G. Abraham: 'Tchaikovsky', 249–334; rev. and repr. 1944 as *Tchaikovsky: a Short Biography*]

R. Fiske: 'Tchaikovsky's Later Piano Concertos', *MO*, lxii (1938), 17, 114, 209

G. Abraham: *On Russian Music* (London, 1939) [incl. 'The Programme of the *Pathétique* Symphony', 143; '*Eugene Onegin* and Tchaikovsky's Marriage', 225]

——: 'Tchaikovsky: some Centennial Reflections', *ML*, xxi (1940), 110

V. M. Bogdanov-Berezovsky: *Opernoye i baletnoye tvorchestvo Chaykovskovo* [Tchaikovsky's operas and ballets] (Leningrad and Moscow, 1940)

I. Glebov: *Pamyati P. I. Chaykovskovo* [Memories of Tchaikovsky] (Leningrad and Moscow, 1940)

Bibliography

I. Kolodin, ed.: *The Critical Composer: the Musical Writings of Berlioz, Wagner, Schumann, Tchaikovsky and Others* (New York, 1940)

A. I. Shaverdyan, ed.: *Chaykovsky i teatr* [Tchaikovsky and the theatre] (Moscow, 1940)

J. Westrup: 'Tchaikovsky and the Symphony', *MT*, lxxxi (1940), 249

V. V. Yakovlev: *Chaykovsky na moskovskoy stsene: pervïye postanovki v godï evo zhizni* [Tchaikovsky on the Moscow stage: first performances during his life] (Moscow and Leningrad, 1940)

SovM (1940), nos.5–6 [special Tchaikovsky issue]

B. V. Asaf'yev: *'Evgeny Onegin': opït intonatsionnovo analiza stilya i muzïkal'noy dramaturgii* [An attempt at intonation analysis of style and musical dramaturgy] (Moscow and Leningrad, 1944)

G. Abraham, ed.: *Tchaikovsky: a Symposium* (London, 1945)

H. Weinstock: *Tchaikovsky* (London, 1946/*R*1980)

D. Shostakovich and others: *Russian Symphony: Thoughts about Tchaikovsky* (New York, 1947)

B. Yarustovsky: *Opernaya dramaturgiya Chaykovskovo* [Tchaikovsky's operatic dramaturgy] (Moscow and Leningrad, 1947)

E. Orlova: *Romansï Chaykovskovo* [Tchaikovsky's songs] (Moscow and Leningrad, 1948)

A. A. Nikolayev: *Fortepiannoye naslediye Chaykovskovo* [Tchaikovsky's piano legacy] (Moscow and Leningrad, 1949, 2/1958)

D. V. Zhitomirsky: *Baletï P. Chaykovskovo* [Tchaikovsky's ballets] (Moscow and Leningrad, 1950, 2/1958)

A. A. Al'shvang: *Opït analiza tvorchestva P. I. Chaykovskovo* [An attempt to analyse Tchaikovsky's works] (Moscow and Leningrad, 1951)

B. V. Asaf'yev: *Izbrannïye rabotï o P. I. Chaykovskom* [Selected works on Tchaikovsky], Izbrannïye trudï, ii, ed. E. Orlova (Moscow, 1952)

V. Ferman: '*Cherevichki (Kuznets Vakula)* Chaykovskovo i *Noch' pered rozhdestvom* Rimskovo-Korsakova: opït sravneniya' [Tchaikovsky's *The Slippers* and Rimsky-Korsakov's *Christmas Eve*: an attempt at comparison], *Voprosï muzïkoznaniya*, i, ed. A. S. Ogolevets (1953–4), 205

A. A. Nikolayev: *Fortepiannoye proizvedeniya P. I. Chaykovskovo* [Tchaikovsky's piano works] (Moscow, 1957)

V. V. Protopopov and N. V. Tumanina: *Opernoye tvorchestvo Chaykovskovo* [Tchaikovsky's operas] (Moscow, 1957)

K. Yu. Davïdova and V. V. Protopopov: *Muzïkal'noye naslediye Chaykovskovo* [Tchaikovsky's musical legacy] (Moscow, 1958)

G. S. Dombayev: *P. I. Chaykovsky i mirovaya kul'tura* [Tchaikovsky and world culture] (Moscow, 1958)

N. S. Nikolayeva: *Simfonii P. I. Chaykovskovo* [Tchaikovsky's symphonies] (Moscow, 1958)

L. N. Raaben: *Skripichnïye i violonchel'nïye proizvedeniya P. I. Chay-*

kovskovo [Tchaikovsky's violin and cello works] (Moscow, 1958)

A. A. Al'shvang: *P. I. Chaykovsky* (Moscow, 1959)

E. Gershkovsky: 'Novïye materialï o P. I. Chaykovskom' [New material on Tchaikovsky], *SovM* (1959), no.1, p.73

G. Abraham: 'Russia', *A History of Song*, ed. D. Stevens (London, 1960), 338

A. N. Dol'zhansky: *Muzïka Chaykovskovo: simfonicheskiye proizvedeniya* [Symphonic works] (Leningrad, 1960)

D. Brown: 'Balakirev, Tchaikovsky and Nationalism', *ML*, xlii (1961), 227

A. Dol'zhansky: *Simfonicheskaya muzïka Chaykovskovo* [Tchaikovsky's symphonic music] (Moscow, 1961, 2/1965)

G. V. Krauklis: *Skripichnïye proizvedeniya P. I. Chaykovskovo* [Tchaikovsky's violin works] (Moscow, 1961)

G. Abraham: 'Tchaikovsky's First Opera', *Festschrift Karl Gustav Fellerer* (Regensburg, 1962), 12

E. E. Bortnikova and others, eds.: *Vospominaniya o P. I. Chaykovskom* [Reminiscences of Tchaikovsky] (Moscow, 1962)

Yu. L. Davïdov: *Zapiski o P. I. Chaykovskom* [Notes on Tchaikovsky] (Moscow, 1962)

N. Tumanina: *Chaykovsky: put' k masterstvu* [Path to mastery] (Moscow, 1962)

——: *Chaykovsky* (Moscow, 1962–8)

I. F. Kunin, ed.: *P. I. Chaykovsky o simfonicheskoy muzïke* [Tchaikovsky on symphonic music] (Moscow, 1963)

B. I. Rabinovich, ed.: *P. I. Chaykovsky i narodnaya pesnya* [Tchaikovsky and folksong] (Moscow, 1963)

K. E. von Mühlendahl: *Die Psychose Tschaikowskis und der Einfluss seiner Musik auf gleichartige Psychotiker* (diss., U. of Munich, 1964)

A. Yakovlev: *Izbrannïye trudï o muzïke* [Selected works on music], ed. D. Zhitomirsky and T. Sokolova (Moscow, 1964)

J. Clapham: 'Dvorak's Visit to Russia', *MQ*, li (1965), 493

K. Davïdov: *Klinskiye godï tvorchestva Chaykovskovo* [Tchaikovsky's works in his Klin years] (Moscow, 1965)

A. Al'shvang: *P. I. Chaykovsky* (Moscow, 1967)

R. Thomas: 'Tschaikowskys Es-Dur-Sinfonie und Idee einer Sinfonie "Das Leben"', *NZM*, Jg.128 (1967), 160

G. Abraham: *Slavonic and Romantic Music* (London, 1968)

V. Fédorov: 'Tchaikovsky et la France', *RdM*, liv/1 (1968), 16

D. Lloyd-Jones: 'A Background to Iolanta', *MT*, cix (1968), 225

J. Friskin: 'The Text of Tchaikovsky's B flat minor Concerto', *ML*, l (1969), 246

L. Koniskaya: *Chaykovsky v Peterburge* [Tchaikovsky in St Petersburg] (Leningrad, 1969)

Bibliography

J. Warrack: *Tchaikovsky Symphonies and Concertos* (London, 1969)

Chaykovsky i zarubyozhnïye muzïkantï: izbrannïye pis'ma inostrannïkh korrespondentov [Tchaikovsky and foreign musicians: selected letters from foreign correspondents] (Leningrad, 1970)

V. Blok: 'Na puti k *Pateticheskoy*' [On the path to the *Pathétique*], *SovM* (1970), no.9, p.78

G. Pribegina: Preface and commentary to *Pyotr Tchaikovsky, Sixth Symphony: Pathétique* (Moscow, 1970) [facs. score, Eng. and Russ. text]

E. Balabanovich: *Chekhov i Chaykovsky* (Moscow, 1973)

E. Garden: *Tchaikovsky* (London, 1973, rev. 2/1984)

G. von Meck: *As I Remember them* (London, 1973)

J. Warrack: *Tchaikovsky* (London, 1973)

E. Garden: 'Tchaikovsky and Tolstoy', *ML*, lv (1974), 307

U. Niebuhr: 'Der Einfluss Anton Rubinsteins auf die Klavierkonzerte Peter Tschaikovskys', *Mf*, xxvii (1974), 412

V. Volkoff: *Tchaikovsky* (Boston and London, 1974)

G. Norris: 'Tchaikovsky and the 18th Century', *MT*, cxviii (1977), 715

D. Brown: *Tchaikovsky: a Biographical and Critical Study*, i: *The Early Years (1840–74)* (London, 1978)

E. Garden: 'Three Russian Piano Concertos', *ML*, lx (1979), 166

J. Warrack: *Tchaikovsky Ballet Music* (London, 1979)

I. Berlin: 'Tchaikovsky, Pushkin and Onegin', *MT*, cxxi (1980), 163

G. Norris: *Stanford, the Cambridge Jubilee, and Tchaikovsky* (London, 1980)

E. Garden: 'A Note on Tchaikovsky's First Piano Concerto', *MT*, cxxii (1981), 238

——: 'The Influence of Balakirev on Tchaikovsky', *PRMA*, cvii (1981), 86

A. A. Orlova: 'Tchaikovsky: the Last Chapter', *ML*, lxii (1981), 125

R. C. Ridenour: *Nationalism, Modernism, and Personal Rivalry in Nineteenth-century Russian Music* (Ann Arbor, Mich., 1981)

D. Brown: *Tchaikovsky: a Biographical and Critical Study*, ii: *The Crisis Years (1874–1878)* (London, 1982)

——: 'Tchaikovsky's Marriage', *MT*, cxxiii (1982), 754

H. Zajaczkowski: 'The Function of Obsessive Elements in Tchaikovsky's Style', *MR*, xliii (1982), 24

H. Macdonald: 'Tchaikovsky: Crises and Contortions', *MT*, cxxiv (1983), 609

N. Sin'kovskaya: *O Garmony P. I. Chaykovskovo* [On Tchaikovsky's harmony] (Moscow, 1983)

D. Brown: 'Tchaikovsky's *Mazeppa*', *MT*, cxxv (1984), 696

R. J. Wiley: 'The Symphonic Element in *Nutcracker*', *MT*, cxxv (1984), 693

D. Brown: 'Tchaikovsky and Chekhov', *Slavonik and Western Music: Essays for Gerald Abraham* (Ann Arbor and Oxford, 1985), 197

R. J. Wiley: *Tchaikovsky's Ballets* (Oxford, 1985)

D. Brown: *Tchaikovsky: a Biographical and Critical Study*, iii: *The Years of Wandering (1878–1885)* (London, in preparation)

Index

Aachen, 5, 205
Abraham, Gerald, 164, 209
Alapayevsk, 147
Alexander II, Tsar of Russia, 10, 55, 80, 123
——, family of, 80
Alexander III, Tsar of Russia, 200, 202, 215, 224
Andreyev, I. P., *122*
Antonova (later Kleinecke), Avdot'ya Konstantinovna [Borodin's mother], 45
Antwerp, 56
Antwerp Exhibition, 56
Argenteau, 56
Arkhangel government, 88
Artot, Désirée, 156–7, 173, 207
Asaf'yev, Boris Vladimirovich, 130
Assier, Alexandra Andreyevna: *see* Tchaikovskaya, Alexandra Andreyevna
Assier, Andrey Tchaikovsky's grandfather], 146
Assier, Michel d' [Tchaikovsky's great-grandfather], 145
Auber, Daniel-François-Esprit: *Le domino noir*, 157
Auer, Leopold, 190
Avdotya Ivanovna [Glinka's nurse], 1

Bach, Johann Sebastian, 26, 48, 131
Baden-Baden, 48, 54
Bakhturin, Konstantin, 14
Baku, 82
Balakirev, Alexey Konstantinovich [father], 77, 84
Balakirev, Mily Alexeyevich, 1, 30, 49, 50, 60, 77–106, 110, 111, 112, 115, 117, 120, 132, 145, 152, 157, 158, 161, 162, 170, 202, 203

——, Requiem [projected], 81, 90
Balakireva, Anna: *see* Gusseva, Anna
Balakireva (née Yasherova), Elizaveta Ivanovna [Balakirev's mother], 77
Balakireva, Mariya [Balakirev's sister], 85
Balaneva, Liza: *see* Dianin, Liza
Baltimore, 217
Bartók, Béla, 229
Basili, Francesco, 5
Basle, 221
Batum, 204, 211
Bayreuth, 178
Bedniy, Demyan, 50
Beethoven, Ludwig van, 1, 4, 46, 65, 77, 110, 131
——, Piano Concerto no.5 in E♭, 80
——, Piano sonatas, 78
——, String Quartet in B♭ op.130, 52
——, String quartets [transcr. Musorgsky], 115
——, Symphony no.1, 78
——, Symphony no.4, 78
——, Symphony no.8, 78
Belgium, 56, 148
Bellini, Vincenzo, 5, 58, 146
Belyayev, Mitrofan Petrovich, 57, 126
Berlin, 5, 7, 8, 27, 208, 211
Berlioz, Hector, 6, 21, 59, 82, 84, 91, 92, 131, 150, 157, 203
——, *Grand traité d'instrumentation et d'orchestration modernes*, 60
——, *Harold en Italie*, 86, 203, 204
——, *Roméo et Juliette*, 203
——, *Symphonie fantastique*, 203
Bernard, Nikolay, 123

251